# Evil Lost, But Her Destiny Won!

By: Destiny Allen

# ACKNOWLEDGMENTS
## With Special Thanks

### To my Heavenly Father

Thank You, Lord, for being the father I always longed for. Your unwavering love, protection, and guidance have been my anchor through life's storms. I am eternally grateful for how You have carried me, giving me the strength to endure, the courage to persevere, and the faith to trust in Your plan. Jesus, thank You for Your unconditional love and for walking with me through every challenge. You gave up Your life so that I could have mine, and I am forever indebted to You. You are my Savior, my strength, and my hope.

### To my beloved children

I am incredibly blessed to be your mother. You are my greatest joy, and I thank God for the privilege of raising you. I pray that you never experience the hardships I faced but instead live lives filled with love, faith, and purpose. May you always know Jesus as your protector, friend, and Savior, walking with you every step of the way. I cherish the small moments that make our lives so meaningful. Lord, I pray that their minds be protected from evil, their hearts are still steadfast in love for You, and their identity in Christ always shines brightly. Thank You, Jesus, for blessing me with them.

## To my family and friends

Your support, prayers, and encouragement have meant so much to me. To my mother, I love you. To my sisters and brother, I pray for God's guidance and wisdom in your lives. "Dear Lord, may You be with them on their journeys, protecting and strengthening them. Let our bond reflect Your unconditional love, and may no weapon formed against them prosper."

## To those who doubted me

Your disbelief fueled my determination and pushed me closer to God's purpose for my life. I pray that you come to know His love, peace, and guidance. Thank you for being part of my story, even in ways you may not realize. I love you, and Jesus loves you even more.

**Finally,**

To everyone who picks up this book, I pray that it touches your heart and inspires you to begin or deepen your spiritual journey. Never give up, for God has greater plans for your future. Keep carrying your cross, trusting that His love and purpose for your life will prevail.

# ABOUT AUTHOR

Destiny Allen is a passionate storyteller whose journey is a testament to resilience, faith, and hope. Through life's many challenges, she has found strength in God and a desire to inspire others by sharing her story. With a deep belief in the power of faith, Destiny hopes her book *Evil Lost But Her Destiny Won!* will encourage readers to trust in God's plan, even in the darkest moments. When she's not writing, Destiny enjoys spending time with her children, reflecting on life's blessings, and helping others navigate their spiritual journeys.

# CONTENTS

# INTRODUCTION

L ife is a journey, filled with peaks of joy and valleys of despair. Along the way, we face trials that challenge our faith, test our resilience, and shape our identity. My journey has been anything but easy, marked by heartbreak, betrayal, and seemingly insurmountable obstacles. Yet, it is also a story of redemption, healing, and unshakable faith.

This book is my testimony—a raw and honest account of the battles I have faced, the lessons I have learned, and the unrelenting power of God's grace. It is not just a collection of stories but a roadmap for those who feel lost, broken, or unworthy. Through every challenge, I discovered that God was with me, even in my darkest moments, guiding me toward His greater purpose.

If you've ever felt rejected, abandoned, or misunderstood, know that you are not alone. My prayer is that as you turn these pages, you find hope, encouragement, and a reminder that you are deeply loved by a God who sees you, knows you, and has a plan for your life.

Each chapter is a glimpse into a season of my life—some filled with sorrow, others with triumph—but all pointing back to the relentless love of Jesus. My story isn't perfect, but it's a testament to the beauty that comes from ashes and the strength that arises from pain.

So, as you read, I invite you to reflect on your own journey. Where have you seen God's hand? How has He carried you through? Whether you're standing in the light of victory or walking through a shadow of despair, this book is for you.

Let this be a reminder: no matter what you've been through, your story is not over. Evil may try to win, but with God, victory is always assured.

Welcome to the journey. Let's walk it together.

CHAPTER

# THE CINDERELLA
# EXPERIENCE

*"God is with her, she will not fail, God will help her at break of day" (Psalms 46:5)*

## Early Childhood: A Fragile Start

**L**ife was challenging for me at a young age, filled with uncertainty and emotions I didn't yet have the words to describe. My mother was battling drug addiction—a battle I was too young to understand but could feel the weight of in my surroundings. In an effort to help her regain control of her life, my grandmother made the difficult decision to place me and my little sister in foster care. Her intentions were meant to teach my mother a lesson, to force change through separation. But for me, it became an experience of navigating a world that felt cold, unstable, and unfamiliar. I was only four years old, too young to grasp why my world had been uprooted, yet old enough to feel the sting of abandonment.

With each new foster home, I carried a fragile hope that this might be the place where I could stay, but that hope was often met with disappointment. Every transition left me feeling like I was drifting further and further from any sense of home. My sister and I, being the youngest, were placed together, which brought a small measure of comfort amidst the chaos. Meanwhile, my older siblings were taken in by family, which left me questioning why we couldn't all be together. Did something make us less worthy of that stability? At five years old, a glimmer of hope appeared when my sister and I were placed in a loving foster home. For the first time, I experienced what it felt like to be part of a family—not just a group of people sharing space, but a family that shared warmth, kindness, and laughter. We went on trips, celebrated small joys, and created memories that, even though fleeting, remain etched in my heart. It was a brief chapter in my life where I felt seen, valued, and loved—something I had craved for so long. However, life has a way of pulling the rug out from under you when you least expect it. That fleeting peace shattered when my mother passed away while my sister and I were still in foster care. It was a loss I struggled to comprehend.

I was too young to remember her face clearly, apart from a single photograph someone showed me. It was strange to grieve someone I hardly knew but still felt connected to. A part of me felt like I had lost something I never truly had—a mother's love, a sense of belonging that only she could have provided. Three years later, my grandmother made the decision to bring my sister and me out of the foster system. I remember feeling a mixture of hope and anxiety. Maybe this time, life would settle into something more stable. Maybe this time, I would find the home and family I had longed for. But behind that hope was also fear—fear that this new chapter might not be as smooth as I desperately wanted it to be

## Overcoming the Pain

Looking back, I can see that it wasn't easy, but it was possible to overcome those early challenges. I didn't realize it at the time, but each difficult experience was shaping me into someone stronger, someone who could face life's storms with faith instead of fear. My strength came from holding onto hope, even when everything around me seemed broken. Hope that things will get better. Hope that, even when people failed me, God never would. I found comfort in my faith, especially in scriptures that reminded me I wasn't alone. *"Though my father and mother forsake me, the Lord will receive me"* (Psalm 27:10) became more than just words; it became a promise I clung to. Even when I felt abandoned by the world, I began to see how God was stepping in to fill the void. He placed people in my life who showed me kindness and love when I needed it most. He gave me moments of joy that reminded me life wasn't just about pain—it could also be about healing and renewal. Overcoming wasn't just a one-time event; it was a process. There were days when I felt like giving up, but something deep inside kept pushing me forward. I didn't want my story to end in defeat. I wanted to rise above the circumstances that tried to break me. One of the most important lessons I learned during this time was to forgive—not just those who hurt me, but also myself. I had to let go of the anger and bitterness that threatened to consume me. Forgiveness didn't mean forgetting what happened, but it meant freeing myself from the burden of carrying those hurts. By forgiving, I allowed room in my heart for healing and for God's love to take root.

## Encouragement For You

If you've ever faced similar struggles, whether it's feeling abandoned, unloved, or uncertain about your future, I want you to know that you're not alone. Your past doesn't define your future. Just as I found a way to overcome through faith, hope, and perseverance, so can you. God sees your pain, and He cares about your story. He has a plan for you, even when it feels like everything is falling apart. Trust that He is guiding you, even when you can't see it. Hold onto hope, because better days are ahead. And most importantly, never give up on yourself or on the beautiful future that God has prepared for you

## The Shadow Of Discipline

Reuniting with my siblings was supposed to be a blessing, a chance to finally feel whole again, to recapture some sense of family after years of separation. For a brief moment, I felt that joy, but it didn't take long for that joy to unravel into something entirely different. What began as hope soon turned into fear and confusion. The grandmother I once looked up to, who I believed would offer comfort and stability, became someone I feared. Her presence, which should have been a refuge, instead became a constant reminder of pain and harsh discipline. There were no gentle corrections or attempts to understand me—only rigid rules and punishments that felt disproportionate to my actions. She didn't ask questions about how I was feeling or why I acted the way I did. Instead, she responded with severity, using wooden paddles, extension cords, and switches to discipline me. I vividly remember the times she would send me out to pick the switch myself. As a child, I thought I could lessen the pain by choosing a small one, but that only seemed to infuriate her more. She would make me go back and choose a bigger one, her anger growing with every failed attempt to meet her unspoken expectations. There were moments when the punishments went beyond just physical. Being forced to strip down before the beatings added layers of humiliation to the pain. It wasn't just my body that hurt—it was my spirit, my sense of self. I began to feel like I was constantly disappointed, like nothing I did could ever be good enough. The home I had once hoped would be a sanctuary became a place I dreaded returning to. School wasn't just about learning anymore, it became a temporary escape, a brief respite from the fear of what awaited me when I got home. Each day after school, I would walk home with a pit in my stomach, dreading what was to come. I didn't always know what I had done wrong, but I knew that punishment was waiting for me. It was as if the air in the house grew heavier with every step I took toward the front door. I stopped expecting love or kindness and started to believe that I was somehow inherently bad, that I was the reason for all her anger. This belief planted seeds of resentment deep in my heart—resentment toward my grandmother, resentment toward my situation, and even resentment toward myself. I couldn't understand why things were this way. I had longed for this reunion, for this chance to be with family again, and now that I had it, I felt more alone than ever. The Bible says, "Fathers, do not provoke your children to anger, but bring them up in the discipline and instruction of the Lord" (Ephesians 6:4). At the time, I didn't know this verse, but I felt its truth in my heart. Discipline is meant to teach, to guide, to help a child grow—not to break them. Yet, I felt broken. I felt unloved. I felt like a target for all the anger and frustration my grandmother carried, and it weighed on me heavily. In those moments, I began to question everything—my worth, my place in the world, and even God. I wondered why He would allow me to endure such hardship. Was I being punished? Had I done something wrong in His eyes too? The Bible promises in Hebrews 12:11, "No discipline seems pleasant at the time, but painful. Later, however, it produces a harvest of righteousness and peace for those who have been trained by it." But at that young age, I couldn't see any harvest. All I could see was pain and confusion. I didn't yet know that God was using those difficult moments to mold me, to strengthen me, and to prepare me for a testimony that would one day inspire others. Even though I didn't understand it then, God was with me through it all. His presence may have felt distant, but it was constant. Each time I endured another punishment, each time I cried myself to sleep, He was there, keeping my heart from hardening completely, keeping me from giving up entirely. "The Lord is close to the brokenhearted and saves those who are crushed in spirit" (Psalm 34:18). That was me—brokenhearted and crushed in spirit. But God's hand was upon me, even when I couldn't feel it. Looking back now, I realize that those moments of harsh discipline taught me something I couldn't see at the time: resilience. They taught me to endure hardship, to keep going even when everything around me felt hopeless. They also taught me the importance of showing love, compassion, and understanding, something I promised myself I would always give to my own children. God was shaping me into someone who could rise above her circumstances, who could find strength in Him even when the world seemed determined to break her. The Bible says in Romans 5:3-4, "Not only that, but we rejoice in our sufferings, knowing that suffering produces endurance, and endurance produces character, and character produces hope." Though I didn't rejoice in my sufferings as a child, I can now see how those difficult times built my character. They made me who I am today—a woman who walks by faith, who refuses to give up, and who finds hope in the promises of God. I've learned that while life may place us in difficult situations, we don't have to stay there emotionally or spiritually. We can rise above them, not through our own strength, but through the strength God provides. He is our refuge and strength, an ever-present help in times of trouble (Psalm 46:1). No matter how dark those early years were, they didn't define me. God did. And through His grace, I found healing, purpose, and the courage to share my story.

## The Burden Of Being Misunderstood

At school, I acted out—not because I was inherently bad, but because I was hurting, confused, and desperate for someone to see beyond my behavior. The world around me didn't ask why I was lashing out. They only saw a "problem child." The truth was, I longed for love, structure, and guidance, but I didn't know how to express it. Instead, my frustration and longing for attention manifested in ways that others couldn't understand. Children don't always have the words to articulate their pain. I certainly didn't. I didn't know how to tell anyone that I felt abandoned, unloved, and constantly afraid. So, I acted out— throwing tantrums, refusing to listen, and doing anything that might get someone to pay attention. I was trapped in a cycle of misunderstanding, where my cries for help were mistaken for defiance. The Bible says, *"Foolishness is bound up in the heart of a child, but the rod of discipline will drive it far from him"* (Proverbs 22:15). But what I needed wasn't punishment, I needed someone to reach out with love, patience, and understanding. One day, my frustration reached its peak. Something triggered me—I can't even recall what it was—but at that moment, I acted impulsively and bit my teacher. It was an action born from a place of deep inner turmoil, but the world didn't see that. All they saw was a child who couldn't control her anger. I knew this incident wouldn't end at school. There would be consequences far beyond the classroom. Later that day, the teacher came to my grandmother's house to report the incident. As soon as I saw her at the door, my heart sank, and a cold wave of fear washed over me. I knew what was coming. I had been through this routine before—an incident at school, a report made to my guardian, and then the inevitable punishment. But this time it felt different. This time, I feared the punishment would be worse than any I had experienced before. I braced myself as my grandmother listened to the teacher recount what had happened. Each word felt like a nail being driven into my fate. My grandmother didn't ask for my side of the story. She didn't try to understand what led to my outburst. Her mind was already made up. To her, I was just being bad again, and bad behavior warranted a severe response. After the teacher left, I stood in silence, waiting for the storm to come. My heart pounded in my chest as my grandmother's anger boiled over. The beating that followed was harsh, and with each strike, it felt like more than just punishment—it felt like rejection. It felt like I was being told, once again, that I was unlovable, that my struggles didn't matter, and that my pain was invisible to the world around me. Those moments, I began to internalize the belief that there was something wrong with me. I started to believe that I was inherently bad, that no matter how hard I tried, I would always fall short. The Bible says in *Psalm*

*34:18, "The Lord is close to the brokenhearted and saves those who are crushed in spirit."* But at that young age, I didn't feel close to the Lord. I felt isolated, misunderstood, and utterly alone.

Looking back now, I realize that what I needed most during those difficult years was grace. I needed someone to see beyond my actions and recognize the hurting child beneath. I needed someone to offer not just correction, but compassion. The Bible teaches in *Colossians 3:21, "Fathers, do not provoke your children, lest they become discouraged."* Discipline without love and understanding only breeds resentment and discouragement. It can crush a child's spirit, leaving wounds that take years to heal. That day was a turning point for me—not in the sense that things got better, but in the sense that something inside me began to harden. I started to build walls around my heart, determined to protect myself from further pain. I didn't want to feel anymore, because feeling only led to hurt. I became more withdrawn, more guarded, and more convinced that I had to navigate this world on my own. Yet even in those dark moments, God was planting seeds of strength within me. Though I didn't know it at the time, He was preparing me for something greater. He was teaching me resilience, endurance, and the importance of seeking Him in times of trouble. The Bible says in *Isaiah 41:10, "Fear not, for I am with you; be not dismayed, for I am your God. I will strengthen you; I will help you; I will uphold you with my righteous right hand."* Though I felt abandoned by those around me, God never left my side. He was there, quietly working behind the scenes, shaping my character and laying the foundation for the person I would one day become. The burden of being misunderstood is a heavy one, especially for a child. It can leave scars that last well into adulthood. But God has a way of turning our deepest wounds into sources of strength. He has a way of taking what was meant to break us and using it to build us up. I learned that no matter how misunderstood we may feel by the world, God sees us. He knows our hearts, our struggles, and our pain, and He offers a love that heals and restores. If you are reading this and you've ever felt misunderstood, know that you are not alone. Know that your worth is not defined by how others see you, but by how God sees you. He calls you, His child. He sees your pain, and He cares. The Bible says in *1 Peter 5:7, "Cast all your anxiety on Him because He cares for you."* I encourage you to cast your burdens on Him, for He is faithful to carry them. Today, I carry the lessons of my past not as a burden, but as a testament to God's faithfulness. I carry them as a reminder that even in our darkest moments, God is at work, bringing light and hope. And I share my story not to dwell on the pain, but to testify to the healing and transformation that is possible through Jesus Christ. *What the enemy meant for harm; God has used for good (Genesis 50:20).* And for that, I will always give Him praise

## Searching for Love in Loss

The absence of my mother loomed large in my life. I longed
for her presence and love, feeling the weight of her absence in
every painful moment. I imagined what life might have been
like if she were still here—maybe I would have felt safer, more
cherished, or at least less alone. I clung to fleeting memories and
the few stories I heard about her, trying to piece together who
she was and why she was no longer with me. My heart ached for
a connection I could never truly have. The Bible says in Jeremiah
1:5, "Before I formed you in your mother's body, I chose you.
Before you were born, I set you apart to serve me." Those words
were meant to bring comfort, a reminder of God's purpose and
love, but in my youthful mind, I couldn't understand why being
"set apart" came with so much pain. If God had chosen me, why
did I feel so rejected by the world around me? I struggled with
feelings of abandonment, unworthiness, and confusion about
my place in life. Instead of finding solace at home, I faced more
rejection. My grandmother, who was supposed to fill the void left
by my mother's death, only deepened my wounds. She frequently
told me that I was the problem, calling me "dumb" and hurling
cruel words that cut deep into my self-worth. Her harsh criticism
became a constant echo in my mind, making it difficult to see
myself as anything more than the negative labels she assigned

to me. She introduced me and my brother to my dad, a moment that should have brought a sense of belonging and joy. Instead, it only added to my trauma. My time with him wasn't filled with the love or protection I had hoped for. Rather, it was a reminder that even the people who were supposed to care for me didn't always know how to show it. Every visit left me feeling more broken, as if I were grasping at fragments of a love that could never be whole. In my quiet moments, I wrestled with my emotions—anger, sadness, longing, and a desperate need to feel valued. I sought love in the absence of it, hoping that someone, anyone, would see past my pain and recognize the person I was trying to become. Yet, even in the darkest moments, there was something within me that refused to give up entirely, a flicker of hope that perhaps one day, things could change. The Bible promises in Psalm 34:18, "The Lord is close to the brokenhearted and saves those who are crushed in spirit." Though I didn't fully grasp it at the time, God was planting seeds of resilience in me. Even when I felt unseen and unloved by the people around me, He saw my heart and heard my cries. Looking back now, I realize that His presence was there all along, guiding me through the storm, even when I couldn't feel it.

## A Lonely Black Sheep

In my family, I felt like the black sheep—unwanted, misunderstood, and unloved. No matter how hard I tried to be good or to fit in, it seemed like I was always on the outside looking in. My heart longed for a place where I could feel safe, accepted, and valued, but instead, I was met with cold stares, harsh words, and a sense of isolation. I craved comfort and understanding, but I found none. The loneliness weighed heavily on me, like an invisible burden I couldn't put down. At night, when the world grew quiet, I would cry myself to sleep, questioning why my life was so full of pain. I asked myself over and over: Why me? What did I do to deserve this? It seemed as though no one noticed the silent battles I was fighting. The emotional wounds went unseen, and yet, they cut deeper than any physical scar ever could. I wanted someone to reach out, to see my pain and tell me it was going to be okay. But that moment never came. Even though my grandmother took us to church every Sunday, I struggled to connect with God. The sermons, the hymns, and the prayers seemed like distant echoes in a life that felt void of real love and hope. The teachings felt hollow against the backdrop of my daily suffering. How could a loving God allow a child to endure so much? I felt lost in a sea of faith that others seemed to grasp effortlessly, while I remained adrift, searching for something real. Yet, even in my confusion and despair, there was a small part of me that refused to let go completely. That part of me clung desperately to a single verse I had learned: *"I can do all things through Christ who strengthens me"* (Philippians 4:13). Those words became a lifeline, a whisper of hope in the darkest moments when I felt like giving up entirely. Though I didn't fully understand what it meant at the time, something about those words made me believe that, perhaps, one day I would find the strength to rise above my circumstances. Looking back, I realize that God was always there, even when I couldn't feel Him. He was the silent presence that kept me holding on when everything else in my life told me to let go. Though I didn't see it then, He was working behind the scenes, shaping me, strengthening me, and preparing me for a purpose far greater than the pain I was enduring. In those lonely nights, when tears stained my pillow, He saw me. He heard the cries that no one else did, and though I didn't know it, He was already writing a better story for my life. The Bible promises in Psalm 147:3, *"He heals the brokenhearted and binds up their wounds."* At the time, I didn't know how to trust that promise, but today, I can testify to its truth. Even when you feel like the black sheep—unwanted, forgotten, or unloved—God's love never fails. He sees what others overlook. He knows the battles you fight silently and the tears you cry in secret. And in His perfect time, He will lift you up and turn your pain into purpose. If I could speak to the little girl I was back then, I would tell her: Hold on. You are not forgotten. You are not unloved. You are seen, and you are held by a God who loves you more than you can imagine. One day, you will see that everything you endured was not in vain. It will shape you into someone stronger, wiser, and filled with a love that only God can give.

## Seeds of Strength Amid the Struggle

Despite the pain, God was always present, even when I couldn't feel Him. He was watching over me, placing angels in my path to encourage me to keep going. I didn't understand the depth of His plan, but I began to realize that the trials I faced were forging a strength within me. The Bible says in **Isaiah 41:10**, "Fear not, for I am with you; be not dismayed, for I am your God; I will strengthen you, I will help you, I will uphold you with my righteous right hand." I clung to this promise, even when everything seemed hopeless. There were moments when I questioned why I had to endure so much suffering. The whispers of doubt told me I wasn't strong enough, but something greater within me whispered back, "Keep going." Each tear shed in pain was watering the seeds of resilience and faith in my heart. It wasn't easy, but I began to trust that God was shaping me into someone who could withstand life's storms and still remain standing. Looking back, I see that those dark days were preparing me for something greater. My story wasn't over, and my faith was the key to moving forward. In those moments of silence and despair, God was at work, weaving together a story of redemption, hope, and purpose. The Bible in **Romans 8:28** reminds us, "And we know that in all things God works for the good of those who love Him, who have been called according to His purpose." Every setback I endured was shaping me into the woman I am today, someone capable of finding light in the darkest places. I now understand that God doesn't waste our pain. He transforms it into strength, wisdom, and purpose. Every difficulty I faced became a lesson, every tear a prayer, and every scar a reminder of His unfailing love. He never left my side, even when I thought I was alone. I grew stronger not by my own will, but through the grace and mercy of a loving Father who was guiding me through each storm. If you find yourself in a season of struggle, know that it isn't the end of your story. God is working behind the scenes, preparing you for a greater purpose. Hold on to your faith and trust His plan, even when it doesn't make sense. You are being refined, strengthened, and prepared for something more beautiful than you could ever imagine. Never forget that with God, your pain has a purpose, and your struggles will lead to your greatest testimony

## Isolation And The Weight Of Neglect

Everybody seemed to think negatively of me and my behavior, which only deepened my sense of isolation. I hated the life I was living because I felt so alone in that house. Why was I always the one being picked on? My uncle used to call me "Cinderella," a nickname that puzzled me at first. Over time, I realized it wasn't a term of endearment, but a reflection of my reality life filled with heartache and unfair treatment, minus the fairy tale ending. Instead of being cared for, I felt like an outsider in my own family. I longed for connection, for someone to see beyond my outward behavior and understand the turmoil within. But the more I sought acceptance, the more I was met with judgment and criticism. I became the scapegoat, the one who was blamed for everything, and that weight was unbearable. I carried the burden of neglect, of being misunderstood, and it chipped away at my sense of self. I was desperate for a mother's love, but she was no longer there. My mom had passed away, leaving me to navigate this painful existence alone. I was mad, searching for a mother I could never find. Why was this my reality? Why was I left with a grandmother who seemed determined to torment me? I wrestled with these questions daily, feeling abandoned and unloved. The Bible says, "Before I formed you in your mother's body, I chose you. Before you were born, I set you apart to serve me" (Jeremiah

1:5). Yet, I struggled to understand what I was set apart for, as my life felt like an endless cycle of pain. How could I be chosen when I felt so rejected by those around me? I didn't feel special, I felt forsaken. I often wondered if there was something inherently wrong with me. Was I too difficult to love? Too flawed to deserve kindness? My heart ached with these unanswered questions. But even in my despair, there was a flicker of hope that maybe, just maybe, my suffering had a purpose. Maybe God saw something in me that I couldn't yet see in myself. In moments of reflection, I would remind myself of the promise in Romans 8:28, "And we know that in all things God works for the good of those who love him, who have been called according to his purpose." I didn't understand how, but I began to cling to the idea that my pain would not be in vain. Perhaps one day, God would use my story to help others who felt just as alone as I did. As much as I struggled to feel God's presence in those dark times, He was there, sustaining me in ways I couldn't comprehend. Every tear I cried, every sleepless night spent wondering why, was shaping me into someone stronger. Though I couldn't see it then, God was preparing me for a purpose far greater than my pain. If you've ever felt like the world is against you, know that God sees you. He sees your suffering, your heartache, and He hasn't abandoned you. It may feel like you're walking this road alone, but He's walking right beside you, guiding you through the storm. Trust that your story is still being written, and the ending will be more beautiful than you could ever imagine.

## The Black Sheep Of The Family

At this point, I felt like the black sheep of the family—unwanted, unloved, and completely out of place. I wanted love and comfort so badly that it consumed my thoughts. Not once did my grandmother tell me she genuinely loved me, and her actions only reinforced the belief that I was a burden. I cried myself to sleep countless nights. My house wasn't a home, it was a horror story I desperately wanted to escape. I didn't understand what love felt like, but I knew I was missing it. I felt like my own family didn't love me, and that realization broke me in ways words could never fully capture. It wasn't just emotional pain; it was a deep, gnawing void that affected every part of my being. Even when surrounded by people, I felt alone. The weight of rejection hung over me like a dark cloud, and I carried that burden into every interaction. I often asked myself, *why wasn't I good enough? Why couldn't I be loved like other children?* I didn't realize at the time that these feelings would become wounds I would need to heal from later in life. Despite the emptiness, there was a part of me that held onto hope that one day, I would know what it was like to be genuinely loved and accepted. The Bible says, "God is our refuge and strength, a very present help in trouble" (Psalms 46:1-3). Even then, I clung to this verse, hoping for refuge, but it felt like the mountains were crashing down around me. Little did I know that God was quietly working behind the scenes, building within me a resilience I couldn't yet understand. Though the love I craved didn't come from those around me, I would later learn that God's love was constant, unconditional, and always present. While I may not have felt it in those dark moments He was there, holding me up when I was too weak to stand on my own. The black sheep I once saw myself as would one day transform. The pain I carried would lead me to a deeper understanding of compassion, empathy, and faith. But at that time, all I could do was cry, pray, and hope that one day, life wouldn't feel so heavy

## The Illusion of Church as a Sanctuary

My grandmother took me and my siblings to church every Sunday. It was supposed to be a place of peace and comfort, but I struggled to connect. The sermons felt distant, and the joy others seemed to feel was something I couldn't relate to. I would sit in those pews, wondering why I didn't feel the love of God the way everyone else claimed to. I Only knew how to pray because that's what I was told to do. Prayer felt like a ritual—an obligation rather than a heartfelt conversation with God. The depth of God's love was something I couldn't comprehend amidst my suffering. *How could a loving God allow me to endure so much pain? Why didn't He intervene when I cried out in silence, longing for relief* The Bible states, "Be careful that you don't look down on one of these little ones. I say to you that their angels in heaven are always looking into the face of my Father who is in heaven" (Matthew 18:10). Yet, I felt invisible, even in the house of God. The people around me were too focused on their own lives to notice a broken child searching for solace. I felt unseen, unheard, and unimportant, even in a place that was supposed to represent hope and healing. Despite my lack of connection, I never completely gave up. There was a faint flicker of hope buried deep within me—a belief that maybe, just maybe, God would hear me one day. Philippians 4:13 became my lifeline: "I can do all things through Christ who strengthens me." I didn't fully understand what it meant back then, but it became my mantra, a reminder that somehow, I could keep going. Looking back, I see that while I didn't feel His presence then, God was still there. He saw me, heard my cries, and began planting seeds of strength and endurance in my heart. Though I didn't recognize it at the time, every whispered prayer and tearful plea was drawing me closer to the moment when I would truly encounter Him.

## The Burden of Inequality

My grandmother's favoritism was glaring. She treated my sisters better than she treated me, showing them the love and care I so desperately craved. It was infuriating to watch and deeply unfair. The disparity in her treatment left me feeling invisible and unworthy of affection. I longed for her approval, but no matter what I did, it seemed like nothing was ever good enough. Every smile she gave them felt like a knife cutting deeper into my already wounded heart. I couldn't understand why she treated us so differently. *Was I not good enough? Did she see something in me that made me less deserving of love?* These unanswered questions weighed heavily on my spirit, planting seeds of anger and bitterness that grew with each passing day. My anger at this injustice manifested in my behavior at home and school. I felt trapped in a world where nothing made sense, and I lashed out because I didn't know how else to express the pain I was carrying. I acted out because it seemed like the only way to release the frustration building inside me. My behavior spiraled out of control, making me an unruly and disobedient child in the eyes of those around me. Teachers labeled me a troublemaker, and at home, I was viewed as a problem child. At the time, I didn't care about anything or anyone because I felt as though nobody truly cared about me.

The Bible says, "Children, obey your parents in the Lord, for this is right" (Ephesians 6:10). It also says, "Children, obey your parents in all things, for this is well-pleasing unto the Lord" (Colossians 3:20). But how could I obey when my heart was so heavy with resentment and my soul so battered by rejection? It was difficult to honor someone who seemed to view me as an inconvenience rather than a blessing. In those moments, I felt trapped in a cycle of rebellion and rejection. Yet, even in my disobedience, there was a part of me that longed for something more. I yearned for peace, for a life where I didn't have to act out to be noticed, and for a love that didn't feel so conditional. Looking back, I realize that those turbulent years were shaping me. They were teaching me to find strength in adversity and to seek a love that could never be earned through performance. I didn't know it then, but God was working behind the scenes, preparing me for a greater purpose. While I was fighting battles I didn't fully understand, He was laying the foundation for the strength and resilience that would one day carry me through even greater trials.

## A Diagnosis that Changed Everything

At just nine years old, my life was turned upside down when I was diagnosed with type 1 juvenile diabetes. The news hit me like a storm, shattering any sense of normalcy I had managed to cling to. It was terrifying. I thought my life would never be normal again. Questions swirled in my mind: *Why me, God? Why does my life seem to be falling apart? What did I do to deserve all of this at such a young age? How much more can I endure?* Living with diabetes wasn't just a medical condition; it became a daily battle. I suddenly found myself having to monitor my blood sugar, take insulin shots, and watch what I ate—all things no child should have to worry about. While other kids played without care in the world, I carried the weight of this disease like an invisible burden that I couldn't set down. The Bible reminds us, *"You shall not curse God, nor curse a ruler of your people"* (Exodus 22:28), and *"For God gave us a spirit not to fear but of power and love and self-control"* (2 Timothy 1:7). Yet, as a child grappling with so much, it was hard to find comfort in those words. I felt powerless, confused, and isolated, unable to understand why God had allowed such hardship into my life. One morning, my worst fears became reality—I slipped into a diabetic coma because my blood sugar was dangerously low. I didn't see it coming. One moment I was awake, and the next, everything went dark. My oldest sister, who was in the room with me, sprang into action. She quickly gave me a shot that saved my life. When I woke up, paramedics were surrounding me, their concerned faces hovering over mine. I was confused and scared, struggling to comprehend what had just happened. But amid the fear and confusion, one truth stood out clearly in my mind: God had spared my life. Even in my young heart, I understood that something greater had been at work that day. My life could have ended, but it didn't. God wasn't finished with me yet. The Bible says, *"Spare my life, O God, and save me, and I will gladly proclaim your righteousness. Help me to speak, Lord, and I will praise you. My sacrifice is a humble spirit"* (Psalms 54:14-17). That day marked a turning point—a second chance at life. But having a second chance didn't mean the road ahead would be any easier. If anything, it felt even harder. I had to learn how to live with this illness, how to accept it as part of my story without letting it define who I was. I began to realize that while I couldn't control what happened to me, I could control how I responded. Slowly, I started to see that God was using even this difficult part of my life to shape me, to build resilience and perseverance in my spirit. Though I was young, I carried a burden that forced me to mature quickly, to learn how to lean on God even when I didn't understand His plan

## The Weight of Embarrassment

As if managing diabetes wasn't challenging enough, life threw another curveball my way—I was diagnosed with scoliosis. The doctors told me I needed to wear a back brace to prevent my spine from curving further. For a young girl trying to fit in, this was beyond humiliating. I was already carrying the weight of being different, and now, this bulky, uncomfortable brace made me feel like I was being singled out even more. I remember the first time I saw the brace. It looked like something out of a medical experiment, stiff and restrictive. Wearing it made me feel trapped—not just physically, but emotionally. I didn't want to be "the girl with the brace. I tried everything to avoid wearing it, but the consequences of disobedience always found me. The brace became a symbol of everything I hated about my life, a constant reminder of my struggles and the lack of control I felt over my own body. Wearing the brace was supposed to help me, but to me, it only brought shame. I was terrified of being ridiculed by my peers. I didn't want to be stared at or laughed at, so I found ways to avoid wearing it. Every morning, I would leave the house with it on, but as soon as I was out of sight, I would sneak behind the neighbor's house, take it off, and hide it. I thought I was clever. I thought I could outsmart the situation. But each day was a cycle of anxiety—hiding the brace, rushing to retrieve it before returning home, and pretending I had worn it all day. One day, the inevitable happened. As I stepped off the school bus, my uncle was waiting for me. He looked me up and down and asked the dreaded question, "Where's your back brace?" My heart dropped. I froze, unable to think of a single excuse. I didn't know how to explain the lengths I had gone to just to avoid the stares and laughter of my classmates. I was already starved for love and acceptance at home—how could I endure the mockery of strangers, too? In that moment, I felt utterly exposed, as if all my efforts to hide my pain had been for nothing. I was caught between two worlds: a home where I felt unloved and a school where I feared being ridiculed. It felt like there was nowhere I truly belonged, nowhere I could be myself without judgment or rejection. The Bible says, *"Come to me, all who are weary and burdened, and I will give you rest"* (Matthew 11:28). But at that time, I didn't know how to come to God with my burdens. I didn't know how to seek the rest He promised. All I knew was that I wanted to be free—free from the brace, free from the shame, and free from the weight of feeling different. Looking back, I now see that even in those moments of hiding and fear, God was with me. He was there, whispering strength into my heart, even when I didn't recognize it. The back brace may have been a symbol of my pain, but it also became a part of the story that shaped me—a story of learning to stand tall, even when life tried to bend me.

## An Anointing I Didn't Yet Understand

I didn't know it at the time, but God's hand was always on me, guiding me through the darkest moments, even when I couldn't see or feel Him. The Bible says, *"Even when I walk through the darkest valley, I will not be afraid, for you are close beside me. Your rod and your staff protect and comfort me"* (Psalms 23:4). Those words, though distant to me then, would later become a source of hope and strength as I reflected on my journey. Even in what seemed like insignificant moments, God was showing me His presence and planting seeds of faith in my life. One day, I went fishing with my aunt and uncle. It was supposed to be a fun day, a distraction from the troubles I faced at home. My uncle tried casting his line repeatedly but couldn't catch a single fish. As frustration set in, my aunt looked at me and said, *"Pray for him."* Her request caught me off guard. I didn't understand why prayer mattered in such a trivial situation. Why would God care about whether or not we caught fish that day? When I hesitated, unsure and confused, my aunt grew stern. She didn't explain further—she demanded obedience. Punishing me for my reluctance, she forced me to pray through my tears. It felt like such a small, strange thing to pray about, and I didn't understand why it mattered. But in my innocence and fear, I closed my eyes and uttered a simple prayer, through sobs and trembling words. The moment I finished praying, something incredible happened—my uncle caught the biggest fish of the day. It wasn't just any fish; it was the kind of catch that left everyone amazed. I stood there, wiping my tears, not quite sure how to feel. On the surface, it seemed like a mere coincidence, but deep inside, I felt something stirred. It was as if God was gently whispering, *"I have my hands on you. I will see you through when you cry. I am holding you."* Even then, I couldn't fully grasp the anointing on my life. I didn't understand that God was planting moments like these as reminders that He was always near, even when I felt abandoned and unloved. In that small act of obedience, through a tearful prayer for something as simple as catching a fish, God was showing me His power. He was teaching me that prayer isn't just for life's big battles—it's for everything, big or small. He wanted me to know that He cared about the details, even the ones that seemed too trivial for His attention. The Bible says, *"For I know the plans I have for you, declares the Lord, plans for welfare and not for evil, to give you a future and a hope"* (Jeremiah 29:11). Looking back, I see that this moment wasn't just about fishing—it was about faith, obedience, and the beginnings of understanding God's presence in my life. It was a lesson that, even in the smallest requests, God listens. Even when I felt unworthy and overlooked, He was shaping me for a purpose far greater than I could comprehend. I didn't know it at the time, but those moments were building my faith. Each tear-filled prayer, every whispered plea, was drawing me closer to God. Though I wouldn't fully understand the depth of His love and the anointing on my life until much later, He was already laying the foundation. Through every trial and every tear, He was preparing me for something greater life of purpose, strength, And Unwavering Faith.

## The Hunger for Sweets and Belonging

Diabetes brought more challenges than I could have imagined. At nine years old, I wasn't just battling a disease—I was fighting a sense of isolation within my own family. My relatives, in their misunderstanding of my condition, banned me from eating sweets altogether. To them, it was a necessary rule to protect my health, but to me, it felt like an unfair punishment that singled me out. Watching my siblings enjoy candies and desserts while I sat on the sidelines was heartbreaking. Every bite they took felt like a reminder of what I couldn't have. It wasn't just about the sweets—it was about belonging, feeling included, and being treated equally.

One night, driven by an unbearable longing for what I was forbidden, I decided to sneak some pies up to my room. I didn't plan it in advance, it was a moment born out of desperation. I ate them quickly, savoring every bite like it was a forbidden treasure. Afterward, I hid the remains under my bed, hoping no one would find out. To others, it might have seemed like a minor act of rebellion, but for me, it was a way of reclaiming a little joy in a world that often felt joyless. I didn't fully understand my diabetes or why I had to endure such strict restrictions. In my young mind, it felt cruel and unnecessary. Watching everyone else enjoy sweets freely while I was constantly told "no" made me feel excluded, less than, and punished for something I had no control over. Inside, I was crumbling under the weight of it all. I longed for someone to see my pain; to understand how difficult it was to be a child living with an illness I didn't fully comprehend. Sneaking sweets became my small, secret act of defiance—a way to reclaim something that had been taken from me. For a brief moment, it gave me a sense of normalcy and control over my life. But it didn't last. One night, my uncle discovered my secret stash. His anger was swift and unforgiving. He didn't ask why I had done it or tried to understand what I was feeling. He only saw disobedience and reacted accordingly.

What followed crushed me. My aunt and uncle decided that I could no longer stay in the house at night. They claimed they couldn't monitor me while they slept and that I was a danger to myself. Their solution? I had to sleep in the garage. It didn't matter that it was cold or that I was just a child seeking comfort in the only way I knew how—they saw no other option. That night in the garage, I lay awake on a makeshift bed, shivering both from the cold and from the weight of my emotions. I felt rejected, unwanted, and deeply misunderstood. I stared at the ceiling, tears streaming down my face, wondering why life was so harsh for me. *Why couldn't anyone see that I wasn't trying to be rebellious—I was just trying to feel normal, to experience a small piece of the joy that seemed reserved for everyone else but me?* In that moment of despair, I clung to the only thing I could—the hope that God hadn't forgotten me. The Bible says, *"The Lord is near to the brokenhearted and saves the crushed in spirit"* (Psalms 34:18). I didn't fully understand the depth of this promise then, but I desperately wanted to believe it. I wanted to believe that someone, somewhere, cared about my pain and that this wasn't the end of my story. Looking back now, I see that those nights in the garage were more than just moments of pain, they were moments that taught me resilience. They forced me to turn inward and seek strength beyond myself. Though it felt like rejection, it was also a chapter that would one day be part of my testimony. God was working, even in the silence, even in the darkness of that cold garage. He was planting seeds of perseverance, faith, and endurance in my heart. The Bible says, *"Consider it pure joy, my brothers and sisters, whenever you face trials of many kinds, because you know that the testing of your faith produces perseverance"* (James 1:2-3). At the time, it was impossible to see any joy in what I was going through, but now I understand that those trials were shaping me into the person I am today. They were preparing me for a future where I would have the strength to face even greater challenges and the wisdom to help others who felt alone and misunderstood. Those nights in the garage were some of the hardest moments of my childhood, but they didn't break me. Instead, they became part of the foundation that taught me how to trust God in the midst of suffering. They taught me that even when the world seems cold and unforgiving, God's love is constant. He never left me, even when it felt like everyone else had.

## The Darkness Of Rejection

As I stood in that cold garage, clutching my blanket, I felt the weight of complete abandonment. The door locked behind me, and I was left alone in the darkness. Tears streamed down my face as I whispered to myself, *"They don't love me."* The Bible says, *"Even if my father and mother abandon me, the Lord will hold me close"* (Psalms 27:10). In that moment, I longed for my mom. But she was gone, and the reality of my loneliness hit harder than ever. I questioned everything: *Why doesn't my family love me? Why am I treated so badly? Why do I have to bear the burden of these health issues on top of everything else?* I wanted to give up, but somehow, God kept me going. A Glimpse of Hope Yet, through it all, God was with me. The Bible says, *"If God is for us, who can be against us?"* (Romans 8:31). Though my life was filled with challenges,

I began to realize that God's plan for me was greater than the pain I was enduring.

## A Return To Familiar Pain

Eventually, they let me back into the house and into my room, but the emotional scars remained. The garage had been a temporary punishment, but it felt like a lifetime of rejection compressed into one dark night. I started expecting the worst in every situation. I longed for my mom, but she was gone. I couldn't call on her for comfort or protection. I felt like an orphan in every sense, abandoned by the people who were supposed to care for me. The Bible promises, *"As I was with Moses, so I will be with you; I will never leave you nor forsake you"* (Joshua 1:5). But at that moment, I couldn't feel it. I questioned everything—my family, my worth, and my purpose. At school, my behavior became more disruptive. Teachers and counselors called my uncle, trying to address my actions, but it didn't lead to change. Their words only reinforced the narrative. *"God has truly been a blessing to me"* (Genesis 2:18). I didn't fully understand it yet, but God was walking with me, holding me together when I felt like falling apart.

## Isolation and the Mental Hospital

Time passed, and my behavior spiraled further out of control. My family decided they couldn't handle me anymore. Their solution was to place me in a mental hospital. The decision felt like the ultimate betrayal. The Bible says, *"Don't let your hearts be troubled. Trust in God and trust also in me"* (John 14:1). But trusting was hard. The hospital was a cold, sterile place, filled with people who didn't understand me. I felt like I was being punished for simply existing. When my family visited, the pain only deepened. Seeing my sisters free, living their lives while I was trapped, made me feel forgotten and unloved. I hated them for watching me suffer and not speaking up for me. The isolation was unbearable. I was often put in a secluded room, restrained in a straitjacket, and given shots to calm me down. My anger flared at anyone who crossed me. I was fighting for my dignity, for a voice in a place where no one seemed to listen.

## The Long Road to Freedom

After about a year, I was finally released. Walking out of those hospital doors should have felt like a victory, but instead, it left me feeling scared, bitter, and deeply hurt. The weight of the experience hung over me like a dark cloud. It wasn't just the hospital stay that had wounded me, it was the betrayal of being placed there by the very people who were supposed to protect and love me. I couldn't shake the feeling that I had been cast aside, as if I didn't matter. I didn't belong in that hospital, and every day I spent there only reinforced the belief that I was unworthy of love. I carried that anger with me, unable to understand how my family could have abandoned me like that. *Did they not see my struggles? Did they not care about the pain I was enduring?* These thoughts swirled in my mind, fueling a resentment that felt impossible to let go of. I had been locked away, isolated, and treated as if I were broken beyond repair. The wounds weren't just physical or mental, they were spiritual, too. My faith had been shaken by the experience, but it wasn't completely destroyed. The Bible reminds us, *"The Lord does not see as man sees; for man looks at the outward appearance, but the Lord looks at the heart"* (1 Samuel 16:7). Even when the world saw a troubled child, God saw something deeper. He saw my pain, my brokenness, and my potential. He saw a child yearning for love and acceptance, a child who didn't fit the mold but who was still worthy of compassion. While my family may have misunderstood me, and while I felt rejected by everyone around me, God knew my heart. He saw what no one else could see—the strength that was being forged through every tear, every moment of isolation, and every trial. Despite the anger and confusion, there was a small flicker of hope within me, though I didn't recognize it at the time. That flicker was

God's presence, gently reminding me that I wasn't alone, even when it felt like the whole world had turned its back on me. I didn't yet understand that He was preparing me for something greater. What felt like rejection was, in fact, redirection. He was guiding me down a path that would one day reveal His greater purpose for my life. Looking back now, I can see that God's hand was on me, even in that dark season. He was molding me, shaping me into someone who could endure, someone who could overcome. The Bible says, *"And we know that in all things God works for the good of those who love him, who have been called according to his purpose"* (Romans 8:28). At the time, I didn't understand why I had to go through so much pain, but today I know that God was using every struggle to bring me closer to Him. It's hard to explain how I survived that period of my life, but I know it wasn't by my own strength. Every day was a battle, yet somehow, I kept going. I didn't give up, even when everything inside me wanted to quit. That resilience wasn't something I created—it was something God placed within me. He gave me the strength to endure the darkest nights, even when I couldn't see the light. As I stepped back into the world, scared but free, I realized that freedom was more than just leaving a physical place, it was about finding freedom in my heart and mind. It was about letting go of the anger and embracing the healing that only God could offer. I wasn't there yet, but I was on the path, and that was enough.

The journey ahead wouldn't be easy, but I was learning that with God, I could face anything. The Bible promises, *"He heals the brokenhearted and binds up their wounds"* (Psalms 147:3). Though my wounds ran deep, I held onto the hope that one day, God would heal every part of me—my heart, my mind, and my spirit. And with that hope, I took my first steps toward a new chapter of my life.

## Finding Strength in God's Plan

Even after leaving the hospital, life didn't suddenly get easier. The pain lingered, and the rejection felt like an unshakable shadow, following me wherever I went. Every day felt like a reminder of what I had endured and the emotional scars I carried. I often wondered if things would ever change, if I would ever experience the kind of love and peace that I longed for. Yet, even in my lowest moments, there was a quiet whisper in my heart, telling me not to give up. The Bible promises, "If God is for us, who can be against us?" (Romans 8:31). Though I didn't fully understand it at the time, those words began to plant seeds of hope within me. It wasn't an overnight transformation, but slowly, I began to find strength in the belief that God had a plan for me, even if I couldn't see it yet. The hardships I faced weren't for nothing— they were shaping me in ways I didn't yet comprehend. They were building a foundation of resilience and faith that would one day carry me through even greater challenges. I began to realize that the trials I endured weren't meant to break me but to refine me. The Bible says, "Consider it pure joy, my brothers and sisters, whenever you face trials of many kinds, because you know that the testing of your faith produces perseverance" (James 1:2-3). I didn't fully grasp it then, but every tear, every moment of heartache, was teaching me how to persevere. I was learning that faith isn't about having a perfect life: it's about trusting God even when life feels anything but perfect. There were days when I wanted to give up, when the weight of my circumstances felt too heavy to bear. But in those moments, I found myself turning to God in prayer. Even when I didn't have the words, I would cry out, trusting that He understood my pain. The Bible says, "In the same way, the Spirit helps us in our weakness. We do not know what we ought to pray for, but the Spirit himself intercedes for us through wordless groans" (Romans 8:26). This became my comfort—that God knew my heart even when I couldn't find the right words to express what I was feeling. While my life was still filled with pain, I held onto the hope that God's purpose for me was greater than my suffering. I began to see that even though my earthly family might have rejected me, my Heavenly Father never would. He had been with me in the darkest moments, sustaining me when I felt like I couldn't go on. The Bible says, "The Lord is close to the brokenhearted and saves those who are crushed in spirit" (Psalms 34:18). These words became a lifeline for me, a reminder that I wasn't alone. Looking back now, I see that those painful experiences were not wasted. They taught me how to rely on God, how to find strength in Him when I felt weak. They helped me understand that true strength doesn't come from our circumstances but from our faith in the One who holds all things together. The Bible reminds us, "And we know that in all things God works for the good of those who love him, who have been called according to his purpose" (Romans 8:28). Though I didn't understand it at the time, God was working behind the scenes, preparing me for something greater. I clung to the belief that my story wasn't over, that God had a greater purpose for my life beyond the pain I was experiencing. And with each passing day, I took small steps forward, trusting that He was guiding me toward something better. Though the road ahead was uncertain, I knew one thing for sure—I wouldn't walk it alone. God was with me, and that gave me the strength to keep going

CHAPTER

2

# GROUP HOME AND
# FOSTER CARE TRAUMA

*Lord, you are my God; I will exalt you and praise your name,*

*for in perfect faithfulness you have done wonderful things, things*

*planned long ago. (Isaiah 25:1)*

## A Cycle of Rejection

I was placed back in foster care because my family didn't want to care for me after I left the hospital. The rejection stung deeply, leaving me with a sense of unworthiness that I couldn't shake. It felt like I was being punished, not just for my behavior, but for existing. The pain of being abandoned by the people who were supposed to love me created a wound that seemed impossible to heal. Moving from one foster home to another only amplified my instability, reinforcing the belief that

I wasn't wanted anywhere. At every home, I faced mistreatment or misunderstanding. Many foster parents didn't know how to handle a child carrying so much trauma. They saw my outbursts as defiance, not realizing they were cries for help from a heart that had endured more pain than it could bear. They didn't understand my pain, my loss, or the turmoil within me. When I acted out, they would call my caseworker and demand that I be moved to another home. I felt like an unwanted package being passed around with no real destination or purpose. The Bible says, *"Though my father and mother forsake me, the Lord will receive me"* (Psalms 27:10). At the time, it was hard to believe that anyone could receive me with open arms, let alone God. I felt invisible misunderstood by the foster families and forgotten by my own. Yet, looking back, I can see that God's hand was quietly guiding me through each transition, keeping me from completely falling apart There were fleeting moments when I encountered kindness—small glimpses of hope in an otherwise bleak situation. A kind word from a foster sibling or a moment of compassion from a foster parent gave me brief relief, but they were rare. Most days, I felt like I was on my own, constantly bracing for the next rejection, the next call to my case worker, the next move to a different house. The cycle seemed endless, and I started to wonder if I would ever find a place where I truly belonged. The Bible promises, *"He heals the brokenhearted and binds up their wounds"* (Psalms 147:3). Though I didn't realize it then, God was beginning to work on my heart, slowly binding the wounds that rejection had left behind. Every home, every painful experience, was shaping me in ways I couldn't understand at the time. He was preparing me for a future where I would find my worth not in people's acceptance, but in His unfailing love. As I moved from place to place, I started to build a kind of resilience. It wasn't easy, and it didn't take away the pain, but it gave me a reason to keep going. I began to hold onto a faint hope that maybe, just maybe, one day I would find a place where I was truly wanted, where I could experience the love and stability I longed for. Until then, I held onto the only thing I could—survival. Despite the constant upheaval, I began to develop an inner strength. The Bible reminds us, *"The Lord is my strength and my shield; my heart trusts in him, and he helps me"* (Psalms 28:7). Though my circumstances were difficult, something inside me kept pushing forward. I didn't know it then, but that strength wasn't my own—it was God carrying me through, sustaining me when I felt like giving up.

## A Glimmer of Hope

Eventually, I was placed with a kind-hearted woman who welcomed me with open arms. She accepted me for who I was, flaws and all. In a world where I had often felt like an outcast, her acceptance was like a balm for my weary soul. For the first time in a long while, I felt valued—not because I had to prove my worth, but simply because I existed. Her home became a refuge where I could breathe, a place where I didn't have to be on guard every moment. She had two daughters, and I connected deeply with one of them. We bonded quickly, sharing laughter, late-night talks, and little moments that brought me peace amidst the chaos of my life. For a brief time, I felt like I belonged. It wasn't just a house, it began to feel like a home. That sense of belonging, however fleeting, was something I had longed for without even realizing it. But life has a way of shaking us awake just when we're beginning to dream again. The news of my grandmother's death arrived, bringing with it a flood of complicated emotions. She had succumbed to cancer, and while others might expect grief, I felt relief. That might sound cold to some, but for me, her memory was stained with pain and harshness. The relationship I had with her was not one that evoked fond memories or tender moments, it was one marked by survival, by enduring rather than enjoying. I couldn't muster sorrow for the loss. Instead, I wrestled with guilt over my relief, wondering if that made me a bad person. Was I wrong for feeling this way? The weight of those questions sat heavy on my heart, and for a while, they consumed me. The Bible says, *"Put up with each other, forgive one another if you are holding something against someone. Forgive, just as the Lord forgave you"* (Colossians 3:13). But forgiveness was a journey I hadn't yet started. How do you forgive someone who never asked for forgiveness? How do you let go of pain that shaped so much of who you are? I knew that forgiveness was more for my healing than for her, but that knowledge didn't make the process easier. It felt like climbing a mountain barefoot—every step was painful, and I wasn't even sure where the top was. Yet, something within me whispered that this was a journey I couldn't avoid forever

## The Group Home Nightmare

When it was time to leave that foster home, my heart broke in ways I hadn't thought possible. Saying goodbye to the one person who truly understood me felt like having my fragile sense of stability ripped away. I wasn't just losing a home, I was losing a safe space, a rare connection that had given me hope amidst the chaos. Once again, I was thrust into the unknown, forced to start over in a new environment. This time, it was a group home—a place that promised structure, safety, and healing but instead delivered a harsh reality of survival. The initial days were jarring. I had hoped for a sense of stability, but it quickly became clear that this wasn't the sanctuary I had imagined. The staff, though present physically, seemed distant emotionally. Their interactions felt robotic, as if we were mere tasks on a checklist. Motivated by their paychecks rather than genuine compassion, they rarely offered the care or support we desperately needed. Our stories didn't matter; we were just another set of case files to manage until their shifts ended. It didn't take long for me to realize that I couldn't rely on anyone but myself. The other girls in the home were hardened by their own trauma, each carrying emotional scars that shaped how they interacted with the world. Instead of drawing strength from shared struggles, jealousy and envy fueled tension among us. Friendships were rare and fragile. Every day felt like a new battlefield—fights broke out regularly, and I often found myself caught in the middle of conflicts I didn't start but couldn't avoid. Survival here wasn't just physical; it was emotional and mental, too. Every moment was a test of endurance, a relentless challenge to see how much I could endure before finally breaking. *"Even though I walk through the darkest valley, I will not be afraid. You are with me. Your shepherd's rod and staff comfort me"* (Psalms 23:4). I had memorized this verse long ago, but in those moments, it felt hollow. I struggled to feel God's presence in a place so devoid of peace and safety. I wanted to believe He was there, watching over me, but it was hard to feel comforted when every day brought new battles and fresh wounds. My heart grew heavy with anger—anger at my family for putting me here, anger at the world for being so cruel, and anger at God for allowing it all to happen at night, I would lie awake in the darkness, staring at the ceiling and wondering if life would ever get better. Loneliness wrapped around me like a heavy blanket, suffocating me with despair. I missed having someone to talk to, someone who genuinely cared about me as a person. Yet, even in those moments of overwhelming isolation, a small voice deep within whispered that I wasn't truly alone. I didn't fully understand it then, but that voice was God, gently reminding me that He was still with me—even when I couldn't feel His presence. One particularly rough day, after an altercation that left me feeling defeated, I retreated to a quiet corner of the room and cried silently. In that moment, I felt utterly broken. But as the tears fell, I remembered another verse: *"The Lord is close to the brokenhearted and saves those who are crushed in spirit"* (Psalms 34:18). It didn't erase the pain, but it gave me a flicker of hope—a reminder that maybe, just maybe, there was a greater purpose to all of this suffering. Despite the harsh environment, something remarkable began to happen. Slowly, I started to develop a resilience I hadn't known I possessed. Each day I survived in that group home became proof that I was stronger than I had ever believed. Without realizing it, I was learning how to fight—not just for survival, but for my identity and my future. Looking back now, I can see that God's hand was guiding me, even when it felt like everything was falling apart. He was molding me, preparing me for something greater. I didn't understand it at the time, but I held on to a fragile hope that one day, I would. That group home experience, as painful as it was, taught me invaluable lessons. It forced me to depend on God in ways I hadn't before, and it gave me a testimony to share with others who might feel trapped in their own dark walls. What once felt like an ending became a chapter in a greater story—one of faith, strength, and redemption. *"And we know that in all things God works for the good of those who love Him, who have been called according to His purpose"* (Romans 8:28). I couldn't see it then, but now I understand that even in that difficult season, God was working for my good. He was shaping me, strengthening me, and preparing me for the purpose He had in store.

## The Weight of Isolation

I wanted to escape, but I couldn't. I wasn't old enough to make my own decisions, and no one seemed to care about my wishes. Every day in the group home felt like a battle for survival. The environment was tense, and every interaction felt like walking on eggshells. The staff, instead of offering support, often took sides in conflicts, which only deepened the divisions among us. Rather than mediating, they became part of the problem, fueling tension and mistrust. Trust was a fragile commodity, and in that kind of atmosphere, it was almost impossible to feel safe. I longed for connection, yet it was hard to build meaningful relationships in a place where everyone was fighting their own battles. Friendships were fleeting, built on convenience rather than trust. Loyalties shifted quickly, like sand beneath my feet. One day, someone would sit next to me during meals, and the next, they'd avoid me, swept up in a new wave of drama or conflict. It left me feeling isolated, uncertain of where I stood with anyone. When I transitioned to another group home, I clung to the hope that things might improve—that maybe, in a new environment, I'd finally find the connection I so desperately needed. But that hope quickly faded. The experience was just as isolating, if not worse. The faces were different, but the struggles remained the same. I found myself in unfamiliar surroundings, facing new challenges with no sense of support. I wasn't allowed to call my family, and that severed connection broke me in ways I couldn't articulate. The absence of their presence, even if imperfect, left me feeling utterly abandoned, like I had been thrown away and forgotten. The Bible says, *"The Lord is near to the brokenhearted and saves the crushed in spirit"* (Psalms 34:18). I wanted to believe those words, to trust that God was near, but in those moments, it was hard to feel His presence. The weight of isolation pressed down on me heavily, making it difficult to hold on to hope. I felt trapped in a cycle of rejection, where no matter how hard I tried,

I couldn't escape the loneliness that surrounded me. Night after night, I lay awake in bed, staring into the darkness and wondering what life would be like if I had someone who genuinely cared. The silence of the night amplified my thoughts, and with each passing hour, the ache in my heart grew heavier. I longed for a sense of belonging, for someone to tell me that I mattered, that I wasn't invisible. Looking back, I realize that even in those moments of deep despair, God was with me. Though I couldn't feel His presence then, He was sustaining me, quietly giving me the strength to endure each day. I didn't know it, but He was carrying me through every moment of isolation, holding me together when I felt like falling apart. The Bible reminds us, *"Even to your old age and gray hairs I am He, I am He who will sustain you. I have made you, and I will carry you; I will sustain you and rescue you"* (Isaiah 46:4). He was carrying me through those dark days, even when it felt like I was utterly alone. Over time, I began to see that my story wasn't over. Yes, I was isolated, but I was also being prepared. God was building something in me—resilience, endurance, faith. He was teaching me how to navigate life's hardships with strength and courage. It wasn't easy, but it was necessary. Every lonely night, every tear shed in silence, was shaping me into someone stronger than I ever thought I could be.In the midst of that isolation, I learned how to rely on God in ways I never had before. Though I didn't fully understand it then, He was working behind the scenes, preparing me for something greater. Those days were painful, but they weren't wasted. They became part of the testimony I now carry, a story of strength, hope, and faith in a God who never abandons His children—even when they can't feel His presence.

## A Self-Destructive Pattern

As I moved from group home to group home, my behavior became increasingly erratic. I was angry, hurt, and overwhelmed by a deep sense of abandonment. Each new placement felt like a temporary stop where I was tolerated rather than wanted. I began to act out, almost as if I was daring those around me to reject me. Deep down, I wanted to prove to myself that love and acceptance were never meant for someone like me. It was easier to believe that lie than to hope for something that constantly eluded me. In my mind, if they felt even a fraction of the pain I carried, maybe they would understand what it was like to feel unloved and misunderstood. But no one saw beyond my outbursts; they only saw a rebellious, difficult child. I didn't know how to process my emotions in a healthy way, so I channeled my anger into rebellion. I rejected authority, pushed boundaries, and often landed in trouble. At times, I convinced myself that I didn't need anyone—that being alone was better than facing more disappointment. But the truth was, I longed for someone to see past my behavior, to see the broken child behind the anger and reach out with patience and love. The Bible teaches, *"Whoever spares the rod hates his son, but he who loves him is diligent to discipline him"* (Proverbs 13:24). Discipline, when rooted in love, can guide and heal. But what I experienced was far from that. The kind of discipline I received came without compassion—it was punishment devoid of empathy, correction without understanding. What I truly needed wasn't stricter rules or harsher consequences; I needed someone to listen, someone to offer guidance and care. Every time I was moved to another group home, it felt like confirmation that I wasn't worth the effort. Instead of helping me heal, the constant upheaval only deepened my wounds. Each move reinforced the lie that if no one cared enough to stay, maybe I wasn't worthy of love at all. But even in my darkest moments, God never abandoned me. Though I couldn't see it at the time, His hand was on my life, protecting me from situations that could have ended far worse. *"The Lord is close to the brokenhearted and saves those who are crushed in spirit"* (Psalms 34:18). Looking back, I can see that God was working behind the scenes, preparing me for something greater. Every painful experience was shaping me, building resilience, endurance, and a deeper understanding of what it means to rely on Him. Despite my destructive behavior, a small part of me still clung to hope that one day, things could be different. That one day, I would find a place where I truly belonged, where I could finally feel safe and loved. Until that day came, I carried my burdens alone, unaware that God was walking with me every step of the way

## Keeping Up Appearances

Despite the mistreatment and instability, I worked hard to present myself as put together. I was determined not to let my circumstances define how I appeared to the world. On the outside, I seemed confident and polished—my hair always neat, my clothes clean, my posture upright. But inside, I was crumbling under the weight of rejection, loneliness, and the persistent feeling of being unloved and unseen. Maintaining this facade became a survival mechanism. I believed that if I looked okay on the outside, maybe people wouldn't notice the brokenness within. Maybe they wouldn't see how fragile I felt. But this outward effort often backfired. Instead of understanding, I was met with disbelief and judgment. People assumed that because I appeared put together, I couldn't possibly be struggling. They couldn't comprehend that behind the neat exterior was a heart burdened by pain. The Bible reminds us, *"For the Lord sees not as man sees man looks on the outward appearance, but the Lord looks on the heart"*

(1 Samuel 16:7). I clung to this verse, knowing that while people might judge me by what they saw, God saw my heart—my pain, my effort, and my desire to find peace amidst the chaos. The constant judgment only deepened my sense of isolation. How could anyone understand what I was going through if they didn't believe me? Their inability to see past my polished exterior made me feel even more invisible. I often thought to myself, *if they only knew how much strength it takes to smile through the pain, they wouldn't be so quick to judge.* Still, I kept going. I worked harder to present an image of someone who had it together because admitting how broken I truly felt too vulnerable. I wanted people to see me as resilient, even when I felt anything but. What I didn't realize then was that this journey wasn't just about appearances, it was about finding real strength. Little did I know, God was teaching me that true strength isn't about hiding your pain—it's about leaning into Him. *"So do not fear, for I am with you; do not be dismayed, for I am your God. I will strengthen you and help you; I will uphold you with my righteous right hand"* (Isaiah 41:10). Though I couldn't see it at the time, God was holding me up through every battle, every judgmental glance, and every silent tear I cried when no one was watching. I kept up appearances because I was afraid of what would happen if I didn't. But over time, I began to learn that I didn't have to carry that burden alone. God was with me, and though the world might judge me by what they saw on the outside, He knew the truth of my heart. And in His eyes, that was enough.

## Strength in Adversity

Through every challenge, I clung to the belief that there was more to life than what I was enduring. The pain of the group homes, the rejection from my family, and the instability of foster care were shaping me in ways I didn't yet understand. Each hardship felt like a weight pressing down on my soul, yet somehow, I kept moving forward. There were moments when I wanted to give up, but something deep inside whispered that this wasn't the end—that there was purpose in my pain. The Bible reminds us, *"The righteous has enough to satisfy his appetite, but the belly of the wicked suffers"* (Proverbs 13:25). At first, I didn't fully grasp the meaning of this verse, but over time, I began to see that my suffering was not in vain. It was building a resilient and strength that would carry me through future storms. Though I couldn't see it then, God was preparing me for battles ahead, fortifying my spirit through every trial.

## Unfair Accusations and Betrayal

The group home environment was toxic for me. The girls and staff often singled me out, not because I had done anything wrong, but because I stood out in ways they didn't understand. My fashion sense, my self-presentation, and the confidence I tried to exude—despite my inner turmoil—made me a target. It seemed that no matter how hard I tried to blend in, jealousy and disdain followed me everywhere. I desperately wanted to fit in, to be accepted, but instead, I was met with rejection and hostility at every turn. Even when I tried to form meaningful connections, I found myself let down time and time again. One such relationship was with a staff member I called my godmother. For a brief moment, I thought I had found someone who truly cared—someone who could offer me the guidance and comfort I so desperately needed. I trusted her, allowed myself to hope, but that hope was shattered when she betrayed me. Her betrayal left a scar deeper than I realized at the time. It reinforced the belief that no one could be trusted and that the support I craved was elusive. With each disappointment, the walls around my heart grew higher, and I retreated further into myself, protecting what little remained of my fragile sense of worth. Things took a dramatic and painful turn when I was falsely accused of vandalizing a staff member's car. The accusations came out of nowhere, blindsiding me. I was bewildered, panicked, and confused—why would someone frame me for something I hadn't done? Fear gripped me as the reality of the situation set in. I knew that no one would believe me. In a place where my reputation was already tarnished by misunderstanding and prejudice, it felt like the final blow. No one from the home came to my defense. It was as though they had already decided who I was—a troubled girl, a problem to be managed, someone who didn't belong. That night, as I lay in bed, trying to calm my racing thoughts, a loud knock at the door startled me. My heart pounded in my chest as I got up to answer, and standing on the other side were the police. They had come to arrest me based on those fabricated claims. I felt betrayed in the deepest way possible. How could the very people who were supposed to protect and care for me, the ones who had seen my struggles firsthand, turn their backs on me without question? The betrayal cut deeper than any punishment ever could. It wasn't just about the false accusations—it was about being utterly abandoned in a moment when I needed someone the most. I felt like I was drowning in a sea of injustice, with no one willing to throw me a lifeline. The Bible says, *"I trust in you, Lord. I say you are my God. My whole life is in your hands. Save me from the hands of my enemies. Save me from those who are chasing me"* (Psalms 31:14-15). That verse became my lifeline. In that moment, all I had was my faith. Climbing to this promise, I tried to remain strong, though my heart was heavy, and my spirit felt crushed. I prayed silently, asking God to protect me, to guide me through yet another storm. Though I didn't understand it at the time, God was using this experience to strengthen me. The rejection, the false accusations, and the betrayal were all part of a greater plan. He was shaping me into someone who would one day rise above the pain, someone who could testify to His power and grace. It was during those moments of feeling completely alone that I began to realize I wasn't truly by myself. Even when no one on earth stood up for me, God was with me. He saw my heart, He knew the truth, and He held me close when the world turned its back on me. Though I didn't yet have the strength to fully understand it, He was planting seeds of resilience and faith within me. Seeds that would one day grow into a powerful testimony of hope, survival, and trust in Him.

## A Moment of Fear, A Glimpse of Hope

I felt my whole world crashing down as I got into the car. In my head, I was thinking: *How am I going to survive in there?* I had seen how they treat people, and I didn't want to go—but I knew I had to. Tears flowed down my face as I felt completely alone, with nobody to call on and no one who had my best interest at heart. It seemed like everyone wanted to see me fail. The Bible says, *"Give me understanding, so that I may keep your law and obey it with all my heart"* (Psalms 119:34). In that moment, I prayed for understanding, for strength to endure what lay ahead. Despite the fear and pain, I clung to the hope that God could still be with me, even in the darkest of places. When we arrived at DeKalb County Jail, my heart felt heavy with shame and worry. I was placed in a holding cell with other women. Looking around, I felt terrified. Their faces seemed hardened by life, and their presence only heightened my anxiety. Someone asked me what I did to end up there. I could barely find the words to explain—I hadn't done anything. I was being blamed for something I didn't do. As I spoke, my heart pounded, and I felt my anxiety take hold. The Bible offers reassurance in moments like this: *"Don't let your hearts be troubled. Trust in God, and trust also in me"* (John 14:1). But it was hard to hold on to that promise when fear surrounded me. Questions swirled in my mind: *Why did these people do this to me? Who would save me from this nightmare?* All I could think about were the horrible things I had seen on TV about life in jail. I didn't want to face that alone. I was the youngest in the cell, and being diabetic only made things worse. I needed to eat, but the food they served looked terrible. I couldn't bring myself to eat any of it, and the thought of staying there any longer was unbearable. I wouldn't wish this experience on my worst enemy. Yet, even in that dark place, I remembered another promise from Scripture: *"Praise be to the God and Father of our Lord Jesus Christ, the Father of compassion and the God of all comfort"* (2 Corinthians 1:3). In my despair, I longed for comfort and a way out. Then came the moment when we were allowed to make one phone call. My cousin immediately came to mind, and I didn't hesitate to dial her number. When she answered, I felt an overwhelming sense of relief. She listened, offering me guidance and encouragement.

In that moment, her words felt like a lifeline, pulling me out of the depths of despair. The Bible reminds us, *"Come to me, all you who are weary and burdened, and I will give you rest"* (Matthew 11:28). Though I was still weary, that phone call gave me a flicker of hope—that maybe I wasn't as alone as I thought. Before long, I was given a signature bond, and I was finally allowed to leave. The relief I felt was indescribable. My cousin came to pick me up, and as I got into her car, joy replaced the fear that had gripped me for so long. She dropped me off at the group home, a place I didn't want to return to. I hated being there, surrounded by people I couldn't trust. To me, they all seemed evil. I was relieved when I was assigned a room by myself. After sharing a room before going to jail, being alone felt like a blessing. I wanted nothing more than to keep to myself. Trusting people wasn't an option anymore. One day, something told me to check the mail. When I did, I was surprised to find an envelope with my name on it. I hurried to my room, opened it, and stared in disbelief—it was a large check from SSI. I had never received that much money before. As I held the check in my hands, I felt a surge of gratitude. It was everything I needed at that moment, a sign that perhaps things were finally turning around. With my 18th birthday approaching, I knew I would soon age out of the system, and this money felt like a fresh start—a glimmer of hope in what had been a long, dark journey.

## Cheers to 18: A New Beginning

I didn't tell anyone much—I was just ready to leave. The thought of finally being free from the group home filled me with excitement and anticipation. After everything I had endured, the idea of stepping out into the world felt like a new beginning, a chance to start over. I approached the staff and informed them that I would be leaving when I turned 18. They gave me the necessary paperwork, and I wasted no time filling it out. It felt so real at that moment, like freedom was just within reach. I counted down the days, unable to contain my excitement. I couldn't stop thinking about what it would feel like to finally leave. Every night, I went to bed happy, and every morning, I woke up even happier. It was as if I could already taste the freedom I had longed for. I imagined what it would be like to live on my own, to make decisions without anyone hovering over me or dictating my life. I had endured so much, and this felt like the reward at the end of a long, hard journey. During that time, I had been talking to a guy I met through one of my group home friends—her brother. We started talking before I got locked up, and somehow, those conversations became a source of comfort for me. It wasn't just about having someone to talk to; it was about feeling seen, feeling like someone cared. Even though my world had been filled with uncertainty and pain, his presence brought me moments of joy. The Bible says, *"The Lord is my strength and shield. I trust him with all my heart. He helps me, and my heart is filled with joy. I burst out in songs of thanksgiving"* (Psalms 28:7). Despite the challenges I faced, that verse reminded me to trust God, who had been my strength through it all. Those moments of joy weren't by accident; they were glimpses of His love and grace, even in the hardest times. Finally, the day came—I turned 18. Cheers to 18! I was officially an adult, and I felt ready to take on the world. I couldn't wait to experience life on my own terms. For the first time, I had the power to make my own choices, and that freedom was exhilarating. I thought, *I don't have to listen to anyone anymore. I'm free.* I was determined to build a life where I didn't have to rely on anyone who didn't truly care about me. The Bible says, *"Because your faith is much too small. What I'm about to tell you is true. If you have faith as small as a mustard seed, it is enough. You can say to this mountain, 'Move from here to there,' and it will move. Nothing will be impossible for you"* (Matthew 17:20). That verse resonated deeply with me. I didn't know what the future held, but I believed that with even a little faith, I could overcome any obstacle. Life had already thrown so much at me, but I was still standing. I trusted that God had a plan for my life, even if I didn't fully understand it yet. But beneath all the excitement, there was still a lingering emptiness that I couldn't shake. No matter how much I tried to distract myself, the longing for a mother's love weighed heavily on my heart. I wanted a mom so badly. I would see people spending time with their mothers—laughing, hugging, sharing special moments—and each time, it felt like a knife to my soul. I wanted that so much. I wanted a mom to hold me when I felt overwhelmed, to celebrate with me on special days, to simply be there when life felt too heavy to bear alone. On Mother's Day, I felt the weight of that longing even more. While others celebrated with their moms, I felt like an outsider looking in. I carried anger and bitterness because I didn't have what they had. I wanted someone to pour love into me, to care for me the way a mother should. That absence left a hole in my heart that nothing seemed to fill. I hated everyone because I didn't have my mom. I hated the world for giving others what I so desperately longed for. Looking back now, I realize that even though I didn't have my mother, God was always there, quietly filling the void in ways I couldn't see at the time. He saw my brokenness, my longing, and my pain. He was the Father who never left, the one who carried me through every storm. The Bible says, *"Even to your old age and gray hairs I am He, I am He who will sustain you. I have made you, and I will carry you; I will sustain you and rescue you"* (Isaiah 46:4). Though I didn't understand it then, He was sustaining me, giving me the strength to endure and the faith to keep moving forward. This new chapter of life was just beginning, and though I carried the scars of my past, I also carried hope. Hope that one day, I will find the love and belonging I longed for. Hope that God would continue to guide me, even when I didn't know where I was going. And most importantly, hope that my story wasn't over—that this was just the beginning of something far greater than I could imagine.

CHAPTER

# EMOTIONAL
# HEARTBREAK

*But while I "This is my command—be strong and courageous!*
*Do not be afraid or discouraged. For the Lord your God is with*
*you wherever you go" (Joshua 1:9).*

## A Step into the Unknown

T his is my command—be strong and courageous! Do not be afraid
or discouraged. For the Lord your God is with you wherever you
go" (Joshua 1:9). As I left, a wave of emotions swept
over me—excitement, nervousness, and the weight of stepping
into the unknown. For years, I had dreamed about what it would
feel like to finally be free from the restrictions of the group
home, and now that moment had arrived. There were no more
staff watching my every move or rules dictating every part of

EVIL LOST, BUT HER DESTINY WON!

my day. For the first time, I was in control of my life, and that freedom was exhilarating. The first thing I did was call my guy friend. With excitement in my voice, I told him, *"I'm free! I'm ready to come stay with you until I find a place of my own."* He told me that he was currently staying with his brother and that we would both be staying there for a while. Without hesitation, I told him that it was fine. At that moment, I was just happy to have a plan, a place to stay, and someone I could turn to as I navigated this new chapter of my life. For the first few days, things felt great. Life finally seemed easier, there was no one hovering over me or reminding me of all the things I needed to do. I felt free to live life on my own terms. But even in the midst of that newfound freedom, there was a quiet unease that I couldn't shake. Freedom felt good, but it didn't erase the emotional scars I carried. I wanted so badly for this new chapter to be different, for it to finally bring me peace and happiness. But deep down, I still felt broken. Years of feeling abandoned, rejected, and unloved had taken a toll on me, and those emotions didn't disappear just because my circumstances changed. The Bible says, *"Come to me, all you who are weary and burdened, and I will give you rest"* (Matthew 11:28). At the time, I didn't fully understand what it meant to find rest in God, but I knew that I was weary. My soul was tired, weighed down by years of longing for something I couldn't quite find. I wanted to feel whole, to finally experience the love and stability

I had craved for so long. I hoped that maybe, just maybe, this new chapter would bring me what I had been missing. Looking back now, I see that God was with me, even in those uncertain moments. He didn't leave me to face the unknown alone. Instead, He was guiding me—quietly and steadily—through every fear, every doubt, and every emotional storm. The Bible reminds us, *"The Lord is near to the brokenhearted and saves those who are crushed in spirit"* (Psalms 34:18). Even when I couldn't feel His presence, He was there, offering comfort and strength when I needed it most. Though I didn't realize it then, God was teaching me that true freedom doesn't come from external changes—it comes from allowing Him to heal the broken places in my heart. The journey wasn't easy, and it wasn't quick, but every step I took was part of a greater purpose. He was preparing me for something more, shaping me into someone who could rise above the pain and one day share a testimony of hope. This step into the unknown wasn't just about physical freedom, it was the beginning of an emotional and spiritual journey. A journey that taught me to be strong and courageous, even when life felt overwhelming. And though I didn't fully understand it at the time, God was walking beside me, reminding me that I didn't have to face the unknown alone.

## When Love Turns Cold

We all got along well, and for a while, things seemed perfect. Everyone was in good spirits, and life felt like it was finally coming together. But then, in the blink of an eye, everything changed. My boyfriend, who had once been kind and loving, began to act differently. His attitude and demeanor shifted, and he started acting distant and strange. I had never seen him behave this way before. He became unruly and cruel, picking fights with me over the smallest things. We would argue constantly, often about things that didn't even matter. I tried to make sense of it, replaying moments in my head, wondering what I had done wrong. I didn't understand why he was treating me this way when all I had ever done was the best girlfriend I could be. Feeling hurt and down, I decided to give him space, hoping things would improve. But even after giving him room to breathe, nothing changed. He would come back into the house with the same cold attitude, and no matter how hard I tried, I couldn't figure out why this was happening to our relationship. During this time, I began feeling unwell. At first, I thought it might be my diabetes acting up, so I decided to go to the doctor. What I learned there caught me completely off guard—the doctor told me I was pregnant. I was in shock, but beneath the surprise, I felt a spark of happiness. This was going to be my first child, and despite everything going on, I wanted to believe this was a blessing. I rushed home, eager to share the news with my boyfriend. When I told him I was pregnant, he seemed happy, but something was still off. His behavior didn't change. Days went by, and instead of us growing closer during this special time, the arguments only got worse. Everything was going downhill, and I was left feeling confused, hurt, and isolated. One night, as we sat together in the room, I couldn't hold back any longer. I was tired of the fights, tired of feeling unloved and unwanted. I asked him directly, *"Are you cheating on me?"* I had found out that he was talking to someone else, and though I didn't want to believe it, I needed to hear the truth from him. In that moment, I felt a storm of emotions—fear, sadness, anger, and disappointment. This wasn't how I imagined things would go. I had hoped that starting a family together would bring us closer, but instead, it felt like everything was falling apart. The weight of uncertainty and emotional heartbreak was crushing, and I didn't know what to do next. The Bible says, *"The Lord is close to the brokenhearted and saves those who are crushed in spirit"* (Psalms 34:18). Even though I felt abandoned and alone, I clung to the hope that God saw my pain. I didn't have all the answers, but I trusted that He was near, offering comfort and strength in my weakest moments. Looking back, I realize that this difficult time wasn't meant to break me—it was meant to build me. God was using these trials to teach me resilience and to prepare me for the road ahead. The Bible reminds us in *Isaiah 41:10, "So do not fear, for I am with you; do not be dismayed, for I am your God. I will strengthen you and help you; I will uphold you with my righteous right hand."* Even when it felt like the ground beneath me was crumbling, God was holding me up, giving me the strength to keep going. Though this season of my life was painful, it taught me an important lesson: no matter how dark things get, God's light is always present. He doesn't abandon us in our heartbreak—He walks beside us, guiding us toward healing and hope. I didn't fully understand it then, but I was never truly alone. And though this chapter was filled with sorrow, it became part of a greater story—a story of survival, faith, and ultimately, redemption.

## Broken Trust and Shattered Hearts

He looked at me with a confused expression, as if he didn't know what I was talking about. But I wasn't about to back down—I needed answers. I asked him again, *"Are you cheating on me?"* Instead of responding, he did something I never imagined he would do. He pushed me, and I fell forward onto my stomach. In that moment, disbelief washed over me. How could someone I loved so much someone I trusted with my heart, do something so cruel? And to make it worse, I was carrying his child. The pain wasn't just physical—it cut straight to my soul. We continued to argue, but I was too hurt to make sense of anything. I asked him why he had done it, why he would hurt me like that. He had no answer—nothing to say that could explain or justify his actions. The next day, I couldn't stop replaying the moment in my mind. I kept asking myself, *why would someone I loved so deeply want to hurt me so badly?* I was heartbroken, not just because of what he had done, but because it shattered the dreams I had for our future. I had envisioned us building a life together, raising our child in love, and now that dream felt like it was slipping through my fingers. In my pain, I did the only thing I could think of, I reached out to my cousin. I called her and told her what had happened. I explained that I needed to get away, even if just for a little while. Without hesitation, she said I could come, and I felt a wave of gratitude. In that moment, knowing I had someone to turn to give me a flicker of hope. The Bible says, *"Praise the Lord, my soul; all my inmost being, praise his holy name. Praise the Lord, my soul, and forget not all his benefits—who forgives all your sins and heals all your diseases, who redeems your life from the pit and crowns you with love and compassion, who satisfies your desires with good things so that your youth is renewed like the eagle's"* (Psalms 103:1-5). Even though I was heartbroken, I reminded myself to trust in God's ability to redeem and heal. I didn't know how He would do it, but I clung to the belief that He could take my brokenness and turn it into something beautiful.

When I arrived at my cousin's house, I tried to push the pain aside and focus on finding a moment of peace. But soon after I got there, something happened that shook me to my core. I went to the bathroom, and when I looked down, I saw blood in the toilet. My heart sank. Panic set in as I thought, *I'm pregnant. Why am I bleeding?* Fear gripped me. I knew I couldn't ignore this. Being diabetic already made my pregnancy high-risk, and now I was bleeding. I didn't want to think the worst, but I couldn't help but worry about what was happening to my baby. Without wasting any time, I rushed to the hospital. I needed answers, and more than anything, I needed reassurance that my child was okay. As I sat in the hospital waiting room, I felt completely overwhelmed. The fear of losing my baby, combined with the heartbreak I was already feeling, was almost too much to bear. But even in that moment, I whispered a prayer. I didn't have the words to express everything I was feeling, but I knew God heard the cry of my heart. The Bible reminds us in *Philippians 4:6-7*, *"Do not be anxious about anything, but in every situation, by prayer and petition, with thanksgiving, present your requests to God. And the peace of God, which transcends all understanding, will guard your hearts and your minds in Christ Jesus.* I didn't feel peace immediately, but I trusted that God was with me. He had carried me through so many storms before, and I believed He wouldn't abandon me now. Even though I was scared, I tried to hold on to the promise that He was near, that He saw my pain, and that somehow, He would make a way through this. This experience taught me that life doesn't always go the way we plan, but God remains faithful. Even when trust is broken, hearts are shattered, and fear overwhelms us, He is still present, offering strength and comfort. I didn't know what the outcome would be, but I knew that whatever happened, God would walk with me through it all.

## Loss, Healing, and Crossroads

I needed to see what was going on with my baby and with me. Fear gripped me as I walked into the hospital, my heart racing with anxious thoughts. I tried to prepare myself for the worst, but no amount of preparation could have softened the blow. As I sat in the cold hospital room, waiting for answers, my mind spiraled with fear. Finally, the doctor came in and delivered the news—*I had experienced a spontaneous miscarriage*. My heart dropped, and for a moment, it felt like time stood still. I didn't know how to process what I was hearing. This was my child, my baby, and now they were gone. Why? Why not my baby? Tears streamed down my face as I struggled to grasp the reality of what had just happened. I felt empty, broken, and overwhelmed by a wave of emotions I wasn't prepared for. Anger quickly followed my grief. I felt like I needed someone to blame, and all I could think about was him—my boyfriend. His constant stress, his coldness, and the way he hurt me had weighed heavily on my heart during this pregnancy. I wanted revenge. I wanted him to feel the pain I was feeling because, in my mind, his actions had caused me to lose my baby. It was disappointing and devastating that someone I loved so much had been incapable of offering me even the smallest amount of support during such a crucial time.as the anger faded, guilt crept in. I began blaming myself, wondering if somehow it was my fault. Had I done something wrong? Had I not been strong enough to protect my baby? These questions haunted me as I faced the painful truth—I had lost my child, and there was nothing I could do to change that. The midst of my pain, my brother came to support me. His presence was a small comfort in an otherwise dark moment. I was grateful for him. He helped ease the burden I was carrying, even if just for a little while. The Bible says, *"I call out to the Lord when I'm in trouble, and He will answer me"* (Psalms 120:1). Though I was drowning in sorrow, I whispered a prayer, hoping God would hear my cry and bring me peace. I decided to stay with my cousin for a while. I needed something new, something that didn't remind me of the heartbreak I had just endured. I wanted a fresh start, a chance to rebuild my life. With renewed determination, I went back to school, hoping to finish my classes and earn my diploma. After everything I had been through, I knew I had to make a change.

First, things seemed clear. I had a plan—I would finish 12th grade, get my diploma, and take steps toward a better future. For a moment, life felt manageable. I was determined to stay on track and see it through. But as time went on, distractions crept in. I started talking to one of the guys who had been in the same group home program as me. What started as casual conversations quickly turned into something more. I found myself drawn to him, and before I knew it, my focus shifted entirely. Instead of keeping my eyes on my goal of finishing school, I became consumed with him. My mind wasn't on my future anymore, it was on him. He talked me into leaving my cousin's house and coming to stay with him. Deep down, I knew it wasn't the best decision, but I was caught up in the moment. I wanted to feel loved, to feel wanted, and in that moment, I let those desires take control. Against my better judgment, I packed up my things, left my cousin's house, and stopped going to school. Looking back, I see how easily I allowed myself to be led astray. I was searching for something—love, stability, comfort—but I was looking for it in the wrong places. The Bible reminds us in *Proverbs 3:5-6, "Trust in the Lord with all your heart and lean not on your own understanding; in all your ways submit to Him, and He will make your paths straight."* At that time, I wasn't trusting in God. I was trying to fill the emptiness in my heart with things and people that couldn't truly satisfy. Though I made mistakes, I now realize that

God never gave up on me. Even when I strayed from the path, He was still there, waiting for me to turn back to Him. He saw my brokenness, my longing, and my pain, and He never stopped loving me. The road wasn't easy, but every step I took—even the wrong ones—became part of the story He was writing for my life. This chapter of my life was filled with loss, heartbreak, and poor decisions, but it also taught me valuable lessons. It showed me the importance of staying focused on what truly matters and trusting in God's plan, even when life feels uncertain. I didn't understand it then, but God was using every experience—good and bad—to shape me into the person I was meant to be.

## A Dangerous Path

He said to me that he had a place for us to stay and assured me that I would be okay. I didn't know him well, but something about the way he spoke made me believe him. I was vulnerable, searching for stability and someone to lean on, and in that moment, I chose to trust his word. Against my better judgment, I took a chance and followed him. When we got into the car, there was someone else with us. He drove us to a hotel. As we pulled up, something about the place felt off. It wasn't anything like what I had imagined. The building looked run-down, worn out, and far from a safe place to stay. As I stepped out of the car, he turned to me and said, *"We need to stay here for the night."* I looked around, confused and uneasy, but I told myself to go along with it. I didn't want to seem difficult, so I simply said, *"Okay.* "Still, I couldn't ignore the growing discomfort inside me. The surroundings looked filthy, like something out of a horror film. The people hanging around the hotel didn't look safe—they looked rough, worn, and like they carried stories of their own struggles and survival. Everything about the situation felt wrong. As I continued following him inside, I kept thinking to myself, *what am I doing here? Why did I trust him so easily?* I wanted to leave, but I didn't know how to. I felt stuck, caught in a situation I didn't fully understand. Time passed, and the uneasy feeling in my chest only grew stronger. I kept wondering, *why are we still here? Why hasn't he said anything about what's next?* The longer we stayed, the more I realized that this wasn't just a one-night stop. Something about the way things were unfolding didn't sit right with me. One night, as we sat in the room talking, I noticed him counting pills—preparing them to sell. My heart sank as the reality of my situation began to hit me. I wasn't just in a bad place; I was in a dangerous one. I had trusted someone I barely knew, and now I have found myself in an environment where things could quickly spiral out of control. I felt fear rising within me. This wasn't the life I wanted for myself, and it definitely wasn't where I thought I would end up. The Bible says, *"The Lord is my light and my salvation—whom shall, I fear? The Lord is the stronghold of my life—of whom shall I be afraid?"* (Psalms 27:1). Even though fear gripped me, I tried to hold on to the promise that God was with me. I didn't fully know how I was going to get out of this situation, but I believed that somehow, He would make a way. Looking back, I see that God was there, even in that dark place. He was giving me the strength to stay aware, to recognize when something wasn't right, and to seek a way out. The experience taught me a powerful lesson about trust—not everyone who speaks with confidence has your best interest at heart. I had followed him because I was searching for love and stability, but instead, I found myself in a dangerous situation that threatened my safety. The Bible reminds us in *Proverbs 3:5-6, "Trust in the Lord with all your heart and lean not on your own understanding; in all your ways submit to Him, and He will make your paths straight."* In that moment, I had leaned on my own understanding, and it had led me down a dangerous path. But God was still with me, guiding me back to the right road, even when I couldn't see it. This chapter of my life was a wake-up call. It showed me that not everyone who promises to take care of you can be trusted. But more importantly, it reminded me that God is the only one who can truly provide the safety, love, and stability I was searching for. Though I didn't understand it at the time, He was working behind the scenes, protecting me from greater harm and leading me toward a better future.

## Trapped in Chaos

He asked me to watch over the pills for him while he took a nap. I hesitated, unsure of what to do, but I didn't want to upset him, so I agreed. He told me that if someone came to the door, I should answer and serve them. I didn't know how to do any of this—it was a world I had never been a part of before. This was a new lifestyle for me, one I never imagined I'd find myself in. As I sat there nervously, I heard a knock at the door. My heart raced as I got up to answer it. Standing in front of me were two men. They asked for a specific amount, and though I didn't really know what I was doing, I reached to give them the pills. In a blink of an eye, everything changed—they grabbed everything on the table and ran. It happened so fast that I didn't even have time to react. I stood there in shock, my heart pounding. *This can't be happening,* I thought to myself. I was terrified. He was still asleep, and all I could think about was what he would say when he found out. Fear gripped me as I paced back and forth, replaying the moment over and over in my mind. *How did I get myself into this? What have I done?* This wasn't the life I wanted—it felt like a nightmare, something straight out of a bad movie. My head was pounding, and crazy thoughts began to race through my mind. I felt trapped, with no way out. Soon, he began to wake up. I could barely breathe as he asked me how much I sold. I froze, unsure of what to say. Fear washed over me as he looked at the empty table, realizing everything was gone. His expression changed instantly, and before I could explain, he got up and started swinging on me. He beat me, yelling and asking why I had let them take all his profit. Through tears and pain, I tried to explain, *"I didn't let them do anything! How was I supposed to stop two guys from taking your stuff by myself?"* But he wasn't listening. He was consumed by his anger and frustration. All he cared about was his loss. I felt helpless, trapped in a situation I didn't know how to escape. The blows hurt physically, but the emotional pain was even worse. How did I end up here? How did my life spiral so far out of control? The Bible says, *"The Lord is a refuge for the oppressed, a stronghold in times of trouble"* (Psalms 9:9). Even in that moment of fear and hopelessness, I wanted to believe that God saw my pain. I felt abandoned and lost, but deep down, I clung to the hope that somehow, God would make a way for me to get out of this. I didn't know how or when, but I knew I couldn't stay in this environment. This experience was unlike anything I had ever gone through before. I felt broken, frightened, and defeated. Yet, even in that dark place, something inside me whispered that this wasn't the end of my story. The Bible reminds us in *Isaiah 41:10, "So do not fear, for I am with you; do not be dismayed, for I am your God. I will strengthen you and help you; I will uphold you with my righteous right hand."* Though I felt weak and powerless, I trusted that God would strengthen me.

Looking back, I see that God's hand was on my life, even when I didn't realize it. He was with me in that room, in the chaos, in the fear. Though I didn't know it at the time, He was preparing me for something greater. This chapter of my life was painful, but it taught me that even in the darkest moments, God's light is still present. He doesn't abandon us in our struggles—He walks with us, offering strength, comfort, and a way out. This situation left me questioning everything, but it also planted a seed of determination in my heart. I didn't want to stay in that life. I didn't want to be surrounded by fear, violence, and danger. I wanted more for myself, and I believed that with God's help, I could find a way out and create a better future

## A Life I Never Wanted

I sat crying, overwhelmed by regret and fear, asking myself over and over, *why did I make this horrible decision? How did I end up here? This can't be real—it just can't be.* I wanted to leave so badly, but I didn't have a car, no money, and no one to call for help. Every time I tried to leave, he would block the door and threaten me, making it clear that I wasn't going anywhere. It was terrifying. I had never felt so trapped in my life. I couldn't believe this was happening to me. The fear was suffocating, and I felt utterly helpless. I cried hard because I didn't deserve this. I had tried to be a good person to him, to be loyal, and this was how he repaid me—with cruelty, control, and fear. The Bible says, *"When I am afraid, I will trust you. I praise God for his word. I trust God, so I am not afraid. What can human beings do to me?"* (Psalms 56:3-4). I repeated those words in my mind, clinging to the hope that somehow, God would rescue me from this nightmare. I didn't know how or when, but I needed to believe that He saw my tears and heard my cries. Days went by, and things only got worse. One day, he told me something that shattered what little strength I had left—he said I had to sell my body to help him pay for the room we were staying in. My heart sank. *I can't do this,* I thought to myself. *I've never done anything like this in my life.* The idea made me sick to my stomach, but I was terrified. I had no way out, and I feared what he might do if I refused. We walked outside the room, and he began introducing me to people, letting them know who I was. But the way he introduced me wasn't with kindness or respect—he called me his "b**ch," a word that made me feel small, degraded, and worthless. I was humiliated and embarrassed. This wasn't who I was, and it wasn't the life I wanted. I wanted to scream, to run, to disappear, but I was trapped, and I didn't know how to break free. Among the people he introduced me to was a girl who was already selling her body. She explained how things worked, talking about where to go and how to get the most money, especially from truck drivers.

I stood there, lost in a haze of disbelief. *This can't be my life right now. This can't be real.* She led me from hotel to hotel, showing me the places where she worked. I felt sick, trapped in a situation I didn't know how to escape. My mind kept racing, trying to find a way out, but I couldn't see one. One night, she asked me to walk with her to make our first stop. She explained that we had to bring the money back to our pimps or face punishment. She was used to this life; I wasn't. I just followed her, scared and confused, watching as she got into a truck. I stood outside, trying to process what was happening. I felt like I was watching someone else's life unfold, but it was mine. When she came back out, it was my turn. I was terrified, but I didn't have a choice—I feared getting beaten if I refused. I climbed into the truck, and though everything in me screamed that this was wrong, I went through with it. I wasn't used to this, but I knew I would have to get used to it if I wanted to survive. The entire time, I felt uncomfortable, ashamed, and broken. I wasn't just selling my body—I was losing pieces of my soul. I felt like my worth was being stripped away with every step I took down this dark path. The Bible says, *"The Lord is close to the brokenhearted and saves those who are crushed in spirit"* (Psalms 34:18). In that moment, I felt completely crushed, but I clung to the hope that God was close, even if I couldn't feel Him. This was a life I never wanted, a life I never imagined for myself. I felt trapped, hopeless, and scared, but somewhere deep inside, a small part of me believed that this wasn't the end of my story. Even in the darkest moments, I believed that God could still rescue me. I didn't know how long it would take, but I knew that I had to hold on to hope. Looking back, I see that God's hand was on my life even then. He saw my pain, my fear, and my desperation, and He didn't abandon me. Though I felt trapped in chaos, God was already working on a way out. He was preparing to lead me out of the darkness and into a future filled with healing, purpose, and redemption. This chapter of my life was one of the hardest I've ever faced, but it taught me that even when we feel completely broken, God can restore us. He can take the pieces of our shattered lives and turn them into something beautiful. My story didn't end in that hotel—it was only the beginning of a greater testimony, one that would show others that no matter how far we fall, God's love is strong enough to lift us back up.

## A Nightmare I Couldn't Escape

Night after night, I had to walk up and down the strips, finding strangers to have sex with just to bring money back to him. Every step felt like a nail in the coffin of my hopes and dreams. I was exhausted, terrified, and emotionally numb. I just knew my life was over. He had promised me love and security, but all of those promises were lies. He had used sweet words and false hope to trap me, only to turn me into his rag doll—someone he could control and abuse. I was thrust into an adult life I wasn't prepared for. I continued selling my body, feeling useless and unworthy. Each encounter left me feeling more broken than the last. Fear consumed me as I walked up to strangers and got into cars with them, not knowing if I would make it back alive. It was a constant gamble with my life. I began to witness people getting killed men and women who were trapped in the same nightmare I was living. The streets were dangerous, and the air was thick with the weight of fear. I was ready to go, desperate to escape this horror story I was caught in. But I had no one to call. I had no way to contact anyone who could help me. I felt completely isolated, trapped in a nightmare with no end in sight. I began planning my escape, hoping to sneak away somehow, but I quickly realized that wouldn't work. There were always people watching me—watching for any sign of rebellion. Any attempt to leave could cost me my life. The Bible says, *"You, O Lord, are a shield about me, my glory, and the lifter of my head"* (Psalms 3:3). In those moments of despair, I held on to this verse, even though it was hard to believe. I needed to trust that somehow, God would shield me, that He would lift me out of this darkness. I felt hopeless, but a small part of me still believed that God could make a way, even when I couldn't see it. One day, he told me that we were leaving. At first, I felt a flicker of hope—maybe this was my chance to escape. But in my head, I was thinking, *Wait, what do you mean "we"? I want to get away from you, not go somewhere else with you.* I didn't want to leave with him, but I knew I didn't have a choice. He was so abusive that I feared he would kill me if I disobeyed. We moved from hotel to hotel, never staying in one place long enough to feel stable. Each new place was just another stop in the nightmare. I continued doing what he asked me to do because I didn't see another way out. He was still abusive, still controlling, and every day felt like a battle for survival. One night, we arrived at a new hotel. He told me he was leaving to handle something and would be right back. I said, *"Okay,"* but deep down, I was relieved to have a moment of peace, even if only for a little while. But when he returned, everything changed again. I saw something on his phone that disturbed me deeply. I questioned him about it, and instead of answering, he became enraged. He denied everything I asked and hit me out of anger. At that moment, I knew I was done. I couldn't live like this anymore. I was tired—tired of the abuse, tired of the fear, tired of being controlled. My soul felt crushed, and I didn't know how much longer I could endure this. I longed for freedom, for a chance to start over and reclaim my life. The Bible says, *"The Lord is near to the brokenhearted and saves those who are crushed in spirit"* (Psalms 34:18). Though I felt broken beyond repair, I held on to the hope that God saw my pain. He was near, even when I couldn't feel Him. He hadn't abandoned me, and I believed that somehow, He would save me from this nightmare. Looking back, I see that God was with me even in those moments of darkness. He gave me the strength to keep going, to survive when everything in me wanted to give up. This chapter of my life was one of the hardest I've ever faced, but it wasn't the end. God had a plan, even in the chaos. He was preparing me for something greater, something beyond the pain I was living Though I didn't know it at the time, this experience would one day become part of my testimony—a story of survival, of strength, and of God's unending grace. The nightmare didn't define me; it was a chapter in my life, not the whole story. And in the end, God's light was greater than the darkness I faced.

## An Escape to Freedom

That morning, we left and went to another hotel. The routine had become so familiar—another place, another temporary stop in a cycle that felt endless. After we got settled in, he stepped outside, giving me a brief moment to myself. It was then that a surge of courage hit me. I knew this might be my only chance to escape. With my heart pounding, I grabbed my phone and called my uncle. I told him everything—how I was in danger, how I needed help, and begged him to come pick me up. Without hesitation, he said, *"I'm on my way.* "Hearing those words felt like a lifeline. I clung to the hope that soon, this nightmare would be over. Minutes felt like hours as I waited for my uncle to arrive. I kept looking at the door, half-expecting him to walk back in before I could leave. Then my phone rang—it was my uncle. He told me he was outside. Relief washed over me, but fear still lingered. I knew I had to act quickly before anything went wrong. I gathered my courage and told him, *"My uncle is outside."* He looked at me in shock, clearly surprised that someone had actually come to help me. To my relief, he let me leave. I didn't waste any time—I hurried out of the room, my heart racing with every step. As I approached the car, he stood there, watching me. I could feel his eyes on me, but I didn't turn back. My uncle waved at him, silently letting him know that I was safe now, that his control over me was over. The Bible says, *"The honest person will live in safety, but the dishonest will be caught"* (Proverbs 10:9). In that moment, I felt the truth of those words. After everything I had endured, I was finally stepping into a place of safety. This was my escape to freedom, a chance to start over and leave the darkness behind. As I got into the car, a mix of emotions overwhelmed me. I tried to explain to my uncle what had happened, though the words felt heavy on my tongue. He listened, offering comfort without judgment. Soon, we met up with my aunt and siblings, and we all went out to eat. It was such a relief to be surrounded by people who cared about me, people who didn't want anything from me except to see me safe and happy. Though I was grateful to be free, I couldn't shake the feeling of emptiness inside. The abuse, the neglect, the fear—it had all taken a toll on me. I tried to hold back my tears, not wanting to break down in front of everyone. I wanted to keep it together, to appear strong, but inside, I felt broken. No one could truly understand what I had endured, and even though I was free physically, I knew the emotional scars would take time to heal. The Bible reminds us in *Psalms 147:3*, *"He heals the brokenhearted and binds up their wounds."* Though I didn't feel whole in that moment, I clung to the hope that God could heal what had been shattered. I had survived something that could have destroyed me, and though I still carried the weight of that experience, I believed that one day, I would find peace. Looking back, I see that God's hand was with me throughout that entire ordeal. He gave me the strength to endure, the courage to call for help, and the opportunity to escape. It wasn't easy, and it left me with wounds that needed healing, but it also taught me that God is always near, even in the darkest moments. He sees our pain, hears our cries, and makes a way when we can't see one. That day marked the beginning of a new chapter. It wasn't the end of my struggles, but it was the start of my journey toward healing and wholeness. I learned that no matter how hopeless things seem, God's love is greater than any fear, and His light is stronger than any darkness. He had rescued me—not just through my uncle, but through His unending grace—and for that, I was deeply thankful

## A New Beginning: Finding My Way

After everything I had been through, I knew I needed a fresh start. I needed a place where I could rest my head, clear my mind, and begin to rebuild my life. I got in contact with a family friend on my cousin's mom's side and explained my situation. I told her I needed a place to stay, and to my relief, she welcomed me with open arms. She told me I could stay there while I got myself together, and for the first time in a while, I felt a glimmer of hope. I was so happy—this was exactly what I needed. It wasn't just about having a roof over my head; it was about having a safe space where I could begin to heal from everything I had endured. Life finally felt a little calmer. I enjoyed spending time with her and her daughter, who was so sweet and full of joy. Watching her play and being around her brought me moments of peace and happiness, something I hadn't felt in a long time. It reminded me that life could be beautiful, even after so much pain. As I settled in, I started thinking about my future. I knew I wanted more for myself. I wanted to finish school and finally obtain my diploma. It was a goal I had put on hold for too long, and now felt like the right time to pick it back up. I got in contact with someone from the Department of Human Services, and they were incredibly helpful. They listened to my story and pointed me in the right direction. Soon after, I was connected with a man who introduced me to Job Corps. He explained what it was—a program that would pay for me to attend, cover my expenses, and even pay for my transportation. As he described it, I felt a spark of excitement. This was the opportunity I had been waiting for—a chance to do something for myself, to work toward a better future. He asked me which location I wanted to go to, listing a few options. I knew right away that I didn't want to stay in Atlanta. I needed a complete change of environment, a fresh start away from everything that reminded me of my past. I chose the location in North Carolina, feeling hopeful about what was ahead. The thought of moving to a new state and starting a new chapter in my life filled me with excitement. For the first time in a long time, I felt like I was taking control of my life. I wasn't running from my past—I was walking toward a better future. The Bible says, *"For I know the plans I have for you," declares the Lord, "plans to prosper you and not to harm you, plans to give you hope and a future"* (Jeremiah 29:11). This verse echoed in my heart as I prepared for this new journey. I believed that God had a plan for my life, and this was part of it. I gathered all my paperwork, and two weeks later, I was ready to get on the bus to North Carolina. The drive was long, but every mile felt like a step closer to a new beginning. I looked out the window, thinking about everything I had been through and how far I had come. I wasn't the same person I had been—I was stronger, wiser, and ready to embrace the future with hope. Though the road ahead was uncertain, I knew one thing for sure: I was making a change for the better. This was my chance to rewrite my story, to rise above the pain of my past, and to build a life I could be proud of. And with God by my side, I knew I could do it

CHAPTER

# HURT PEOPLE
# HURT PEOPLE

*"We can make our plans, but the Lord determines our steps"*

*(Proverbs 16:9).*

I finally arrived at Job Corps, and as the bus pulled up, I looked out of the window and smiled to myself. This was a new start—one I desperately needed. After everything I had been through, this place represented more than just an opportunity; it represented hope, healing, and a future. I had made it here despite everything that had tried to break me. I could feel the weight of my past beginning to lift, even if only for a moment. As soon as we got off the bus, the staff guided us to the check-in area. Other students who had ridden with me stood nearby, their faces a mixture of excitement and nervousness. There were boys on one side and girls on the other, and I noticed a few people already there to greet us. The atmosphere felt like a fresh beginning. I said to myself, *this feels like a mini college."* A sense of joy filled me—I couldn't help but smile from ear to ear. This was everything I had dreamed of. I had a purpose, a goal, and a plan, and I was determined to make it happen. No more distractions, no more setbacks, this was my time to rebuild and move forward. During orientation, we were told that each of us had to choose a trade. When my turn came, I didn't hesitate. I chose culinary arts. Cooking had always been something I loved something that brought me peace even in my darkest moments. It felt like second nature to me. The idea of turning something I loved into a skill I could use to build a future excited me. I couldn't wait to get started. I began my classes for both school and my trade, and for the first few days, everything seemed to be going perfectly. I was focused, determined to stay on track and make the most of this opportunity. But then, something—or rather someone—caught my eye. There was this guy. He was a painter, and his trade was painting. The moment I saw him, I felt something shift. He was attractive, and something about him caught my attention in a way I couldn't explain. I tried to ignore it at first, reminding myself that I had come here for a reason—to finish school, to learn a trade, and to create a better life. But no matter how hard I tried to stay focused; I kept thinking about him. I started asking people about him, trying to find out his name and learn more about him. It felt like I couldn't help myself. Even though I knew I had to stay on track, part of me was curious—maybe even a little hopeful—that getting to know him wouldn't be such a bad thing. After all, I had been through so much, and for once, I wanted to experience something light, something new. But as the days went on, I realized how easy it was to get distracted. I reminded myself of why I was really here. The Bible says, *"We can make our plans, but the Lord determines our steps"* (Proverbs 16:9). I had plans when I came here—to stay focused, to grow, and to create a future I could be proud of. But life has a way of throwing unexpected situations our way, and I knew I had to trust God to guide me, even when I felt pulled in different directions. I had come too far to lose sight of my purpose. Yes, life had been hard, and yes, I wanted to experience love, joy, and connection. But I also knew that I couldn't let anything, or anyone, derail me from what I had set out to accomplish. This was my time to heal, to focus on myself, and to trust that God had something greater in store for me. Looking back, I realize that this experience taught me an important lesson: sometimes we think we know what's best for us, but God sees the bigger picture. He knows the steps we need to take, even when we don't understand them. And while I didn't fully see it at the time, God was working in my life, leading me down a path that would ultimately bring me closer to the future

He had planned for me. Job Corps wasn't just a place to learn a trade—it was a place where I began to find myself again. It was where I started to believe that I was capable of more than just surviving. I could thrive, I could grow, and I could become the person God created me to be.

## Love-Struck and Vulnerable

I started hearing from people around campus that he was talking to another girl. At first, I felt a little disappointed, but that didn't stop me. *Dang, I still want him though,* I thought to myself. Something about him had caught my attention, and I wasn't ready to let it go just because of a rumor. So, I started doing little things to get his attention, hoping he would notice me. One day, I gathered my courage and walked up to him. My heart was racing, but I tried to stay calm. I started a conversation, asking him if he was talking to someone. He admitted that he had been talking to a girl before but that it wasn't anything serious anymore. In that moment, I felt a sense of relief—I was right. He wasn't committed to anyone. We continued talking, and he asked me where I was from and what my trade was. As he spoke, my heart fluttered. I couldn't help but think, *He's falling for me.* I looked at him, taking in his voice, his style, and his perfectly built physique. Butterflies swirled in my stomach, and I found myself blushing. He was everything I wanted, and I couldn't believe we were having this conversation. By the end of that conversation, we had exchanged numbers, and I walked away feeling on top of the world. Job Corps was starting to feel even better than I imagined. I was excited about being here, about learning my trade, and now, I was excited about him. His voice, the way he dressed, his confidence, everything about him made me feel giddy inside. I've always loved hard. It's just who I am. When I see someone, I like, I pour my heart into them, hoping they'll love me back the same way. And with him, it wasn't any different. I felt like I needed to go out of my way to do things for him, to show him how much I cared, so that he would love me in return. We started talking more and more. He would call me, and we'd have conversations that made me feel like I was in a dream. Then one day, he told me to meet him outside early in the morning—before the staff and other students came out for breakfast. He wanted to see me alone, and I couldn't say no. I told him, *"Okay.* "The next morning, he called me as planned, telling me to come outside. I got ready, feeling nervous and excited at the same time. As soon as I saw him, I smiled. *Yes, this is about to be my man,* I thought. We stood outside, talking quietly before everyone else woke up. I felt like I was in my own little world with him, and everything else faded away. At one point, I gathered my courage and told him, *"I really like you.* "In that moment, I felt vulnerable, but it didn't matter—I was caught up in the excitement of being noticed by someone I liked so much. The Bible says, *"Above all else, guard your heart, for everything you do flows from it"* (Proverbs 4:23). Looking back, I realize how unguarded my heart was. I wanted so badly to be loved that I was willing to give my heart away quickly, without truly knowing what was in store. At that time, I didn't fully understand the importance of guarding my heart, but God was still with me. He saw my longing for love and acceptance, and even though I was caught up in my emotions, He was guiding me through it all. This experience taught me that it's okay to love, but it's also important to take time to truly know someone before giving away your heart completely.

## When Love Became Control

At first, everything felt perfect. We were inseparable—sharing meals, walking to class, and spending every free moment together. Being with him gave me a sense of belonging, something I had craved for so long. I felt like I finally had someone who saw me, cared for me, and loved me back. But what I didn't realize then was how quickly my feelings for him had begun to consume me. I became so focused on him that my goals started to fade into the background. I had come to Job Corps with a plan—

to finish school, learn a trade, and build a future for myself. But somewhere along the way, I lost sight of that plan. Instead, my entire world revolved around him. His presence made me feel whole, and I didn't want to do anything without him. The intensity between us grew, but so did something else—his control over me. At first, it seemed harmless. He would ask where I was going, who I was with, and what I was doing. I didn't think much of it because I liked the attention. But over time, his questions became more demanding, and I felt like I had to report my every move. I didn't want to upset him, so I went along with it, thinking that this was what it meant to be in love. Things got even more complicated when jealousy entered the picture. He started getting upset if I talked to other guys, even if it was just friendly. I tried to reassure him that he was the only one I wanted, but it didn't seem to help. His jealousy made me feel guilty, like I was doing something wrong even when I wasn't. The Bible says, *"Love is patient, love is kind. It does not envy, it does not boast, it is not proud. It does not dishonor others, it is not self-seeking, it is not easily angered, it keeps no record of wrongs"* (1 Corinthians 13:4-5). At that time, I didn't know what true love was supposed to look like. I thought that love was supposed to be intense, all-consuming, and even a little jealous. But real love, the kind of love that God designed, isn't about control or possession—it's about kindness, respect, and trust. One night, after dinner, we went back to his dorm room to hang out. Things felt normal at first, but as we talked, something shifted. He seemed distant, like something was bothering him. I asked him if everything was okay, but instead of answering, he got upset. His anger caught me off guard. I tried to calm him down, but he started accusing me of talking to other guys again. I felt helpless—I hadn't done anything wrong, yet here I was, trying to defend myself against something I didn't even do. That night, I went back to my dorm feeling confused and hurt. I had given so much of myself to him, yet it felt like no matter how hard I tried, it wasn't enough. I started questioning myself—*Was I doing something wrong? Was I not good enough?* I loved him deeply, but the more I tried to hold on, the more it felt like I was losing myself. Looking back, I realize that I had placed my worth in his hands. I believed that if he loved me, I was valuable. If he didn't, I wasn't. The Bible says, *"Fear of man will prove to be a snare, but whoever trusts in the Lord is kept safe"* (Proverbs 29:25). At that time, I didn't trust in God—I trusted in this relationship to define my value. And because Of that, I allowed myself to be controlled by fear—fear of losing him, fear of not being enough, fear of being alone. This wasn't love, it was dependent. I didn't understand that then, but God was still with me, watching over me even as I navigated a situation that could have broken me. He saw my heart, my longing to be loved, and He never left me. Though I was searching for love in the wrong place, God was patiently waiting for me to turn back to Him—the only one who could truly satisfy the longing in my hear

## Blinded by Desire

One morning, he called me and told me to come outside. Without hesitation, I got up and went to meet him. We walked quietly behind one of the buildings where it was more private. I could feel my heart racing, anticipating what was about to happen. He leaned in close, his voice soft yet commanding, and told me to turn around and pull my pants down. In that moment, something shifted in me. What I felt for him grew even stronger—not because of who he was, but because of how he made me feel physically. I fell in love with him even more. I didn't want him to stop, but deep down, I knew we couldn't keep going. We were out in the open, and the risk of getting caught was too high. After a few moments, he kissed me softly and whispered, *"I'll see you later."* I stood there for a moment, feeling overwhelmed by emotions I couldn't fully understand. I felt so loved by him—not in a way that nurtured my soul, but in a way that fed my flesh. Afterward, I went back to my dorm, took a shower, and met him at the breakfast table. Sitting across from him, everything felt so real. He was mine, and I was his. Every morning, we continued to feed our desires, meeting in secret places to be together. What started as an attraction quickly became an obsession. I craved his presence, his touch, and the way he made me feel. One morning, in the midst of our routine, I told him something bold—I wanted to have a baby. I wanted to create something that would bond us forever. I was shocked when he agreed, and in that moment, my happiness soared. I felt like I had everything I ever wanted. We continued meeting up, finding any place we could to be alone together. Nothing else mattered to me. My goals, my future, my plans—they all faded into the background. He was my world, and I couldn't see anything beyond him. The Bible says, *"The heart is deceitful above all things and beyond cure. Who can understand it?"* (Jeremiah 17:9). Looking back, I realize how blinded I was by my emotions. I mistook physical attraction and obsession for love. I thought that being with him, giving myself to him, and even planning a future with him was what love looked like. But real love isn't about losing yourself in another person—it's about growing together in a way that honors both God and yourself. At the time, I didn't see how distracted I had become. I had come to Job Corps with a purpose—to change my life, to gain an education, and to build a better future. But somewhere along the way, I lost sight of that purpose. My focus shifted entirely to him, and I didn't realize how much of myself I was giving away. As the holidays approached, we were told that we could choose anywhere we wanted to go. I should have been thinking about my goals, my future, and what I needed to do to stay on track. Instead, all I could think about was him—being with him, spending time with him, and keeping the love, I thought I had found. The Bible reminds us in *Proverbs 4:23*, *"Above all else, guard your heart, for everything you do flows from it."* At that time, I didn't know how to guard my heart. I wanted love so badly that I gave my heart away too easily. I let my emotions lead me, not realizing that true love is more than physical attraction—it's about respect, trust, and growing together in a healthy way. Though I couldn't see it then, God was still with me. He saw how lost I was in my emotions, and He didn't abandon me. He was patiently waiting for me to turn back to Him, to seek His love, the only love that truly satisfies. Looking back, I realize that this chapter of my life taught me an important lesson: love isn't about losing yourself; it's about becoming the best version of yourself while being with someone who helps you grow. I didn't know it then, but God was using this experience to shape me, to teach me what real love looks like, and to prepare me for something greater.

## The Highs and Lows of Family

After everything I had been through, I needed a break, a chance to clear my mind and spend time with people who cared about me. I called my aunt and uncle, asking if I could come and stay with them for the holidays. When they said yes, I felt a wave of relief and excitement. I packed my things, knowing that this time away would give me a chance to reset. He went to stay at his mother's house during the holiday break, and though I missed him, I wasn't worried. I knew we would see each other again soon, so I didn't panic. This time apart felt necessary, and it gave me something to look forward to when we reunited. I got on the Greyhound bus and headed to Virginia, where my aunt and uncle lived. It was a long ride, but my heart was filled with anticipation. I couldn't wait to see them. When I arrived at the station, they were there waiting for me, and as soon as I saw them, a big smile spread across my face. It felt so good to be welcomed by family, to be surrounded by love during the holidays. After picking me up, we went out to eat and then did some shopping for holiday meals. Being able to spend quality time with my family meant so much to me because family was something I had always longed for. Growing up, I had faced so much instability, and all I ever wanted was to feel that sense of belonging. During my time with them, I got to see and experience things I hadn't before. They took me sightseeing. I saw the White House and explored different parts of the city. It was exciting and refreshing, a brief moment where life felt light and carefree. I was truly enjoying myself, soaking in every moment of this special time with family. But just when everything seemed perfect, things took a sudden turn. Out of nowhere, my aunt snapped at me. Her tone was sharp, and her words stung. I was confused, I didn't know what I had done to upset her. I tried to replay everything in my mind, searching for a reason, but nothing made sense. The exchange of words between us left me heartbroken. It was like a wound from my past had been reopened. Her reaction brought back memories of how I was treated as a child—times when I felt misunderstood, unloved, and rejected. It was as if I had been transported back to a place, I thought I had escaped. In that moment, all the joy and excitement I had felt vanished. I was ready to leave. I didn't want to stay any longer, but I knew I couldn't leave until the holiday break was over. I felt trapped trapped in a place that was supposed to bring me comfort but instead brought me pain. My living area was downstairs, so I went down, needing space to process everything. I sat there, still in disbelief. I didn't understand why things had escalated so quickly or why my aunt had reacted that way. The situation felt unfair and overwhelming. The Bible says, *"The Lord is close to the brokenhearted and saves those who are crushed in spirit"* (Psalms 34:18). In that moment, I felt crushed—emotionally drained from everything I had endured in the past and now facing a situation that mirrored those old wounds. But I tried to hold on to the belief that God was near, that He saw my heart and understood my pain even when no one else did. Though I didn't have answers, I knew I had to keep going. I reminded myself that this was just a moment—a difficult one, yes, but not the end of my story. I had come too far to let this setback derail me. The Bible says, *"Cast all your anxiety on Him because He cares for you"* (1 Peter 5:7). So, I prayed silently, asking God to help me navigate this situation, to give me peace and strength to endure until I could return to Job Corps.Looking back, I realize that experiences like this taught me resilience. They taught me that life won't always go the way we expect, and sometimes, even those we love can hurt us. But through it all, God remains constant—offering comfort, healing, and the strength to keep moving forward. This moment was painful, but it didn't define me. It became another part of my journey, another lesson in trusting God even when things don't make sense. And though it hurt, it also reminded me of how far I had come. I wasn't the same person I had been—I was growing, learning, and becoming stronger with each challenge I faced

## Longing for Love and Peace

I felt so incomplete all over again. My mind was racing, filled with thoughts I couldn't quiet. *I didn't come here for this,* I thought bitterly. This trip was supposed to be a peaceful getaway, a time to relax and feel safe with family. Instead, it had turned into yet another painful experience that left me feeling more alone than ever. As I sat downstairs, trying to hold back tears, I couldn't stop thinking about my boyfriend. I wanted to be back in his arms, to feel the love and warmth I had grown used to receiving from him. That love, however flawed, had become a source of comfort for me, something that made me feel whole in a way nothing else had. I was ready to get back to him, to Job Corps, to a place where I felt like I belonged. I hated being there. What was supposed to be a joyful holiday with family had turned into a reminder of old wounds. All I wanted now was to get far away from my aunt. The way she snapped at me for no reason hurt deeply. I kept thinking, *Why did I come here? Why did I think this would be different?* But as much as I resented her in that moment, I knew I couldn't carry that bitterness in my heart. The Bible says, *"Three things will last forever: faith, hope, and love—and the greatest of these is love"* (1 Corinthians 13:13). Though it was hard, I told myself that I had to accept her for who she was. Maybe she didn't mean to hurt me, or maybe she did, but either way, I couldn't let her actions steal my peace. Finally, the day came for me to return to Job Corps, and I was happier than anything. My aunt and uncle dropped me off at the Greyhound station, and as I boarded the bus, I felt a sense of relief wash over me. I was ready to leave all of this behind. I needed to breathe again, to feel free from the heaviness that this trip had brought. As the bus pulled away, I silently promised myself that I wouldn't go back to her house again. *I don't care about spending the holidays with family anymore,* I told myself. *I won't put myself in a position to be hurt like that again.* The disappointment was too much, and I didn't want to risk feeling that way again. When I finally returned to Job Corps, I felt a surge of happiness. Stepping onto the campus felt like coming home. I was back in a place where I felt like I belonged, where I had people around me who made me feel wanted. Most importantly, I got to see my boyfriend again. As soon as I saw him, all the tension and sadness I had been carrying melted away. Being with him made me feel complete, and I realized just how much I had missed him. I was also happy to see the rest of the people I had grown close to at Job Corps. It felt like I had been gone forever, even though it had only been a short time. The familiar faces, the laughter, and the energy of the campus were exactly what I needed to lift my spirits. The Bible reminds us in *Isaiah 26:3, "You will keep in perfect peace those whose minds are steadfast, because they trust in you."* Though I had placed a lot of my peace in being with my boyfriend and being back at Job Corps, I knew that true peace could only come from God. He had brought me through another storm, and even though I didn't fully understand everything, I trusted that He was leading me toward something greater. This experience taught me a valuable lesson: sometimes, the places and people we expect to bring us joy can disappoint us, but that doesn't mean we stop hoping or stop loving. It just means we learn to place our trust in God, who never fails us. I may not have had the perfect holiday, but I had a chance to reflect, grow, and come back stronger. I was ready to refocus on my goals, surround myself with people who lifted me up, and continue moving forward on the path God had set before me.

## A New Chapter: Expecting Hope

Spending time with him made everything feel complete. His presence had a way of lifting my spirits, turning my sadness into happiness. All the disappointment and hurt I had felt during the holidays seemed to fade away in his presence. The love he gave me made me feel secure and cared for, and I cherished every moment we spent together. Life felt peaceful again, and I was loving every bit of it. We continued doing everything together, sharing moments that made me believe we were building something real. Months went by, and everything seemed perfect. Then, one day, I noticed that I hadn't had a period in a while. My mind started racing with possibilities. *Could I be pregnant?* I wondered. I decided to take a pregnancy test, and when I saw the positive result, excitement filled my heart. This was something we had talked about, something we had both wanted. We had planned for this moment, hoping that one day we would have a child together—a daughter. And now, it was happening. I immediately called him to share the news, barely able to contain my excitement. *"I'm pregnant!"* I told him, my voice filled with joy. He was excited too, thrilled at the idea of becoming a father. This was our first child together and knowing that he shared my excitement made the moment even more special. I became pregnant with my daughter at the age of 19, and though I didn't fully understand what lay ahead, I felt a sense of hope and purpose growing within me. The Bible says, *"Give praise to the God and Father of our Lord Jesus Christ. He has blessed us with every spiritual blessing that comes from the heavenly world. They belong to us because we belong to Christ. God chose us to belong to Christ before the world was created. He chose us to be holy and without blame in his eyes. He loved us"* (Ephesians 1:3-4). In that moment, I felt truly blessed. Despite all the trials I had faced, God had chosen to bless me with this child—a gift of love and hope. News of my pregnancy quickly spread, and soon, everyone knew that we were expecting. It felt good to have something positive to share with others, something that gave me hope for the future. My boyfriend was almost finished with his trade, and it felt like everything was falling into place. We were young and in love, about to welcome a new life into the world. Though life hadn't been easy, this moment gave me something to hold on to, something to look forward to with joy. Looking back, I realize that even in the midst of uncertainty, God's hand was guiding me.

Becoming a mother at 19 wasn't part of the plan I had when I first came to Job Corps, but it became part of the story God was writing for my life. The Bible reminds us in *Jeremiah 1:5*, *"Before I formed you in the womb, I knew you; before you were born, I set you apart."* God had a purpose for my daughter's life, and He had a purpose for me too. This new chapter of my life was filled with hope, excitement, and a sense of responsibility. I didn't know what the future held, but I trusted that God would lead me through it. Though I was young, I was determined to do my best—to love and care for my child with everything I had.

## Betrayed and Broken

He started Job Corps way before me, so naturally, he finished before me. I knew this day would come, but I didn't expect it to bring so much pain. As soon as he was close to finishing, everything changed. He started acting distant, and suddenly, lies were being thrown at me. He accused me of talking to someone else, which wasn't true. The only person I ever gave my heart to was him, so I didn't understand where these accusations were coming from. *Why is he doing this?* I kept asking myself. We had talked about this—we had planned our future; we had created a life together. How could he question my loyalty now? Then he said something that shook me to my core. He told me he wasn't sure the baby was his because of what someone else had told him. I couldn't believe what I was hearing. *After everything we've been through, after all we planned, how could you even say that?* I tried to reason with him, begging him to see the truth. *"You know what we planned. You know this baby is yours. Why are you doing this to me?"* I pleaded, hoping he would realize how much his words were hurting me. But he remained cold, insisting that he wanted a DNA test. I was shocked that he would even suggest such a thing after all we had shared. We stayed arguing, going back and forth over things that didn't even matter, until it was time for him to leave. His transition marked the end of our time together, and I felt completely broken. He was supposed to be my partner, the father of my child, the person I trusted the most. But instead, he left me with nothing but pain and unanswered questions. I felt misled, abandoned, and betrayed. My heart ached with the weight of everything I had gone through—not just with him, but with life in general. *How could he leave me like this?* I thought over and over again. I wanted to hurt him the way he had hurt me. I wanted him to feel the same pain, the same heartbreak that was tearing me apart. The love of my life, the person I trusted the most—had turned his back on me, just like so many others before him. Darkness crept over me, and I felt myself sinking into despair. It felt like every painful experience I had ever endured was happening all over again. I couldn't escape the cycle of hurt, betrayal, and rejection. I wanted to give up. *Why does this keep happening to me?* I asked God, desperate for an answer. The Bible says, *"The Lord is close to the brokenhearted and saves those who are crushed in spirit"* (Psalms 34:18). In that moment, I felt crushed in every way possible—emotionally, mentally, and spiritually. But even in the midst of my darkness, I tried to remind myself that God was still near. Though I couldn't see His hand at work, I believed He hadn't abandoned me. This experience left me feeling betrayed and empty, but it also taught me something important: people will fail us, but God never will. I had placed all my hope, trust, and love in someone who wasn't capable of carrying that weight. I had made him the center of my world, and when he left, my world crumbled. But God was still there, waiting for me to lean on Him instead. The Bible reminds us in *Isaiah 41:10, "So do not fear, for I am with you; do not be dismayed, for I am your God. I will strengthen you and help you; I will uphold you with my righteous right hand."* Though I felt weak, abandoned, and broken, I knew that God was my strength. He would uphold me when no one else could. I didn't understand it at the time, but this was a turning point in my life. It was a moment that forced me to confront the emptiness I felt and begin searching for something greater—something that wouldn't leave me feeling abandoned. Though I didn't know how, I trusted that God could use even this pain to shape me into someone stronger, someone who could rise above the hurt.

## Broken Yet Determined

I tried so hard to be good to him. Even while I was still broken inside, I gave him my love wholeheartedly. I wanted to be there for him, to show him the kind of love I always longed to receive. But loving someone who didn't love me back in the same way only deepened the wounds I was already carrying. I didn't deserve the way he treated me. I felt anger rising within a mix of betrayal, hurt, and frustration. *Why does this keep happening to me?* I wondered. I had poured so much of myself into this relationship, only to be left feeling unworthy and discarded. There was a part of me that wanted to hurt him the way he hurt me, to make him feel the pain I was carrying. But the Bible says, *"Don't be upset, it only leads to trouble. Evil people will be sent away. But those who trust the Lord will inherit the land"* (Psalms 37:8-9). Those words reminded me that holding onto anger would only harm me in the end. I didn't want to become bitter or allow this pain to define me. Instead, I needed to trust that God had a greater plan for my life—a plan far beyond the heartache I was feeling. When he finally left Job Corps and returned to Miami, I was overcome with sadness. Despite everything we had been through, I still loved him. His absence left a void, but it also gave me clarity. I reminded myself of the reason I came to Job Corps in the first place: to finish my classes, complete my trade in culinary arts, and build a better future for myself. I threw myself into my work, determined to finish strong. And when the time came, I achieved what I had set out to do. I completed all my classes, obtained my high school diploma, and earned my culinary arts certificate. Holding those accomplishments in my hands, I felt an overwhelming sense of pride. *I did it.* Despite all the challenges, distractions, and setbacks, I stayed on the course and achieved my goals. The Bible says, *"And we know that for those who love God all things work together for good, for those who are called according to His purpose"* (Romans 8:28). I held on to that verse as a reminder that even the pain and trials I had faced were part of God's plan. He was working everything together for my good, preparing me for the next chapter of my life. When it was time for me to transition out of Job Corps, I had a big decision to make. The staff asked me where I wanted to go, and they would cover the cost of my travel. I wasn't sure what to do or where to go. Part of me felt lost, unsure of what the future held. In a moment of vulnerability, I picked up the phone and called him. Despite everything we had been through, my heart still longed for him. I told him that I had finished my program and needed a place to go. He said he would ask his brother, and when he called me back to say his brother had agreed, I felt a wave of excitement. Even though he had hurt me, I still loved him. I was willing to give him another chance, hoping that this time things would be different. Deep down, I wanted to believe that love could heal the brokenness between us, that we could rebuild what had been lost. Looking back, I realized how much I was still searching for love and validation from people who couldn't give it to me. But even in my brokenness, God was with me. He saw my heart, my struggles, and my desire to move forward. The Bible reminds us in *Isaiah 41:10*, *"So do not fear, for I am with you; do not be dismayed, for I am your God. I will strengthen you and help you; I will uphold you with my righteous right hand.* Though I didn't have all the answers, I trusted that God would guide my steps. He had brought me this far, and I knew He wouldn't leave me now.

## A Journey of Hope and Heartache

With all my things packed and my heart full of hope, I was ready to start a new journey with my child's father. Job Corps had arranged my flight to Miami and even provided me with some money to help me transition. As the plane descended, I stared out of the window, thinking about what awaited me. I told myself this was my chance for a fresh start, a chance to build the family I had always dreamed of but never truly had. When I stepped off the plane and saw his face, my heart skipped a beat. His smile felt warm, his embrace comforting. In that moment, I believed that everything would finally fall into place. I wanted nothing more than to create a loving, stable home safe haven for me and my child. He took me to his family's house, where I was introduced to his sisters, his mom, and his brother. They seemed welcoming, and for the first time in a long time, I felt like I belonged somewhere. His brother showed us the room where we would be staying. It wasn't much, but it felt like home simply because I was with him. The dream of being a family was finally starting to feel real. But as the days turned into weeks, things began to shift. I caught him texting other women, and my heart shattered. *How could he do this?* I thought. I had come all this way, given him all of me, and yet he betrayed my trust. I confronted him, hoping for honesty, but instead, the arguments began. We went back and forth, our voices rising until it felt like there was no love left between us. I didn't know his family well, and I felt uneasy involving them in our issues. But with no one else to turn to, I decided to talk to his brother and sister about what was happening. I hoped they could offer some insight or guidance, but even with their support, the situation didn't improve. Two months passed, and the arguments continued. Each fight left me feeling more broken, more defeated. Being pregnant only added to the weight I was carrying. I was overwhelmed, stressed, and emotionally drained. My mind raced constantly, filled with thoughts of failure and heartbreak. I kept asking myself, *why does this keep happening to me? Why can't I have the love I deserve?* One day, the arguments escalated to a point where he walked out. He left me at his brother's house, alone with his brother and his brother's girlfriend—people I barely knew. I felt abandoned, discarded like I didn't matter. I tried calling him, desperate to hear his voice, to understand why he had done this. But he didn't answer. Days turned into nights, and still, no word from him. The silence was deafening. I couldn't understand how someone who had promised to love me, someone who was supposed to be my partner and the father of my child, could leave me like this. The loneliness was suffocating. I was in a city where I knew no one, surrounded by strangers, carrying a life inside me, and yet I felt completely alone. The Bible says, *"The Lord is close to the brokenhearted and saves those who are crushed in spirit"* (Psalms 34:18). In those moments, I clung to that verse, hoping that God was near even when I couldn't feel His presence. I tried to hold myself together, but the weight of everything was too much to bear. I felt foolish for believing this could work. *Why did I come here? Why did I think he would change?* I questioned myself repeatedly. The reality of my situation hit me hard: I was in Miami, far from home, with no one to comfort me, no one to lean on. This pregnancy was supposed to be a joyful time, but instead, it became a season of pain and isolation. I cried myself to sleep many nights, praying for strength to make it through. The Bible says, *"Cast all your anxiety on Him because He cares for you"* (1 Peter 5:7). Though I felt alone, I tried to trust that God was watching over me, even if I didn't fully understand His plan. Despite the pain, I knew I couldn't give up. I had a child depending on me, and I had to find a way to keep going. The Bible reminds us in *Isaiah 41:10, "So do not fear, for I am with you; do not be dismayed, for I am your God. I will strengthen you and help you; I will uphold you with my righteous right hand.* Looking back, I see that this season of heartache was shaping me, strengthening me for what was to come. It was a reminder that even when people fail us, God never will. He remains constant, loving, and faithful, carrying us through the storms of life when we can't carry ourselves. Though I felt abandoned and unloved, God was using this time to teach me that His love was enough. He was showing me that my worth wasn't determined by anyone else's actions or approval—it came from Him. And even in the darkest moments, His light was guiding me forward.

## Breaking Free from the Darkness

I was alone, with nobody to run to. The man who was supposed to stand by me, the father of my child, was running from his responsibilities. I was left in a house with people I barely knew, feeling isolated and heartbroken. Every day was a reminder of how far I had fallen from the life I had imagined for myself. When he finally returned, I thought things might get better—that he would see the pain he caused and take responsibility. But instead, he turned his family against me. He told them lies, claiming that he wasn't sure if the baby I carried was his. His words cut deep, reopening wounds that were already raw. I couldn't understand why he would say such hurtful things, especially when he knew the truth. He knew this was his child, yet he chose to deny it, pushing me further into despair. The Bible says, *"He has delivered us from the power of darkness and conveyed us into the kingdom of the Son of His love"* (Colossians 1:13). In that moment, I clung to the promise that God would deliver me from the darkness I was living in. I prayed for strength, for clarity, and for a way out of the toxic situation I was trapped in. His denial and accusations made me feel so small, so unwanted, that I began to question everything about myself. How could someone I loved so deeply treat me this way? How could someone so close to me inflict so much pain? The atmosphere became so unbearable that I knew I had to leave. Florida no longer felt like a place of hope—it felt like a prison. The decision to leave wasn't easy. Part of me wanted to stay and fight for what I thought was love. But deep down, I knew I deserved better. I deserved peace, stability, and a life free from the chaos that surrounded me. I couldn't raise my child in this environment. I couldn't continue to sacrifice my own well-being for someone who clearly didn't value me. I picked up the phone and called my aunt and uncle. I was desperate, and I needed their help. I explained everything to them, pouring out my heart, and asked if they could send me money to buy a ticket back to Atlanta. Without hesitation, they agreed. Their willingness to help me felt like a lifeline in a storm that was threatening to drown me. When I told him I was leaving, he tried to convince me to stay. But his words no longer held power over me. I had made up my mind. I was done living this crazy, chaotic life. I was done trying to force someone to love and care for me. I packed my things, said goodbye to the hurt and betrayal, and boarded a bus back to Atlanta. Coming back to Atlanta wasn't easy. I didn't have a stable place to stay, so I moved from house to house, relying on the kindness of friends and family. Each place I stayed felt temporary, like I was floating without a true home. But even in instability, I began to feel a glimmer of hope. The Bible reminds us, *"Come to me, all you who are weary and burdened, and I will give you rest"* (Matthew 11:28). I was exhausted—physically, emotionally, and spiritually—but I held on to the promise that God would provide rest for my weary soul. Leaving Florida was one of the hardest decisions I ever made, but it was also one of the most necessary. It was a step toward reclaiming my life, a step away from darkness and toward the light of God's love and grace. Though the road ahead was uncertain, I trusted that God was guiding me, one step at a time.

## Betrayed and Broken

When I returned to Atlanta, I didn't know where to go. The weight of being alone and pregnant was crushing, but I was determined to find a way. I asked my brother if I could stay with him and his girlfriend for a while until I could get on my feet. At first, things seemed fine. It wasn't ideal, but I was grateful to have a roof over my head and a little time to figure things out. But as the days passed, tension started to build between me and my brother. Our relationship, which had always been strong, began to strain under the weight of unspoken emotions. One day, everything came to a head. We got into a heated argument, and the situation escalated quickly. He told me to leave his house. I couldn't believe what I was hearing. *Leave? Where would I go?* I pleaded with him, trying to make him understand that I had nowhere else to turn. But my words fell on deaf ears. He insisted that I leave, and when I refused, he opened the door and pushed me out. I fought back, desperate and hurt, but his anger consumed him. Before I knew it, he dragged me down the stairs—while I was pregnant. My heart shattered. This wasn't just anyone—this was my brother, my ride-or-die, someone I had always trusted and loved deeply. How could he do this to me? How could he betray me like this? As I lay there, tears streaming down my face, I felt a mix of emotions—pain, anger, betrayal, and disbelief. I hated him in that moment. I wanted revenge; to make him feel the same hurt he had inflicted on me. And before I knew it, I blinked out, letting my emotions take control. The next thing I knew, blood had been shed. When the dust settled, I was left with an overwhelming sense of guilt. I couldn't believe what had happened between us. I loved my brother, but this situation left me broken. I didn't speak to him for a long time after that. The pain was too fresh, too deep to even begin to mend. I picked up the phone and called my cousin, desperately seeking help. When I told her what had happened, she didn't hesitate to offer me a place to stay. For the first time in what felt like forever, I felt a glimmer of hope. She gave me a roof over my head and even offered me a job to help me get back on my feet. But despite her kindness, the pain I carried was unbearable. I couldn't escape the hurt and betrayal I had endured. It was like a storm raging inside me, and I didn't know how to stop it. Instead of dealing with the pain, I began to take it out on the people around me. My family bore the brunt of my anger and frustration. My attitude became a shield, a way to protect myself from further hurt. But it only pushed people away. My family always had something negative to say about me—criticizing my behavior, judging me for my actions. What they didn't understand was that I was damaged on the inside. I was carrying so much pain, so much trauma, and I didn't know how to release it in a healthy way. The Bible says,

*"The Lord is close to the brokenhearted and saves those who are crushed in spirit"* (Psalms 34:18). I was crushed, broken in ways that words couldn't fully express. But even in my pain, I began to realize that God was still with me. He saw my hurt, my struggles, and my efforts to keep going despite it all. Looking back, I see how important it is to deal with the pain we carry instead of letting it consume us. The Bible reminds us in *Ephesians 4:31-32, "Get rid of all bitterness, rage, and anger, brawling and slander, along with every form of malice. Be kind and compassionate to one another, forgiving each other, just as in Christ God forgave you."* I wasn't there yet—I wasn't ready to forgive my brother or anyone else who had hurt me. But God was planting seeds of healing in my heart, preparing me for the journey ahead.

This chapter of my life was one of the darkest, but it taught me that even in the midst of pain, there is hope. God's love is greater than any hurt we face, and His grace is enough to carry us through.

## A Mother's Strength: Fighting for My Child

When I started working, I was grateful for the opportunity to save money. My cousin's generosity in allowing me to save every penny was a blessing I didn't take for granted. It gave me hope that, despite my struggles, I was taking small steps toward stability for myself and my baby. But even as I worked, the heaviness of my situation weighed on me. I was pregnant, miserable, and carrying the emotional scars of abandonment and disappointment. My baby was due in January 2014. I had envisioned the final weeks of my pregnancy as a time of joyful preparation—setting up a space for her, imagining the life we would share, and eagerly counting down the days until I could hold her in my arms. But life had other plans. One day, I found myself in the hospital due to dangerously high blood sugar levels. The doctors told me I was a high-risk pregnancy, and I needed to be closely monitored. Fear gripped me as they explained the risks, but I tried to stay calm, trusting that everything would work out. Then, they told me something I wasn't prepared to hear they needed to induce labor. Hearing those words shattered the vision I had for my daughter's birth. I still had a month to go, and I wasn't ready—not physically, emotionally, or mentally. I prayed silently, asking God to guide the doctors and protect my baby. The Bible says, *"When I am afraid, I will trust you. I praise God for His word. I trust God, so I am not afraid"* (Psalms 56:3-4). I clung to those words, willing myself to trust God even as fear threatened to overwhelm me. As the labor progressed, the contractions became more intense. The physical pain was unlike anything I had ever felt, but the emotional pain was even greater. I was about to bring my daughter into the world, but the person who was supposed to be by my side her father wasn't there. I was grateful for my cousin, who stayed with me and offered her support, but it didn't fill the void left by his absence. I was angry at him, hurt that he had chosen not to share this moment with me. When my daughter was born, all the pain and fear melted away for a moment. She was so tiny, so delicate, and yet so beautiful. I was overwhelmed with love for this little life I had carried inside me. But my joy was short-lived. The doctors told me that she needed to stay in the hospital because her lungs weren't fully developed, and she couldn't breathe or eat on her own yet. Hearing those words felt like a punch to the chest. This was my first baby—why did she have to go through this? Why couldn't I take her home and hold her close? The thought of leaving her in the hospital while I went home alone was unbearable. But the doctors assured me that this was what she needed and that she would be in good hands. Walking out of the hospital without her was one of the hardest things I've ever done. My heart broke into pieces as I left her tiny, fragile body behind. I cried the entire way home, praying for her strength and health. The Bible says, *"Cast all your anxiety on Him because He cares for you"* (1 Peter 5:7). I poured out my fears to God, asking Him to protect her and help her grow strong. Every day, I visited her in the hospital. Holding her tiny hand, singing to her, and whispering prayers over her brought me some comfort, but it wasn't enough. I wanted her home with me, where she belonged. Then, on December 24, 2013—Christmas Eve—I received a call that shook me to my core. The nurse on the other end of the line told me that my daughter had stopped breathing. My heart sank, and fear gripped me like never before. *Stopped breathing? No, this can't be happening,* I thought. The nurse quickly reassured me that she had started breathing again, but the damage was done. My mind raced with thoughts of losing her, and my heart ached with the weight of it all. I dropped to my knees, tears streaming down my face, and cried out to God. *Why, Lord? Why is this happening to her?* I couldn't understand why my innocent baby had to fight for her life. The fear of losing her was unbearable, but I held on to the promise that God was with us. The Bible says, *"The Lord is near to the brokenhearted and saves those who are crushed in spirit"* (Psalms 34:18). In that moment, I was crushed—broken in ways I didn't think were possible. But I reminded myself that God was near, holding both me and my daughter in His hands. As I reflect on that time, I realize how much it taught me about love and resilience. A mother's love is fierce—it fights through pain, fear, and uncertainty. And though I didn't know it then, God was using this trial to strengthen me. He was teaching me to trust Him, even when the path ahead seemed dark and uncertain. Through this experience, I learned to lean on God like never before. His grace carried me through the sleepless nights, the fear-filled days, and the moments when I felt like giving up. He reminded me that His love is greater than any storm, and His plans are always for my good.

## Just Me and My Daughter

I didn't know what to say or how to feel about the situation I was facing. Relief mixed with fear as I processed the nurse's words. My baby girl was alive, but there were challenges ahead. The nurse explained that when it was time for her to be released, she would need to wear a breathing machine to monitor her in case she stopped breathing again. Hearing that felt like a heavy weight on my heart. This was my first child—why did she have to face these struggles so soon after entering the world? I nodded and said, "Okay," trying to stay strong. But inside, I was terrified. All I wanted was for her to be healthy and safe. As soon as I left the hospital room, I called her father. Despite everything that had happened between us, I wanted him to know what was going on. I told him about her condition, about how she had stopped breathing but had started again. I could hear a hint of happiness in his voice when I told him she was okay. He asked me a few questions about her condition, and I answered each one. For a moment, I felt hopeful—maybe this news would bring us closer, maybe he would step up and be the father she needed him to be.

Then I asked him, "Are you going to come and support me? "His answer crushed me. He said he didn't have a way to get there. I couldn't believe what I was hearing. *Your daughter needs you. How can you not find a way?* I told him, "She needs you to stop making excuses and figure it out." But instead of taking action, he made excuse after excuse. Tears filled my eyes as I hung up the phone. In that moment, I realized that I couldn't rely on him. If he couldn't try to be there for her now, when she needed him the most, how could I expect him to be there in the future? I made a promise to myself: no matter what, I would be there for my daughter. Every single day, I would show up for her, because she needed me more than ever. I didn't know if she was going to be okay, and that uncertainty weighed heavily on me. But when I looked at her, so small and fragile, it was clear that she needed my love and presence to fight through this. Her dad never came to visit her in the hospital. No matter how many times I reached out, he didn't make the effort. The realization that it was just me and my daughter against the world hit me hard. I had dreamed of us being a family, of raising her together and giving her the love and stability I had always wanted. But that dream was gone. The Bible says, *"The Lord your God goes with you; He will never leave you nor forsake you"* (Deuteronomy 31:6). In my loneliness, I clung to that promise. Even though I felt abandoned by the one person who should have been by my side, I knew that God hadn't left me. He was walking with me, strengthening me to endure the challenges ahead. Every day, I sat by her side in the hospital. I sang to her, whispered prayers over her, and told her how much I loved her. Even though she couldn't speak, I knew she felt my presence. Holding her tiny hand gave me a sense of peace and reminded me why I had to keep going. At night, when I left the hospital, the silence was overwhelming. I cried myself to sleep, praying for her health and strength. I pleaded with God to watch over her and give her the fight she needed to grow strong. The Bible says, *"Cast all your anxiety on Him because He cares for you"* (1 Peter 5:7). I laid all my fears at His feet, trusting Him to carry both of us through this storm. Looking back, I see how those days in the hospital taught me the depth of a mother's love. It's a love that endures fear, pain, and uncertainty. It's a love that keeps showing up, even when everything feels impossible. And though I was scared and often felt alone, God was with me every step of the way. Through this experience, I learned to rely on God's strength when my own failed. His love carried me through the sleepless nights and the overwhelming days. My daughter's fight became my fight, and I resolved to give her all the love and support I had, even if it meant doing it on my own.

CHAPTER

# HOPE

*"God gives us even more grace, as the scripture says, 'God is*
*against the proud, but He gives grace to the humble.'"*
*(James 4:6)*

I never missed a single day without seeing my daughter. She
was my source of joy when I needed it most, the light that
broke through my darkest moments. Sitting by her side,
holding her tiny hand, and watching her fight to grow stronger
gave me the courage to keep going. Each day brought small
improvements, and with every step forward, my hope grew. The
nurses were kind, keeping me informed of her progress and
encouraging me along the way. One day, after what felt like an
eternity, the nurse told me something I had been longing to
hear: "Your daughter can go home tomorrow. "Hearing those
words filled me with so much excitement, relief, and gratitude

that I could hardly contain myself. After everything we had been through, this was the moment I had been waiting for. The Bible says, *"When my anxious thoughts multiply within me, your comforts delight me"* (Psalm 94:19). God's promise to comfort and sustain me was evident in this moment. All the worry and fear I had carried for so long seemed to melt away, replaced by joy and anticipation. I couldn't wait to take her home, to start the life I had dreamed of for the two of us. Though our circumstances weren't perfect, the thought of holding her in my arms at home, without machines or hospital walls surrounding us, felt like a victory.

## A New Beginning

The nurse explained to me that my daughter would need to always wear her breathing machine. While I was thrilled to finally bring her home, the thought of her stopping breathing terrified me. I promised myself that I would do everything I could to keep her safe. I made sure her breathing machine stayed on, no matter what. My love for her grew stronger with every breath she took, and I became fiercely protective of her. Before we left the hospital, I was required to take a few classes to learn how to properly care for her. I remember sitting in those classes, feeling both overwhelmed and determined. I was grateful for the knowledge, but I also feared making a mistake. Every little thing felt so critical. But with each lesson, I gained more confidence. I reminded myself that these steps were part of giving her the best possible care and ensuring she would thrive. Finally, the day came when I brought her home. That moment felt surreal—like a dream finally coming true. But with the joy came an underlying sense of fear. She was so tiny, so fragile, and every movement she made filled me with both awe and worry. I watched her constantly, as if my eyes alone could keep her safe. Holding her in my arms was a reminder of God's faithfulness, even in the midst of challenges. At the time, I was still staying with my cousin, who had been a blessing to me during this season. Her support allowed me to focus on my daughter's needs without added stress. But deep down, I knew I needed to create a space of my own. I wanted my daughter to grow up in a stable home—a space where it could just be us. I longed to have a place where we could create new memories and start fresh. I started putting in applications for apartments. With every application, I prayed, *Lord, guide me to the right place for us. Open the door You want us to walk through.* I was diligent about saving money, putting aside every penny I could from my job. I kept telling myself, *this is just the beginning. Better days are coming.* Then, after weeks of waiting, I got the call I had been praying for—I was approved for an apartment. The news brought tears of joy to my eyes. For the first time, I would have a space to call my own, a place where I could build a life for my daughter. Signing the lease felt like a turning point. This wasn't just about having a roof over my head; it was about reclaiming my independence and stepping into a new chapter of my life. It was proof that, even in the midst of my struggles, God was working behind the scenes to provide for us. The Bible says, *"And my God will meet all your needs according to the riches of His glory in Christ Jesus"* (Philippians 4:19). I had seen this promise come to life in ways I couldn't have imagined. God had carried me through the darkest moments, and now He was leading me into a season of hope, healing, and restoration. Looking at my daughter, I felt an overwhelming sense of purpose. This wasn't just about me anymore—it was about giving her the life she deserved. Every challenge I faced had prepared me for this moment, and I was determined to make the most of it.

## A Home for Us

I found an apartment close to my cousin's daycare so I could get back and forth to work easily. It was important that it be within walking distance—I needed the convenience to balance my responsibilities. When I finally moved in, it felt like a dream. The space wasn't just a roof over my head; it was the start of something new, a fresh beginning for me and my daughter. As I settled into the apartment, I started thinking about my family and how much I wanted to rebuild what I had lost. My daughter deserved a chance to have both her parents present. Deep down, I still hoped that things could work out with her dad. I picked up the phone and called him, telling him about my new apartment in Atlanta. I asked him to come stay with me so we could work things out for the sake of our child. To my surprise, he agreed. When he arrived and moved in, I felt a wave of relief and joy. *Maybe this is the second chance we need,* I thought. For a short time, it seemed like things were falling into place. We were working together to care for our daughter, and for a brief moment, it felt like we could be a family. But that happiness didn't last long. Slowly, his efforts began to fade. He stopped helping as much as he did in the beginning, and his lack of effort became impossible to ignore. I was the one waking up in the middle of the night with our daughter, the one juggling work, childcare, and the responsibilities of keeping our household running. Exhaustion consumed me. Each morning, I dragged myself out of bed, tired from sleepless nights. It was as if he didn't care about anyone but himself. The man I thought I could depend on was showing me, once again, that his words didn't match his actions. As the days passed, resentment began to build. I was frustrated, annoyed, and feeling completely unsupported. It felt like he was leeching off me, taking up space in a home I had worked so hard to provide without contributing anything meaningful. One morning, as I got up to get ready for work, I looked at him lying there, completely unbothered by the weight I was carrying alone. I got myself and my daughter ready, but inside, I felt like I was reaching a breaking point. I couldn't keep doing this—I couldn't keep carrying the entire burden while he sat idly by. The Bible says, *"Come to me, all you who are weary and burdened, and I will give you rest"* (Matthew 11:28). I held on to that promise, praying for strength and guidance. I didn't know what the next step would be, but I knew I couldn't keep living like this.

## A New Chapter

He didn't even have the money to fix the door he broke. I stood there, furious and heartbroken, as he walked out of our lives, leaving me and our daughter behind. I was angry—not just at him, but at myself for believing that he would change. How could he leave us in this situation, with no regard for how we would manage or even how his daughter would sleep safely that night? But as hurt as I was, I refused to let it stop me. I made the decision to move forward—literally and figuratively. I applied for an apartment complex across the street from where I was staying. It wasn't an immediate process, but I was determined. I needed a fresh start, and I knew that a new space would help me create a better environment for me and my daughter. After some time, my persistence paid off, and I was approved. Moving into that apartment felt like another step toward reclaiming my life. It wasn't just about having a new place, it was about creating stability, something I had been craving for so long. Despite everything I had been through, I kept pushing forward. Every day, I got up, went to work, and did my best to provide for my daughter. It wasn't easy—I had no one to lean on, no one to share the load with. But I was determined to keep grinding because I knew she was depending on me. The Bible says, *"I can do all things through Christ who strengthens me"* (Philippians 4:13), and I clung to that promise. There were ups and downs, as always, but I made it work. Some days were harder than others. Some nights, I cried myself to sleep, wondering if I was doing enough or if things would ever get better. But overall, I was okay. I was surviving, and that alone felt like a victory. During my time at the new apartment, something unexpected happened and I met a friend. She and I connected almost instantly. We bonded over our shared experiences as single mothers, both trying to navigate life while raising two children. We discovered that not only were we going through similar struggles, but we also lived in the same apartment complex—right next to each other. It felt like more than a coincidence. It felt like God had placed her in my life at just the right time. We leaned on each other in ways that only another single mother could understand. We shared stories, laughter, and even tears. She became a source of comfort and encouragement for me, reminding me that I wasn't alone in this journey. One day, I told her about my cousin's daycare and mentioned that they were hiring. She was excited about the opportunity, and before long, she started working there with me. Having her at work made the days feel a little lighter. We motivated each other to keep pushing forward, even on the hardest days. Looking back, I see how God orchestrated those moments. Even in my loneliness and frustration, He was placing the right people in my life to help me carry the weight. The Bible says, *"A friend loves at all times, and a brother is born for adversity"* (Proverbs 17:17). That friendship was a reminder that even in the hardest seasons, we don't have to walk alone. Life wasn't perfect, but it was manageable. With my daughter as my motivation, I stayed in grind mode, focused on building a better future for the both of us. Every step I took, no matter how small, was a step forward, and I trusted that God was guiding me every step of the way.

## Balancing Burdens and Blessings

Everything seemed to be going well. My friendship with my neighbor was growing stronger, and I felt supported in a way I hadn't experienced in a long time. My daughter was approaching a milestone—her first birthday—and I was excited to plan a celebration for her. I wanted this party to be special, something that would show my daughter how much she was loved, even if she was too young to remember it. I called her father, hoping he would help me plan or at least contribute in some way. But as usual, he came up with excuse after excuse. He couldn't make it. He couldn't help. His lack of support left me feeling irritated and frustrated. I couldn't understand how someone could be so absent from their child's life, especially during such an important moment. The Bible says, *"Give generously, for your gifts will return to you later. Divide your gifts among many, for in the days ahead you yourself may need much help"* (Ecclesiastes 11:1-2). I wanted to believe that one day, he would realize the importance of showing up—not just with words, but with actions. But at that moment, I knew I couldn't count on him. So, I did what I always did: I stepped up and handled it myself. I planned the party, bought everything we needed, and made sure the day would be a joyful celebration for my daughter. It wasn't easy, but seeing her smile made every bit of effort worth it. In the middle of planning, I got a call from my uncle. He explained that he needed a place to stay temporarily while he got back on his feet. Without hesitation, I told him he could stay with me, even though I only had a one-bedroom apartment. I knew he would have to sleep in the living room, but I believed it was the right thing to do. At first, I was hopeful that things would go smoothly. But over time, my uncle's actions started to create tension in the apartment. He wasn't respecting my rules, and his behavior didn't align with the boundaries I had set for my home. It made me uncomfortable, but I tried to tolerate it because I knew his stay was only temporary. The Bible says, *"If anyone has material possessions and sees a brother or sister in need but has no pity on them, how can the love of God be in that person? Dear children, let us not love with words or speech but with actions and in truth"* (1 John 3:17-18). I reminded myself that showing love and support, even when it's inconvenient or challenging, is part of what God calls us to do. Even though it wasn't easy, I chose to extend grace and patience toward my uncle. I reminded myself that just as I needed help in the past, there would be times when others would need my help, too. I prayed for strength and wisdom, asking God to guide me in handling the situation with love and understanding. Looking back, I realize that those moments of inconvenience and frustration were teaching me something important. They reminded me of the value of perseverance, grace, and generosity, even when life feels overwhelming. It wasn't just about providing a space for my uncle—it was about growing in faith and trust, knowing that God sees and honors the love we show to others. Through all of this, I continued to focus on my daughter. She was my light, my motivation to keep pushing forward. Despite the challenges, I knew that everything I was doing was for her. And with God's help, I would continue to create a life filled with love, hope, and possibility for both of us.

## Learning to Love Through Pain

As time went by, life settled into a quiet rhythm. It was just me and my daughter. My uncle had finally found a place of his own, and while I was happy for him, I was also relieved to have my space back. For the first time in a long while, my home felt like mine again. The holidays became a special time for me. Having my daughter to share them with made everything feel brighter, even in the midst of my struggles. Her laughter, her smile, and her tiny hands reaching for me brought light to my darkest days. I was determined to make every birthday and holiday memorable for her, filled with love and joy. But no matter how much I tried to focus on her, there was still a part of me that felt incomplete. As her birthday approached, I called her dad to invite him and asked if he could help with the celebration. His response shattered what little hope I had left. He told me he didn't have a way to come, and to make matters worse, he mentioned he was spending time with another woman. Hearing that made my blood boil. I wasn't upset because he was with someone else—I had long since given up on us as a couple. What hurt was his complete disregard for his daughter. How could he prioritize someone else over his child? How could he refuse to show up for her on her special day? It wasn't her fault that things hadn't worked out between us. She deserved better. He never showed up for her birthday. As I looked at my daughter, I felt a deep, aching pain for her. She didn't understand what was happening, she was too young to realize that her father wasn't there. But I knew. And it broke my heart to think that she might grow up feeling the same rejection and abandonment that I had felt throughout my life. The Bible says, *"The Lord is close to the brokenhearted and saves those who are crushed in spirit"* (Psalms 34:18). In that moment, I felt crushed. But I reminded myself that God was near, even when it felt like the world was against me. Despite the pain, I made sure her birthday was filled with love. I decorated, baked, and poured my heart into creating a day that would make her smile. I didn't want her to feel the absence of her father. I wanted her to know that she was loved, even if it was just by me. As a young, single mother, I was still learning who I was while trying to raise a child. Some days, the weight of it all felt unbearable. I was doing my best, but the wounds from my past kept creeping into my present. The pain and rejection I had carried for so long were spilling over, and I didn't know how to stop it. Without realizing it, I started taking my frustrations out on my daughter. It wasn't intentional, but the pain I was carrying left little room for patience and grace. I found myself treating her the way I had been treated all my life—with harshness, frustration, and a sense of inadequacy. One day, as I raised my voice at her over something small, I stopped and saw the fear in her eyes. It was like looking into a mirror. I saw myself as a child, longing for love and kindness but met with anger instead. My heart sank. I didn't want to pass on the same pain I had endured. The Bible says, *"Fathers, do not provoke your children to anger, but bring them up in the discipline and instruction of the Lord"* (Ephesians 6:4). I knew I needed to break the cycle. My daughter didn't deserve to carry the weight of my past. She deserved to be raised with love, patience, and understanding—the very things I had always longed for. From that moment, I committed to doing better. I prayed for God to heal my heart so that I could love her the way she deserved to be loved. I asked Him to help me be the mother she needed—a mother who could nurture and encourage her, even when life felt overwhelming. I didn't have all the answers, and I knew it wouldn't be an easy journey. But I also knew that God was walking with me, guiding me as I learned to parent with grace and love. My daughter became motivated to keep going, to keep striving for better, and to trust that brighter days were ahead.

## Seeking Safety and Self-Love

I loved my daughter deeply, but I didn't know how to fully show it because I didn't love myself. Growing up with so much pain and rejection had left me broken in ways I didn't even understand. Without realizing it, I treated her the way I had been treated as a child—with frustration, impatience, and a lack of tenderness. The Bible says, *"This is my commandment, that you love one another as I have loved you"* (John 15:12). Those words reminded me that God's love is the example we are called to follow. But how could I love her fully when I hadn't yet experienced that love for myself? I began to realize that loving my daughter the way she deserved started with allowing God to heal the wounds in my heart. While I was grappling with these inner struggles, life around me became increasingly difficult. Things in my apartment complex took a turn for the worse. Violence and crime became a regular occurrence, and fear settled over me like a heavy cloud. I had moved to Riverdale without knowing the dangers of the area, but now I saw them firsthand. The sound of sirens became a nightly routine, and every loud noise made my heart race. I was terrified—not just for myself, but for my daughter. I knew this wasn't the environment I wanted to raise her in, but I felt stuck. Without a car, I needed to live close to my job, and finding an affordable place nearby wasn't easy. The Bible says, *"A gentle answer turns away wrath, but a harsh word stirs up anger. Blessed are those who are humble; they will be given the earth"* (Proverbs 15:1). I prayed for humility and patience as I searched for a solution. I knew that God had brought me this far, and I trusted that He would guide me to the next step. Determined to find a safer place for us, I started applying to apartments down the street from where I was.

I didn't know if I'd be approved, but I kept believing that God would open the right door. After some time, I got the news I had been waiting for—I was approved. The new apartment was much smaller than the one I had before, but I didn't care. Safety and stability were more important than space. I packed up everything we had and made the move, thankful for the opportunity to start fresh in a better environment. As I settled into the new apartment, I felt a mix of relief and determination. It wasn't perfect, but it was a step in the right direction. I went back to work, focused on providing for my daughter and creating a better future for us. This new chapter was about more than just a change of address—it was about finding hope in the midst of uncertainty. It was about learning to trust God's timing and provision, even when the path ahead wasn't clear. Looking back, I see how God was working through every challenge, every moment of fear, and every decision I had to make. He was teaching me to lean on Him, to let go of the pain from my past, and to embrace the love He had for me. Through it all, my daughter remained my motivation. Her presence reminded me of God's grace and the incredible gift of life. And as I continued to rebuild, I began to understand that loving her meant learning to love myself, too.

## When Connections Break

I was working as an assistant teacher in the 1-year-old class at the daycare, and I loved being around the children. Each day brought smiles and laughter, even amidst the challenges. It gave me a sense of purpose and a place where I could pour out my love and care. During this time, I connected with one of my students' mothers. We began talking casually, and over time, our conversations grew deeper. She became a friend—someone I could relate to and share parts of my life with. She told me about her struggles, and when she asked if she and her children could stay with me for a while, I didn't hesitate to say yes. I understood what it was like to need help, to feel like you're carrying the weight of the world alone. She didn't have much money, but she promised to help with food. That was enough for me. Having her and her children in my home felt comforting. We formed a small community of support for each other. I was her children's teacher, and after work, we'd all head home together. It felt so nice to have companionship and someone to share the little joys of life with. But as time went on, things began to change. The initial happiness and peace we felt started to fade. We were both emotionally wounded in ways that neither of us fully understood, and instead of healing together, we started unintentionally hurting each other. Small disagreements turned into arguments, and the atmosphere in the house grew tense. The Bible says, *"In everything, do to others what you would want them to do to you"* (Matthew 7:12). I tried to hold on to that principle, but the tension in the house kept building. Both of us were carrying so much pain, and it was spilling over into our relationship. One day, in a moment of frustration, I let my anger get the best of me. I asked her to leave. It wasn't a decision I had made thoughtfully—it was an emotional reaction to everything that had been building up between us. She left, taking her children with her, and we stopped talking. At first, I felt justified. I told myself that it was for the best, that I needed to protect my peace and my home. But as the days went on, guilt began to creep in. I started to question whether I had handled the situation the right way. I had opened my home to her because I wanted to help, but in the end, I let my emotions drive a wedge between us. The Bible says, *"Be kind and compassionate to one another, forgiving each other, just as in Christ God forgave you"* (Ephesians 4:32). I realized that while I had tried to be kind and compassionate initially, I had let my own emotional struggles cloud my judgment. Looking back, I see that the situation wasn't just about her or me—it was about two broken people trying to navigate life's challenges without the tools to fully heal. I learned an important lesson about boundaries, forgiveness, and the importance of addressing my own pain so that it doesn't harm the people around me. Though our friendship ended, I prayed for her and her children, asking God to guide them and provide for them. I also prayed for healing in my own heart, asking Him to teach me how to better manage my emotions and relationships. Life has a way of bringing people into your journey for a reason, even if it's only for a season. While this chapter didn't end the way I had hoped, it reminded me of the importance of grace—not just for others, but for myself as well.

## Lessons in Connection and Chaos

As time went by, I found myself opening my home once again, this time to a friend of the family and her children. At first, it felt like a good decision. We had fun together, partied, and filled the house with laughter. But as the weeks passed, things started to take a turn. Men started coming around frequently, and the peaceful sanctuary I had tried to create for myself, and my daughter began to crumble. My home became chaotic, far from the safe and stable space I had envisioned. What started as lighthearted fun quickly spiraled into disagreements, tension, and messes—both literal and emotional. It became clear that we weren't on the same page, and we began to clash more and more. Eventually, she decided to leave and find somewhere else to stay. I wasn't upset when she left; in fact, I felt a sense of relief. This experience taught me an important lesson: I couldn't keep opening my home to everyone, especially when it came at the expense of my peace. I told myself, *"No more.* My home needed to be a place of rest, not chaos. I resolved to stop letting people move in with me, no matter how much I cared about them. It was time to focus on me and my daughter—to create stability and order we both deserved. I threw myself into work, doing my best to make ends meet. Life wasn't easy, but I was determined to keep pushing forward. Then one day, something—or rather, someone—unexpectedly entered my life. I met him through a connection with one of my homegirls. He was one of her boyfriend's friends, and I first saw him standing in front of my cousin's daycare. He looked so fine, dressed so nicely, and carried himself with confidence. I couldn't help but be drawn to him. In my mind, I thought, *I want him.* I worked up the courage to say something to him, and before long, we exchanged numbers. From there, things happened quickly. He started coming over to my house, and we found ourselves connecting on so many levels. Our conversations flowed effortlessly, and our physical connection was undeniable. It wasn't long before he began spending the night at my house. He brought some of his clothes over, and I made sure he felt at home. I cooked for him, did my best to create a welcoming environment, and treated him the way I thought a man should be treated. I wanted him to feel comfortable, cared for, and valued. The Bible says, *"Above all, love each other deeply, because love covers over a multitude of sins"* (1 Peter 4:8). In those moments, I believed I was showing love through my actions. But looking back, I realized that while I was pouring into him, I wasn't taking the time to pour into myself. Our connection felt intense, fueled by both emotions and physical desires. I began focusing on him completely, to the point where everything else faded into the background. I convinced myself that what we had was love because of the way we made each other feel in that moment. But as much as I loved the way we connected, there was a part of me that knew I needed to be careful. I had been through so much already, and I didn't want to lose myself in another relationship that might not last. This chapter of my life was filled with highs and lows, teaching me the importance of guarding my heart and making sure that my focus stayed on the things that truly mattered. Through it all, I kept reminding myself that God was with me, guiding me toward the lessons I needed to learn.

## When Loneliness Takes Over

At first, it felt so real, so comforting. After spending so much time alone in the house with just me and my daughter, having a man around made the space feel less empty. I liked the idea of not doing everything on my own, and for a little while, his presence made the house feel like a home. Around this time, I started working at Popeyes near my new apartment. I had decided to leave the daycare job because I needed a change. Working with children has become overwhelming, and I wanted a fresh start in a different environment. But even as I tried to create a new routine, things at home began to unravel. My relationship with him, which had felt so promising in the beginning, started to fall apart. The arguments started small but grew bigger and more frequent. I noticed changes in his behavior and routine. He wasn't acting the same, and I couldn't ignore the feeling that something wasn't right. I began questioning him—where he was going, what he was doing—and the more I pressed, the more distant he became. The tension between us became unbearable, and in a moment of anger, I told him to leave. I didn't expect him to actually go. But he did. He packed up his things and walked out, leaving me stunned. I sat there, trying to process what had just happened. At first, I felt justified—I had every reason to be upset. But as the hours passed, my anger faded, replaced by sadness and regret. I hadn't truly wanted him to leave. I had spoken out of frustration, not realizing the weight of my words. Now, the house felt emptier than ever, and I couldn't shake the guilt. I missed him, missed the comfort of not being alone. The Bible says, *"The tongue has the power of life and death, and those who love it will eat its fruit"* (Proverbs 18:21). I reflected on how powerful words can be. In my frustration, I had spoken something I didn't truly mean, and now I was left to face the consequences. As if the loneliness wasn't enough, the apartment complex began to feel more dangerous with each passing day. Crime was becoming more common, and the sense of security I had hoped to find in my new home was slipping away. One night, as I sat in my living room, I heard loud commotion outside my apartment. My heart raced as I went to the window, peering out cautiously. Moments later, I heard the sound of gunshots. Someone had shot through my neighbor's window. Fear gripped me. I held my daughter close, praying that we would be protected. The Bible says, *"The Lord is my light and my salvation—whom shall, I fear? The Lord is the stronghold of my life—of whom shall I be afraid?"* (Psalm 27:1). In that moment, I clung to those words, asking God to shield us from harm. I didn't know what to do. I had just moved, and the thought of uprooting my life again felt impossible. My mind was all over the place, torn between fear, uncertainty, and the overwhelming weight of being the sole protector for my daughter. Through it all, I reminded myself that God was with me. Even in the midst of chaos, I held onto the belief that He was guiding me and that this season, as difficult as it was, would not last forever.

## Living in Fear

That night was terrifying. The sound of gunshots and the chaos outside my window left me shaken to my core. I held my daughter close, praying for our safety as the commotion unfolded around us. By the time the noise had stopped, I was already thinking about leaving. I didn't want to spend another night in a place where my life, and my daughter's life, felt so uncertain. The next morning, with fear still lingering in my heart, I called the leasing office to report what had happened. I explained the situation, hoping they could help me move to a different area within the apartment complex—anywhere that felt safer. One of the ladies at the leasing office listened patiently, but her response wasn't what I had hoped for. She told me that I needed to file a police report in order to take further action. Her words felt like a roadblock. The thought of going through that long and exhausting process overwhelmed me. I didn't want to spend days reliving the fear, explaining it to strangers, and waiting for an uncertain outcome. I just wanted to leave. I wanted safety for me and my daughter, and I didn't want to have to fight so hard to find it. The Bible says, *"I have told you these things, so that you can have peace because of me. In this world you will have trouble. But be encouraged! I have won the battle over the world"* (John 16:33). That verse gave me comfort in a moment of discouragement. Even though I felt trapped and afraid, I reminded myself that God's peace was greater than my fear. As I hung up the phone, I felt stuck. The reality of my situation weighed heavily on me. I couldn't just pack up and leave overnight, and the process of finding somewhere new felt impossible. But I also knew that staying in this unsafe environment wasn't an option. In that moment, I turned to prayer. I asked God for guidance, for protection, and for the strength to make the right decision for my daughter and me. I reminded myself that even in the face of fear, I wasn't alone. God was with me, fighting my battles and lighting the path ahead.

CHAPTER

# BETRAYAL

*"God is our refuge and strength, a very present help in trouble.
Therefore, we will not fear, though the earth gives way, though
the mountains be moved into the heart of the sea, though its
waters roar and foam, though the mountains tremble at its
swelling." (Psalms 46:1-3)*

After the terrifying incident at my apartment, I knew I couldn't stay there any longer. I needed a safe place for me and my daughter, even if it meant starting over once again. I called my friend and explained everything that had happened. She was understanding and kind, and without hesitation, she told me I could come and stay with her. Relieved, I broke my lease, packed up all my belongings, and left the place that had brought so much fear and chaos into my life. Moving in with my friend felt like a fresh start, a chance to regroup and find some peace.

At first, everything was going well. Living together brought us closer, and we started to bond in ways we hadn't before. For a little while, it felt like things were falling into place. But then, she allowed another friend of hers to move in, and that's when things started to change. The apartment was small, and having another person there made the space feel even tighter. At first, I tried to make the best of it, but it quickly became clear that this new dynamic wasn't going to work. Her friend began to act jealous of the relationship I had with my friend. It felt like she was constantly trying to come between us, creating tension where there didn't need to be any. What hurt the most was how she treated my daughter. She started to single her out, treating my friend's children much better than my own. She would lie about me, spreading false stories to my friend, and would even do hurtful things to my daughter out of spite. Seeing my child mistreated in that way made my blood boil. The Bible says, *"Do not repay anyone evil for evil. Be careful to do what is right in the eyes of everyone"* (Romans 12:17). I tried to remind myself of this when my anger began to rise, but it was so hard to stay calm. Watching someone act cruelly toward my daughter, who was completely innocent in all of this, felt unbearable. What made it even worse was that my friend didn't seem to say much about the situation. She didn't address her friend's behavior, and instead, it felt like she was taking her side. The two of them would go places together, leaving me and my daughter behind. It was like we didn't matter anymore. The betrayal stung deeply. This was someone I had trusted; someone I had leaned on during one of the hardest seasons of my life. And now, it felt like she had chosen someone else over me, turning a blind eye to the way her friend was treating my child. The Bible says, *"The Lord is near to the brokenhearted and saves the crushed in spirit"* (Psalms 34:18). I clung to this promise, knowing that God saw my pain and understood the depth of my hurt. Even though I felt abandoned and betrayed, I knew I wasn't truly alone. In those moments of hurt, I turned to God for strength. I prayed for wisdom, for guidance, and for the courage to do what was best for me and my daughter. This situation taught me a painful but important lesson: not everyone who offers help has your best interest at heart. Though it felt like another setback, I reminded myself that this was just a chapter in my story, not the whole book. God was still writing my story, and I trusted that He would lead me to a better place.

## The Weight of Betrayal

It hurt deeply, more than I could put into words. I didn't understand why my friend, someone who knew me and my heart, would allow her mind to be so easily corrupted by lies. Her friend had filled her with bad thoughts about me, twisting her perception of who I was. I kept asking myself, *how could this be happening?* My friend knew me better than anyone—she had seen my struggles, my efforts, my love for my daughter—yet it felt like she was choosing to believe someone else over me. I felt like an outsider in a place that was supposed to be my refuge. The betrayal cut me to my core, and I knew I couldn't stay there much longer. But leaving wasn't as simple as packing up and walking out the door. I had nowhere to go, no clear plan. The Bible says, *"The Lord does not see as man sees. For man looks at the outward appearance, but the Lord looks at the heart"* (1 Samuel 16:7). That verse gave me comfort as I wrestled with the pain of being misunderstood. I knew that God saw my heart. He knew my intentions and my struggles, even when others didn't. Desperation began to set in. I couldn't keep living like this, enduring the tension, the lies, and the constant feeling of being unwanted. That night, I turned to Facebook, hoping to find a room for rent. I spent hours scrolling, searching through posts, looking for any opportunity. I was determined I had to find a way out. All night and into the morning, I searched relentlessly. My eyes burned from staring at the screen, but I didn't stop. I prayed as I searched, asking God to lead me to the right place. Then, finally, I found a post from a girl who said she had just moved into a three-bedroom apartment. I reached out to her immediately, explaining my situation. I told her I needed a place to stay but that I didn't have any money at the moment. I promised her that once I had the money, I would pay her for the room. My heart raced as I waited for her response. To my surprise and relief, she told me it was fine. She didn't hesitate or question me. She simply agreed to let me stay. Her kindness felt like an answered prayer, a light breaking through the darkness. The Bible says, *"The Lord is my shepherd; I shall not want. He makes me lie down in green pastures. He leads me beside still waters. He restores my soul"* (Psalms 23:1-3). In that moment, I felt a sense of peace. I knew that God was leading me to a place of rest, even if only for a little while. Though I didn't know what the future would hold, I felt hopeful for the first time in weeks. This new opportunity was a chance to start fresh, to leave the pain and betrayal behind and focus on building something better for me and my daughter.

## A Fresh Start in a New Home

When I moved into the house, it felt like a weight had been lifted off my shoulders. The house was big and beautiful, with plenty of space for me and my daughter. For the first time in a long while, we had a room of our own—a place that felt like ours. It was spacious, comfortable, and just what I needed to start rebuilding my life. The girl who owned the house was kind and welcoming. She shared with me about a job she was working at and even offered to take me to a job fair. I was excited about the opportunity and hopeful that I'd find work soon. At the job fair, they told me they'd call me when something became available. Though I didn't have anything lined up yet, the possibility of working again gave me a sense of purpose and determination. But as much as I wanted to move forward, there were still challenges I needed to overcome. I didn't know how to drive, and the thought of figuring out transportation weighed heavily on me. I knew that when I started working, I'd need a reliable way to get to and from my job. I kept praying, asking God to make a way and help me find a solution. The Bible says, *"Trust in the Lord with all your heart and lean not on your own understanding; in all your ways submit to Him, and He will make your paths straight"* (Proverbs 3:5-6). I reminded myself of this verse every time doubt crept into my mind. I didn't have all the answers, but I trusted that God was guiding my steps. As I settled into the house, I began to learn more about the woman who had given me a place to stay. She confided in me that she had moved to Atlanta after being banned from her hometown for something she had done. Her past was complicated, and though I didn't know all the details, it was clear that she was trying to leave that chapter of her life behind and start fresh. Hearing her story reminded me that everyone carries their own burdens, their own mistakes, and their own pain. It also reminded me of the importance of grace. None of us are perfect, but we all deserve a chance to grow, change, and rebuild. While there was still uncertainty about what the future held, I felt a glimmer of hope. I had a roof over my head, a safe place for my daughter, and the potential for a job on the horizon. Slowly but surely, I was taking steps toward a brighter future. The Bible says, *"For I know the plans I have for you, declares the Lord, plans to prosper you and not to harm you, plans to give you hope and a future"* (Jeremiah 29:11). I held onto that promise, trusting that even though I couldn't see the full picture, God had a plan for me and my daughter—a plan filled with hope, healing, and new beginnings.

## Revealing True Colors

At first, I was grateful to have a safe place to stay, but it didn't take long for the cracks in the foundation of this arrangement to show. She made me feel small, as if I was nothing compared to her. She had a house, rentals every week, and a lifestyle funded by her father, who seemed to pay for everything. Meanwhile, I had nothing.

She flaunted her material possessions in front of me, as if they defined her worth. It was as though she wanted me to feel inferior, to believe that I needed the same things she had to survive. The constant comparison weighed heavily on me. I started questioning myself, feeling like I wasn't good enough, like I was falling short as a mother and a woman. But deep down, I knew that what she was doing was wrong. Her words and actions were not rooted in kindness or support. Instead of lifting me up during a time when I was trying to rebuild my life, she seemed intent on tearing me down. One of the hardest parts was realizing how self-centered she truly was. I didn't know how to drive, and it was something I desperately wanted to learn so I could become more independent. But despite her resources and connections, she never offered to help me. It was as if she didn't want me to grow, didn't want me to rise above my circumstances. Over time, her true colors began to shine through. I discovered who she really was and what she was up to behind the scenes. She wasn't the person she had first presented herself to be. The house, the rentals, the lifestyle she flaunted—it was all built on lies. Everything she had, she had scammed for. The Bible says, *"The Lord detests lying lips, but He delights in people who are trustworthy"* (Proverbs 12:22). As I reflected on her actions, I couldn't help but feel disappointment. Not just in her, but in myself for trusting someone who wasn't honest. Our relationship began to deteriorate. Arguments erupted over the things she said and did, and I found myself feeling more isolated and unwelcome in the place that was supposed to be my refuge. What hurt the most was how she treated our daughters. She treated her child far better than mine, constantly pointing out what her daughter had and what mine didn't. It felt like a deliberate attempt to make me feel less like a mother. I couldn't take it anymore. The tension, the toxic environment, the constant comparison—it was all too much. I was ready to leave, to find a way out of this situation and create a better life for me and my daughter. The Bible says, *"A heart at peace gives life to the body, but envy rots the bones"* (Proverbs 14:30). I reminded myself not to let envy or resentment take root in my heart. Her lifestyle may have looked glamorous on the outside, but it was built on dishonesty, and I knew I didn't want that for myself. I wanted something real, something honest. I prayed for guidance and strength, asking God to show me the next step. This experience taught me that material things don't define a person's worth. What mattered was my integrity, my faith, and my love for my daughter. Even though I didn't have much, I had the determination to keep moving forward—and that was worth more than anything she could ever flaunt.

## Unmasking the Illusion

At first, I believed the image she presented—that she had worked tirelessly for everything she had. But the reality was far from what I had imagined. All the possessions she flaunted, the house, the rentals—none of it came from hard work. Learning this truth left me disappointed and ready to leave, but I had no plan in place yet. I needed to figure out my next steps carefully. She seemed to think that just because I was staying with her, she had the right to treat me however she wanted. The sense of entitlement in her tone and actions became unbearable. We argued constantly, and the tension in the house made it hard to focus on anything else. I found myself questioning everything. *How did I end up here again? Why do I keep finding myself in situations where I feel unwanted and unappreciated?* These thoughts swirled in my head as I tried to make sense of it all. Her words cut deep, filled with criticism and comparisons. She used her possessions as a weapon, reminding me of what she had and what I didn't. It felt like she took pride in trying to make me feel small. Every insult and dismissive comment were another blow to my spirit, and it hurt more than I could put into words. The Bible says, *"The Lord does not see as man sees; for man looks at the outward appearance, but the Lord looks at the heart"* (1 Samuel 16:7). This verse gave me strength. I reminded myself that my worth wasn't tied to material things. God saw my heart, my struggles, and my efforts, even when others couldn't or wouldn't. Just when I thought I couldn't endure the situation any longer, her cousin came to visit. I wasn't sure what to expect, but her energy was different. She was kind and approachable, and we clicked right away. Talking to her felt like a small glimmer of hope in the midst of my frustration. She didn't treat me with judgment or superiority. Instead, she showed genuine interest and respect. It was refreshing to have someone in the house who wasn't contributing to the tension, and for the first time in a while, I felt seen and heard. Her kindness reminded me that not everyone is out to harm or belittle you. There are still good-hearted people in the world, even when it feels like they're few and far between. I knew I needed to leave that house and find a place where I could rebuild my peace and stability. But for the moment, I held onto the small blessings, like the connection with her cousin, and reminded myself that God was walking with me through it all. The Bible says, *"For I know the plans I have for you, declares the Lord, plans to prosper you and not to harm you, plans to give you hope and a future"* (Jeremiah 29:11). I trusted that this difficult season wouldn't last forever, and that God was preparing a way for me and my daughter to move forward into something better.

## Learning the Hard Way

With the tax money I received, I bought a car. It felt like such an important step forward—a chance to gain the independence I had always wanted. I was determined to learn how to drive. Having a car would mean no more relying on others, no more walking everywhere, and no more feeling trapped by circumstances. I asked her cousin if she knew how to drive. She told me she did, so I asked if she would be willing to help teach me. She agreed, and I was excited to finally take this leap. We got into the car together, and she drove first, demonstrating how to handle everything step by step. Watching her made it seem easy, and I felt confident that I could do it too. When it was my turn, I got into the driver's seat and tried to follow her instructions as best I could. At first, I was doing okay nervous but determined. But then, in a split second, everything changed. I lost control and hit someone's mailbox. Before I could fully react, the car rolled onto the grass. I scrambled to put it in park, my heart racing as I realized what had just happened. Panic set in. I couldn't believe this had happened while I was just trying to learn. It was a mistake—one I hadn't meant to make—but the damage was done. My car was stuck in the grass, and the mailbox was broken. I didn't know what to do. The situation felt overwhelming, and my thoughts were racing. The Bible says, *"The Lord is my light and my salvation—whom shall, I fear? The Lord is the stronghold of my life—of whom shall I be afraid?"* (Psalms 27:1). I clung to this verse, reminding myself that even in moments of fear and uncertainty, God was with me. I knew I couldn't run from the situation. I had to face the consequences, no matter how scared I was. As I was trying to figure out my next step, a woman came outside. My stomach dropped when I realized it wasn't just anyone's mailbox—it belonged to a police officer. At that moment, I felt like everything was crashing down around me. The fear of what might happen consumed me, and I felt completely out of my depth. All I wanted was to learn how to drive and take control of my life, and now I was standing in the middle of a situation that felt like it had spiraled completely out of control. But even in the midst of my fear, I knew I had to take responsibility. The Bible reminds us, *"Be strong and courageous. Do not be afraid or terrified because of them, for the Lord your God goes with you; He will never leave you nor forsake you"* (Deuteronomy 31:6). I prayed silently, asking God to give me the courage to handle the situation with honesty and grace.

## Facing the Fear

This was one of the most terrifying moments of my life. The last thing I wanted was to talk to the police, but I knew I had no choice. My heart was pounding as I tried to gather my thoughts and figure out what to say. Out of fear and panic, I lied about the situation, hoping it might make things easier. When the officer came outside and saw the damage, I braced myself for the worst. But to my surprise, she gave me grace. She listened as I explained, trembling, that I was only trying to learn how to drive and that this had been a complete accident. I apologized repeatedly, my voice breaking as I expressed how sorry I was. Instead of being harsh or angry, she showed sympathy. She told me I just needed to fix the mailbox, and she let me go without any further trouble. I was overwhelmed with relief. What could have been a disastrous situation turned out to be a blessing. The Bible says, *"God is faithful and fair. If we confess our sins, He will forgive our sins. He will forgive every wrong thing we have done. He will make us pure"* (1 John 1:9). Her understanding and compassion reminded me of God's grace—that even in our mistakes, there is forgiveness and a chance to make things right. When I returned home, I thought the worst was behind me, but it wasn't. The girl I was staying with took the opportunity to mock me over the incident. She made fun of me, laughing at what had happened, and tried to make me feel small. At first, her words stung, but then I reminded myself that I had handled the situation with honesty and taken responsibility for my actions. I was good with myself and with God, and her opinion didn't matter. The Bible says, *"The Lord is my strength and my defense; He has become my salvation. He is my God, and I will praise Him, my father's God, and I will exalt Him"* (Exodus 15:2). That verse strengthened me, reminding me that my worth doesn't come from others' opinions but from God's love and grace. Later, I called a friend I had met before to share what had happened. I just needed someone to listen and offer some encouragement. She seemed concerned and asked to speak with the girl I was staying with to figure out what all the confusion was about. I handed over the phone, and they began talking. They exchanged numbers and continued the conversation later. Over the next few days, I noticed they were talking on the phone more and more—far more than I spoke with either of them. At first, I didn't think much of it, but over time, it felt like another shift in my relationships. I wasn't sure what it meant, but I trusted that God was still leading me through this season of growth and change. Even though life was unpredictable, I knew He had a plan for me. The Bible says, *"For the Spirit God gave us does not make us timid, but gives us power, love, and self-discipline"* (2 Timothy 1:7). With this truth in my heart, I pressed forward, determined to continue learning, growing, and trusting God through it all.

## Seeking an Escape

This situation didn't make any sense to me. The girl I was staying with was supposed to be my friend, yet she was constantly mocking me, and now she was forming a bond with my other friend. It felt like betrayal on both sides. I finally confronted my friend and asked her; *how could you be friends with someone like her after everything she's done to me?* Her response shocked me. She told me I should never have found the girl on Facebook in the first place. She said it was stupid and dangerous for me to reach out to a stranger like that. Her words stung, but they also felt hypocritical. In my mind, I thought, *if you feel this way, then why are you building a friendship with her? How is that any different?* The situation left me feeling angry and frustrated. I hated both of them at that point. I felt abandoned, like no one was truly on my side. I knew I couldn't stay there any longer. It was time to leave and find a new place to start over—again. I called my uncle, someone I trusted deeply, and explained what was going on. I asked him if I could stay with him until I got back on my feet. Without hesitation, he told me that I could. Relieved, I called my cousin and asked if she could help me move my things and take me to my uncle's house. She agreed, and soon, I was on my way to what I hoped would be a more peaceful environment. When I arrived at my uncle's house, he welcomed me with open arms. He told me that my daughter and I could sleep in his room, and for the first time in a while, I felt a glimmer of hope. I thought that being with my uncle would bring me comfort and stability I so desperately needed. But even as I settled in, I couldn't shake the weight of everything I had been through. The constant betrayals, the arguments, the feeling of being unwanted—it all weighed heavily on my heart. I was emotionally drained, and my soul felt battered. The Bible says, *"Come to me, all you who are weary and burdened, and I will give you rest"* (Matthew 11:28). I clung to this promise, praying that God would help me find peace and healing in the midst of my struggles. Though I was physically in a new place, the emotional baggage I carried remained with me. I realized that escaping the problems in my life wasn't enough—I needed to face them, heal from them, and learn how to rebuild. This chapter of my life taught me that sometimes the people we expect to support us may let us down, but God's love and guidance never fail. Even when I felt lost and alone, I trusted that He was leading me to a better future—one step at a time.

## Struggling to Hold It Together

As part of my effort to start over, I selected a daycare for my daughter so I could have time to search for a job and begin rebuilding my life. I was determined to get back on the right path, not just for myself, but for my daughter as well. I wanted to provide her with the stability and love she deserved, but nothing about this journey was easy. Despite my efforts, I struggled to find a job. Every rejection chipped away at my confidence, leaving me feeling stuck and defeated. To make matters worse, things with my uncle began to deteriorate. He had his own struggles, and his behavior became unpredictable. He was smoking things that seemed to cloud his judgment and corrupt his mind, and he started getting irritated with everything I did. It didn't matter if I was trying my best—nothing seemed good enough for him. His frustration created a tense atmosphere in the house, and I felt like

I was walking on eggshells every moment of the day. The constant stress weighed heavily on me, both physically and emotionally. I became so overwhelmed that I started neglecting my health. My diabetes, which already required careful management, was pushed to the back of my mind. I wasn't eating properly, my blood sugar was out of control, and I lost a significant amount of weight. On top of everything, my daughter began acting out. She was just a child, innocent and unaware of the depth of my struggles, but her behavior added to the growing pile of challenges I was trying to navigate. I didn't know how to love her the way I wanted to because my heart and mind were consumed with the pain of everything I had endured. The Bible says, *"But you, O Lord, are a shield around me; you are my glory, the one who holds my head high"* (Psalms 3:3). I clung to this verse, praying for God to shield me from the overwhelming weight of my circumstances and to lift me up when I felt too weak to carry on. Every day there was a battle to hold it all together. On the outside, I tried to appear strong, but inside, I was breaking. Depression wrapped itself around me like a heavy blanket, and I felt trapped under its weight. But even in my lowest moments, I reminded myself that God hadn't abandoned me. His presence was still with me, even when I couldn't see or feel it. I prayed for strength, for clarity, and for the ability to move forward despite the challenges. This season of my life was one of the hardest I had faced, but it taught me the importance of perseverance. The Bible says, *"The Lord is close to the brokenhearted and saves those who are crushed in spirit"* (Psalms 34:18). I believed that even though I was crushed and broken, God was working behind the scenes to carry me through. I didn't have all the answers, but I knew that giving up wasn't an option. My daughter needed me, and deep down, I knew that God was preparing me for something greater.

## Living in Darkness

Staying with my uncle felt like living in a constant state of darkness. His mood swings and sudden bursts of anger weighed heavily on me. He would get upset with me over the smallest things, and I never knew what would trigger him. I carried so much hurt and trauma from my past, but I didn't talk about it. Instead, I bottled everything up, and the weight of it all turned into anger. I was angry at the world, at my circumstances, and even at myself. I started taking that anger out on my daughter. She was acting out and getting in trouble everywhere she went, and I didn't know how to handle it. Instead of guiding her with love and patience, I found myself being mean to her, mirroring the way I had been treated throughout my own life. It was a cycle I hated, but I didn't know how to break free from it. The Bible says, *"Cast all your anxiety on Him because He cares for you"* (1 Peter

5:7). I wanted so badly to give all my burdens to God, but the weight of everything felt overwhelming. I was so consumed by anger, sadness, and frustration that I couldn't see a way out. My uncle's behavior only made things worse. Every time he smoked, his spirit would change completely. He became mean, uptight, and impossible to talk to. I didn't understand why he treated me the way he did—it felt like he was angry at me just for existing. The tension in the house grew unbearable, and I started to feel like I couldn't keep going. I needed relief, but I didn't know where to find it. When my other uncle moved in, things got even more chaotic. Both of them would sit and smoke from a can, something I had never seen before. It became clear to me that this was what was controlling them. Whatever they were smoking was stealing their peace, their kindness, and their ability to see me as anything other than a burden. Their anger became overwhelming, and I felt like I was walking on eggshells every moment of the day. One night, things took a terrifying turn. My uncle and I were having a discussion that escalated into an argument. Out of nowhere, he pulled out a gun and pointed it at me. My heart sank, and fear washed over me. I was frozen, staring at him, trying to comprehend what was happening. This was my family, someone who was supposed to love and protect me, and yet here I was, facing the possibility of losing my life at his hands. The Bible says, *"Even though I walk through the darkest valley, I will fear no evil, for You are with me; Your rod and Your staff, they comfort me"* (Psalms 23:4). In that moment, I clung to God's promise of protection. Though I was terrified, I prayed silently, asking God to shield me and my daughter from harm. Thankfully, the situation didn't escalate further, but the damage was done. I was shaken to my core, and I knew I couldn't stay there any longer. This wasn't just about needing my own space anymore— it was about survival. I had to leave for the sake of my safety and my daughter's well-being. The darkness I had been living in felt suffocating, but I reminded myself that God is a light in the midst of even the darkest places. The Bible says, *"The Lord is my rock, my fortress, and my deliverer; my God is my rock, in whom I take refuge"* (Psalms 18:2). I held onto this truth, knowing that God would make a way for me to escape this toxic environment and lead me to a place of peace. This chapter of my life was one of the most terrifying and challenging I had faced, but it reminded me of my strength and resilience. No matter how many times I felt like giving up, God's grace kept me moving forward.

## A Cry for Freedom

The Bible says, *"All praise to God, the Father of our Lord Jesus Christ. It is by His great mercy that we have been born again, because God raised Jesus Christ from the dead. "Now we live with great expectation"* (1 Peter

1:3). But in that moment, I felt anything but hopeful. I was consumed with fear, my heart pounding as I stared at the gun in my uncle's hand. I just knew he was going to pull the trigger. Time seemed to stand still as I wrestled with the terrifying reality that my own uncle, someone who was supposed to protect and care for me, was threatening my life. I couldn't believe it was happening. The person I had trusted enough to turn to in my time of need was now the one endangering me. After what felt like an eternity, the moment passed, and he lowered the gun. But the damage had been done. I was shaken to my core, and the house no longer felt like a refuge—it felt like a prison. How could I sleep under the same roof with someone who had come so close to ending my life? I called my oldest sister and told her what had happened. She rushed over to check on me and make sure I was okay. Having her there brought some comfort, but it wasn't enough to erase the fear and anxiety that had taken hold of me. I didn't just want to leave—I needed to leave. I felt trapped, desperate for someone to rescue me and my daughter from this nightmare. The Bible says, *"Now the Lord is the Spirit, and where the Spirit of the Lord is, there is freedom"* (2 Corinthians 3:17). I clung to this truth, praying for God to deliver me from this situation and guide me to a place of peace and safety. It was insane and completely unfair for me and my child to stay in such a toxic and dangerous environment. No one should have to live in fear of the very people they should be able to trust. I felt like I had been failed on so many levels, and the weight of it all was crushing me. Even though I was terrified, I knew I couldn't let this situation define me or hold me back. God had a plan for my life, and I trusted that He would lead me to freedom. The Bible says, "The righteous cry out, and the Lord hears them; He delivers them from all their troubles" (Psalms 34:17). I cried out to God with everything I had, trusting that He heard me and would make a way. This chapter of my life reminded me of how deeply I needed God's protection and guidance. No matter how dark the situation seemed, I held onto the hope that brighter days were ahead—for me and for my daughter.

## A Light in the Storm

I was ready to leave, ready to escape the pain that had consumed me for so long. My heart ached with the weight of rejection, and I couldn't shake the thought: *Does anyone in my family even love me? Why does it feel like they all want me to suffer?* The questions circled in my mind as I tried to hold myself together for the sake of my daughter. That morning, I woke up, got on the bus, and took my daughter to daycare. The bus ride felt longer than usual, each moment filled with the tension of knowing I had to return to my uncle's house. After dropping her off, I came back to the room where we were staying. I sat there, alone with my thoughts, counting down the hours until it was time to pick her up again. The day grew darker, and I noticed the clouds gathering. Rain was coming, and I needed to hurry. I decided to go to the gas station to get some milk before picking up my daughter. As I started walking, the rain began to fall, and soon it was pouring. I pulled my hood up, bracing myself against the cold drops, and kept moving. Then, through the haze of the rain, I saw a car slow down and stop near me. A woman rolled down her window and called out, *"Do you need a ride?"* At first, I hesitated. I didn't know her, but something about her felt genuine. I nodded and told her yes, and as I climbed into her car, a wave of relief washed over me. For the first time, in what felt like forever, someone cared enough to help me. She drove me to the daycare to pick up my daughter, and then she brought us back to my uncle's house. As much as I dreaded going back to that house, I couldn't help but feel a glimmer of gratitude. Her kindness in that moment felt like a gift from God, a reminder that I wasn't completely alone in this world. The Bible says, *"The Lord is close to the brokenhearted and saves those who are crushed in spirit"* (Psalms 34:18). That woman's act of kindness felt like an answer to my unspoken prayers, a sign that God was still watching over me even in the midst of my pain. She started coming over more often after that day, checking in on me and offering her support. Over time, we became friends, and her presence in my life became a source of comfort and hope. She didn't judge me for my struggles or look down on me for the things I couldn't control. She simply showed up, and that meant more than words could express. I was so happy to have someone like her in my corner. When I needed someone the most, she was there. Her friendship reminded me that there are still good people in the world who care, who are willing to help without expecting anything in return. The Bible says, *"A friend loves at all times, and a brother is born for a time of adversity"* (Proverbs 17:17). Her friendship was a testament to that truth, and I thanked God for bringing her into my life during such a dark and difficult season.

## A New Chapter, A Familiar Pattern

Feeling overwhelmed by everything I was going through; I decided to reach out to an old friend from high school. I needed someone to talk to—someone who might understand or, at the very least, listen. During our conversation, I opened up about my struggles and mentioned that I needed a place to stay. To my surprise, she told me she and her boyfriend had a place just down the street from my uncle's house. Hearing this felt like a small ray of hope. I was excited at the thought of having somewhere else to go, a fresh start away from the tension and fear I had been living with. I moved in with her and her boyfriend, grateful to have a roof over my head and a place to lay my head, even if it meant sleeping downstairs. I didn't mind as long as I had a safe space for me and my daughter. When I met my friend's boyfriend, I noticed he had just gotten out of jail that same day. They spent most of their time upstairs, recording music together. At first, I didn't think much of him, but one evening, we found ourselves in the kitchen at the same time. He was eating chicken, and I jokingly asked if I could have a piece. He handed me some, and we started talking. It was a simple moment, but it felt easy and natural. After that, I started seeing him more often. Little by little, we got to know each other better, and before I knew it, we were spending more time together. There was a mutual attraction, and soon, we both admitted we liked each other. He ended up moving downstairs with me, and for a while, things seemed to be going well. It was comforting to have someone by my side, someone who made me feel less alone. But as time went on, cracks began to show in the foundation of our relationship. I started noticing the way he moved—the secrecy, the constant coming and going, the late-night phone calls. It didn't take long for me to figure out that he was selling drugs. I felt conflicted. On one hand, I wanted to believe in the good I saw in him, but on the other, I couldn't ignore the warning signs. Worse still, I couldn't shake the suspicion that he was talking to other women. His actions made it hard to trust him, and my mind was constantly racing with doubts and insecurities. I felt like I was slipping into an all-too-familiar pattern, drawn to someone who wasn't fully invested in me or my well-being. The Bible says, *"Do not be deceived: 'Bad company ruins good morals'"* (1 Corinthians 15:33). I started questioning whether being in this situation was truly what was best for me and my daughter. Though I tried to make the best of the circumstances, a part of me knew deep down that this wasn't where I was meant to be. I prayed for clarity and strength, asking God to help me navigate the situation and make the right decisions for my future. This chapter of my life reminded me that even when things seem to offer a temporary escape, they're not always the solution we need. It was another lesson in recognizing my worth and trusting that God had something better planned for me.

## Betrayed Again

I started noticing changes in him—subtle at first, but enough to make me uneasy. He wasn't acting like the person I had first gotten to know. His behavior became erratic, and his mood swings were unpredictable. One morning, I was already on edge. My daughter, being a child, was doing things that irritated me, and I let my frustration get the best of me. I yelled at her, overwhelmed by everything I had been holding inside. That's when he snapped.

Before I could process what was happening, he slapped me. The sting of his hand on my face was nothing compared to the shock and rage that surged through me. I couldn't believe it. This man I had trusted, the one I thought cared for me, had just crossed a line I never imagined he would.

I was shaking with anger and hurt, tears streaming down my face as I tried to make sense of what had just happened. *How dare he put his hands on me?* The thought of calling the police flashed through my mind, but I hesitated. I felt trapped, unsure of what to do next. I turned to my friend, hoping she would be there for me, that she would help me find a way out of this situation. But instead of supporting me, she took his side. Her loyalty to him— because he was her boyfriend's friend—came before her loyalty to me. Her response cut deeper than I could have imagined. She dismissed my pain, acting as though what he had done was no big deal. She didn't care about what I was going through or the betrayal I felt. In that moment, I realized I couldn't rely on her. The Bible says, *"The Lord is close to the brokenhearted and saves those who are crushed in spirit"* (Psalms 34:18). I felt crushed, abandoned by the very person I thought would stand by me. To make matters worse, they all left me in the house by myself. They walked to the store together, laughing and carrying on as if nothing had happened. I stood there alone, feeling a mix of anger, sadness, and disbelief. How could they act so casually after what had just occurred? This was yet another reminder of how quickly people could turn their backs on you. It felt like no matter how much I tried to trust or depend on others; I kept finding myself betrayed and hurt.

The Bible says, *"Cast your burden on the Lord, and He will sustain you; He will never permit the righteous to be moved"* (Psalms 55:22). In that moment of despair, I prayed silently, asking God to give me strength and to help me find a way out of this toxic environment. I knew I couldn't stay there much longer. For the sake of my safety and my daughter's well-being, I needed to leave. It wasn't just about what had happened that morning, it was about protecting myself from further harm and breaking free from the cycle of pain and betrayal. This experience opened my eyes to the importance of relying on God above all else. People may fail you, but God's love and protection never will.

## Desperate for Love

I was ready to leave. I was tired of the constant pain, the endless betrayals, and the overwhelming feeling of being unloved. All my life, it felt like I had been searching for something I couldn't seem to find—real love, support, and peace. I kept asking myself, *why*

*am I going through this? Why is my life so full of hurt and disappointment?*
The weight of my past and present struggles made it hard to see
a way forward. The Bible says, *"Those who look to Him are radiant;*
*their faces are never covered with shame"* (Psalms 34:5). I clung to
this verse, reminding myself that God was my source of hope
and that He would never let me be disgraced. In an attempt to
find some stability, my friend helped me get a job at the airport,
working at Five Guys. It felt like a small step forward, something
to keep me occupied and help me provide for my daughter. We
would ride the bus to work together, and for a brief moment, I
thought things might improve. But soon, trouble started brewing.
My friend stirred up drama at the job, creating confusion and
tension that eventually drew the attention of the manager. I
found myself caught in the middle of it all, being questioned and
feeling the weight of someone else's actions. It became clear that
even this small step toward progress was being overshadowed
by negativity. I wanted to leave. It seemed like everywhere I
went, people were cruel, creating chaos and trying to drag me
down. It felt like the world was against me, and I was constantly
fighting just to keep my head above water. Out of desperation,
I called a family friend I had known since childhood. He lived
across the street from where I grew up, and I hoped he could
offer me some help. I told him about everything I was going
through, the toxic situation I was in, the slap, and how I needed

to get out. He agreed to help me, sending someone to pick me up and take me to where he was staying. At first, I felt relieved to have somewhere else to go, but that relief didn't last long. Being around him made me uncomfortable. He was much older than me, and while I looked at him as an uncle or a family figure, it became clear that he didn't see me the same way. He would make comments that hinted at wanting something more, and it made my skin crawl. I only accepted his help because I needed it—he was giving me money, and I felt like I didn't have any other options. But the way he acted made it seem like I owed him something in return. He told me I was grown, as if that justified his advances, but I didn't see him that way. I couldn't. In my eyes, he was like family, someone I should have been able to trust. The situation left me feeling trapped and vulnerable, once again questioning why my life always seemed to lead me into these painful and uncomfortable places. The Bible says, *"The Lord is my rock, my fortress, and my deliverer; my God is my rock, in whom I take refuge, my shield and the horn of my salvation, my stronghold"* (Psalms 18:2). I held onto this truth, praying for strength and guidance as I tried to navigate yet another difficult chapter of my life. I knew this wasn't where I wanted to stay, but I didn't have a clear plan for what to do next. I just kept praying that God would lead me to a place of peace, love, and stability—a place where I could finally feel safe and begin to heal.

## A Temporary Solution

I continued to let him help me because I felt like I had no other options. I didn't trust him completely, but his willingness to give me money and provide some form of support seemed like a lifeline in the midst of my struggles. However, the situation became even more unstable when I realized he didn't even have a secure place to stay himself. He was already living with someone else, and that person eventually told me that I couldn't stay there any longer. Their reasoning was simple: he barely had a place to stay, so there wasn't room for me and my daughter. I was frustrated and defeated. Just when I thought I had found a temporary solution, I was being uprooted again. It felt like every time I took a step forward, something pushed me two steps back. The Bible says, *"The Lord does not listen to the wicked, but He hears the prayer of those who do right"* (Proverbs 15:29). I reminded myself that God was listening to my prayers, even when my circumstances seemed hopeless. He saw my heart and my efforts to do the best I could for my daughter and myself, and I trusted that He would provide a way out. This experience was another reminder that relying on others for help wasn't always the solution. While I was grateful for the help I had received, it was clear that this wasn't a long-term answer. I needed stability, and I needed to find it in a way that didn't compromise my dignity or safety.

## A Glimmer Of Hope In The Chaos

Even though I felt uncomfortable, I continued to let him help me because I didn't know where else to turn. I was desperate for support, even if it came from someone I didn't fully trust. At that moment, his willingness to give me money and provide a temporary place to stay felt like the only option I had. But soon, reality came crashing down. He was already staying with someone else, and that person made it clear that I couldn't stay there. Their reasoning was simple: he barely had a secure place himself, so there wasn't room for me and my daughter. It was yet another door closing in my face, another reminder of how unstable my life had become. I felt defeated, wondering why I kept finding myself in these impossible situations. I questioned God's plan for my life, struggling to understand why I had to endure so much rejection, instability, and heartache. The Bible says, *"The Lord does not listen to the wicked, but He hears the prayer of those who do right"* (Proverbs 15:29). This verse reminded me that even in my darkest moments, God was listening. He saw my efforts, my struggles, and my heart. I wasn't forgotten, even if it felt that way. As I sat and reflected, I realized how far I had come despite everything. Every setback, every betrayal, every moment of uncertainty had taught me something. It taught me resilience, patience, and the importance of leaning on God rather than people. I began to understand that while others could provide temporary help, only God could give me the lasting peace and stability I was longing for. I prayed fervently, pouring out my heart to God. I asked Him for strength to keep moving forward, for wisdom to make the right decisions, and for clarity to see the path He was leading me on. I also prayed for forgiveness—for the mistakes I had made, for the times I had let anger or frustration take over, and for the moments I had doubted His presence in my life. The Bible says, *"For I know the plans I have for you," declares the Lord, "plans to prosper you and not to harm you, plans to give you hope and a future"* (Jeremiah 29:11). This verse became my anchor. Even when my circumstances looked bleak, I trusted that God's plan for me was still unfolding. He wasn't finished with me yet. I began to focus on what I could do, no matter how small. I started thinking about ways to find work, save money, and create a better life for my daughter and myself. I reminded myself that I had overcome so much already, and I could overcome this too. This chapter of my life was painful, but it was also a turning point. It forced me to confront the patterns and choices that kept leading me into toxic situations. It reminded me that I couldn't keep relying on others to rescue me—I needed to rely on God and trust in His ability to lead me out of the chaos. The Bible says, *"The righteous cry out, and the Lord hears them; He delivers them from all their troubles"* (Psalms 34:17). I cried out to God with everything I had, trusting that

He would deliver me once again. Even though I didn't have all the answers, I began to feel a sense of hope. I realized that every challenge was preparing me for something greater. Every closed door was leading me closer to the path God had designed for me. And while the journey was far from easy, I knew I wasn't walking it alone. As I prepared to move forward, I made a commitment to myself: to let go of the pain, the bitterness, and the feelings of unworthiness that had held me back for so long. I wasn't just surviving, I was stepping into a new season of faith, strength, and hope.

CHAPTER

# ENOUGH IS ENOUGH

*"Wait for the Lord; be strong and take heart and wait for the Lord." (Psalms 27:13-14)*

This was the final time I was going to stay with anyone else. I had reached my breaking point and knew that something had to change. I longed for peace, for a safe and stable environment where my daughter and I could finally breathe without the constant stress of uncertainty. I called my cousin and asked if she and her mom would let us stay with them for a little while. It wasn't going to be forever—just until the program that was helping me could finalize everything and get us into our own place. I explained the situation to her, hoping she'd understand how desperate I was for a place to go. After a brief conversation with her mom, she called me back and said yes. A wave of relief swept over me. Finally, there was a light at the end of the tunnel, a temporary solution that would give me the chance to gather myself and prepare for the next step. All I wanted was a peaceful environment where I could regroup and refocus—where my daughter and I could feel safe and stable for a change. I wasn't asking for much, just a chance to breathe and move forward. The Bible says, *"The Lord gives strength to His people; the Lord blesses His people with peace"* (Psalms 29:11). I clung to this promise, trusting that God was providing me with the strength to endure and the peace I so desperately needed. This time, I told myself things would be different. I was determined to make the most of this opportunity, to hold onto my faith, and to keep pushing forward toward a better life for me and my daughter. Enough was enough, I was ready to step into a new chapter and claim the peace I had been searching for all along.

## Confronting The Hurt

I knew I wasn't going to let anyone talk to me any kind of way, not anymore. After everything I had endured, I felt like I had to defend myself at all costs. Whenever someone said something hurtful, I made sure to say something back that would hurt them just as much. It wasn't because I wanted to be mean, but because I was tired—tired of being everyone's target, tired of carrying the weight of constant pain and rejection from my own family and friends. Things escalated when my cousin's mom got involved. Instead of being a voice of reason, she chose to support her daughter's wrongdoings, defending her actions and turning her anger toward me. Her words were sharp, calculated to wound. She told me things I would never forget—cruel accusations about my past, about my mom being a crackhead, and how she didn't love me. Hearing those words felt like a knife twisting in my heart. I had already carried so much hurt from my childhood, and for her to throw that pain back in my face was too much to bear. Meanwhile, she bragged about how much she loved her children, using it as a way to belittle me and make me feel unworthy. I felt rage rise up inside me, a burning anger that threatened to take over. I wanted to hurt her the way she had hurt me, to make her feel the weight of her words. How could someone who claimed to be a Christian speak so much hatred and cruelty? She talked about God, but her actions and words told a different story. The Bible says, *"Out of the same mouth come praise and cursing. My brothers and sisters, this should not be"* (James 3:10). I knew in my heart that her actions were not aligned with the faith she claimed to have. It was clear that something deeper was at play—something spiritual. The words she spoke were filled with bitterness, and it felt like a spirit of darkness had taken hold of her. Her words didn't just hurt, they reopened old wounds. They reminded me of every moment in my life when I felt unloved, unseen, and unworthy. I struggled to hold back my tears, but I also struggled to keep my anger under control. The urge to lash out was strong, but I knew that doing so would only make the situation worse. The Bible says, *"Do not be overcome by evil, but overcome evil with good"* (Romans 12:21). This was a hard lesson to live out in that moment. I wanted so badly to fight back, to defend myself, but deep down, I knew that wasn't the answer. Instead, I turned to prayer. I prayed for strength, for peace, and for the wisdom to navigate this situation with grace. I asked God to help me see beyond her hurtful words and to heal the wounds they had reopened. I also prayed for her, asking God to reveal His love to her and to remove whatever spirit was fueling her cruelty. This moment was a painful reminder of how much work I still needed to do—not just in healing from my own trauma, but in learning to respond to hurt with faith instead of anger. It wasn't easy, but I trusted that God was using even this painful experience to shape me and prepare me for something greater.

## Reconnecting Through Pain

One day, my little sister came to visit me, and it brought a moment of joy to my chaotic life. I loved my sister deeply, but the distance between us had grown over the years because of everything we had been through together. The weight of our shared struggles and unresolved pain had created a wall between us, pushing us further and further apart. Despite all of that, having her there with me meant the world. For a brief moment, it felt like things could be okay again, like the bond we once had could be repaired. Her visit reminded me of the love we shared, even if life had made it hard to express. Later, I decided to call my oldest sister. I told her everything—how I was hungry, where I was staying, and the events that led me to this place. She already knew most of the story because word had spread through the family about my situation. She came to see me, bringing food for me and my daughter. We talked for a while, and I was grateful for the small gesture of kindness. But as much as I appreciated her effort, I couldn't help but feel a deeper hurt. She didn't offer me a place to stay, and that cut me in ways I couldn't even put into words. It wasn't just about needing shelter, it was about feeling rejected, about the realization that even my own sister didn't think I was worth helping in that way. I knew why. People had been talking about me, spreading stories and judgments about my life, my choices, and my struggles. Their words had painted a picture of me that wasn't true, but it was enough to make others hesitate to help. The Bible says, *"The Lord is close to the brokenhearted and saves those who are crushed in spirit"* (Psalms 34:18). I clung to this verse, praying for strength and peace as I wrestled with the sting of rejection from those I loved most. Feeling overwhelmed and unsure of what to do next, I decided to call someone who had been there for me in the past—a staff member from the home I used to stay at. I didn't know if she could help, but I was desperate for guidance and support. This chapter of my life reminded me that even in moments of disappointment, God was still at work. He was teaching me resilience, showing me how to lean on Him when people let me down. Though my heart ached for the love and support of my family, I trusted that God was leading me toward something greater—something that would bring healing and hope.

## A New Beginning

My God mom came to visit me at the hotel and brought me a box of chicken. It was a small gesture, but in my heart, I had hoped for more. I didn't want to stay at the hotel alone with my daughter any longer. It felt like there was no peace, only fear and uncertainty. The isolation was overwhelming, and the nights felt endless as I prayed for safety and strength. People around me would say that my attitude was the reason they didn't want to deal with me. They told me I was too difficult, too angry, and too hard to help. But I didn't see it that way. I didn't need judgment—I needed compassion. I longed for someone to see through my pain, to understand that beneath the frustration and anger was a person desperately searching for love and stability. The Bible says, *"Rejoice always, pray continually, give thanks in all circumstances; for this is God's will for you in Christ Jesus"* (1 Thessalonians 5:16-18). Clinging to this promise, I forced myself to keep going, even when it felt like the world was against me. I had to accept the reality that I would be staying in the hotel until my apartment was ready. It wasn't easy, but I pushed through, reminding myself that this was just a season—one that would eventually pass. Then, out of nowhere, I got the call I had been waiting for. Someone from the program called to tell me that my apartment was ready. I was overjoyed. After months of waiting, praying, and enduring hardship, the moment had finally come. I packed up our belongings and left the hotel with a sense of relief and excitement. When I walked into the apartment, I couldn't believe my eyes. It was a beautiful two-bedroom, fully furnished, with everything me and my daughter needed to start fresh. This was more than just a place to stay—it was a blessing, a gift from God that reminded me of His faithfulness. The Bible says, *"Without faith it is impossible to please God. Those who come to God must believe that He exists, and they must believe that He rewards those who look to Him"* (Hebrews 11:6). I had held onto my faith, even in the darkest moments, and now I was seeing the rewards of that trust. The program didn't just provide me with an apartment; it gave me a foundation to rebuild my life. With their support, I was even able to buy myself a car. I couldn't contain my gratitude. These new blessings were a reminder that God hadn't forgotten about me. Shortly after moving in, I went to Walmart to pick up a few things for the apartment. While I was there, a guy working for Xfinity stopped me and asked what service I had for internet and cable. I told him I didn't have any yet, and we struck up a conversation about setting it up. He ran my name, and to my surprise, everything went smoothly. I left Walmart with a smile on my face, knowing that even the small things were falling into place. With internet and cable now set up, my apartment felt even more like home. For the first time in a long time, I felt a sense of stability and hope. This new beginning wasn't just about having a roof over our heads; it was about stepping into a chapter of possibility, where me and my daughter could thrive. This was God's grace in action, and I couldn't wait to see where He would lead us next.

## New Connections, Old Patterns

We exchanged numbers and started talking regularly. Our conversations were good, and over time, we began to like each other. He was kind, respectful, and had a calm demeanor that stood out to me. But as much as I appreciated him, my heart wasn't fully in it.

Before meeting him, someone else had already caught my attention—a street guy who embodied the type of man I had been drawn to for years. I couldn't help it; I had a habit of being attracted to men from the streets because it was what I was familiar with. It was a pattern that I didn't realize was tied to my past and the comfort I found in chaos. Even though my attention wasn't fully on him, he still went out of his way to help me. He made sure my cable was always on, and I was grateful for his kindness. He never pressured me or made me feel uncomfortable. Instead, he was respectful and patient, which was something I wasn't used to. One day, he asked me if I could refer people to him for his services. He was trying to boost his sales, and I agreed to help. I told friends and neighbors about him, hoping it would help him get more business. It was the least I could do to show my appreciation for all the ways he had been there for me. At the same time, I was adjusting to the rules of my new apartment complex. The program that had helped me secure my place came with strict guidelines. One of the most challenging rules was that we had to inform the staff in the office whenever we were home. On top of that, we couldn't have visitors unless they were pre-approved and added to a visitation list. This was completely new to me, and honestly, it was embarrassing. The idea of having to get approval for someone to come visit felt restrictive and awkward. If a friend or anyone wanted to stop by, I had to go through the process of adding them to the list. Because of this, I stopped inviting people over altogether. The Bible says, *"Therefore, if anyone is in Christ, the new creation has come: The old has gone, the new is here!"* (2 Corinthians 5:17). I was trying to embrace this new chapter of my life, but it wasn't easy. The rules, the changes, and the need to let go of old habits made me feel uncomfortable. Though I wasn't fully invested in him, the man from Xfinity showed me that kindness and respect could exist outside of the chaos I was used to. It was a small glimpse of what a healthier connection could look like, even if I wasn't quite ready to embrace it yet. This chapter of my life was teaching me the importance of breaking patterns and stepping into something new. It wasn't easy, but I knew it was necessary if I wanted to create a better future for myself and my daughter.

## Pushing Through And Reaching For More

I told everyone that I was always busy, which is why I never had company over. It was easier to say that than to explain the rules of the program or the limitations I faced. Deep down, I didn't mind because I knew I wasn't going to be there long. This was just a steppingstone to something greater. I had already put in applications for town homes before I even moved into the apartment. I was determined to find a house for me and my daughter. The Bible says, *"We are God's masterpiece. He has created us anew in Christ Jesus, so we can do the good things He planned for us long ago"* (Ephesians 2:10). I held onto this verse, believing that God had greater things in store for us. I just had to keep moving forward. To support myself and my daughter, I applied for a job at a daycare on Bouldercrest Road. It wasn't my dream job, but it was a start, and I was thankful for the opportunity. I met people and made connections while working there. Things seemed okay at first, and I told myself I'd just focus on doing my job and going home. But the environment wasn't as peaceful as I had hoped. There was a lot of commotion among the staff, and it made work feel tense and uncomfortable. My attitude wasn't as good as it should have been either. I was already carrying so much frustration and unresolved pain, and it was hard to keep that from spilling over into my work. Still, I kept pushing through, reminding myself that this was temporary. I had a goal, and I wasn't going to let anything stop me from reaching it. One bright spot at the daycare was a friend I made who worked in the kitchen. She was kind, and she could cook food so well. We started spending time together outside of work, and she would invite me over to her house. She'd cook for me and my daughter, and it felt good to have someone to connect with. But even that friendship had its challenges. One day, we got into an argument. It started because she asked me to do something I didn't want to do, and I stood my ground. The disagreement escalated, and it left a strain on our relationship. I didn't want to lose the one friend I had made, but the situation reminded me how difficult it could be to maintain connections when emotions and unresolved pain were involved. The Bible says, *"Be completely humble and gentle; be patient, bearing with one another in love"* (Ephesians 4:2). I tried to reflect on this, knowing I needed to work on my reactions and how I handled conflict. This experience taught me that while I was striving for greater things, I also needed to work on myself—on my patience, my attitude, and my ability to forgive. I couldn't move forward into the life God had for me if I was still carrying the weight of my past.

## A Risky Situation

Our argument at the daycare got heated. She told me to clock out, and I was so upset, but I had no choice but to leave. My emotions were running high, and it felt like everything was spiraling out of control. After taking some time to cool down, I returned to work the next day, ready to move past the confusion. In the middle of all this, I told my sister about the daycare and mentioned that they were hiring. She went in for an interview and got the job. I was happy for her—it felt good to see her find an opportunity to work and provide for herself and her family. It also made me feel a little less alone to have her working alongside me. One morning, during my lunch break, my sister asked me for a favor. She wanted me to take her to a house where her child's father was staying. She explained that he was at another woman's house with her son, and she wanted to confront him. I hesitated at first, unsure of how this would play out, but I wanted to support her. She was my sister, and I felt like I needed to have her back. The Bible says, *"Do not make friends with a hot-tempered person, do not associate with one easily angered. Or you may learn their ways and get yourself ensnared"* (Proverbs 22:24-25). Deep down, I knew this situation could escalate, but I chose to push that thought aside. I drove her to the house, unaware of the danger that might follow. She got out of the car and knocked on the door, demanding to see her son. She told her child's father to bring the baby outside, calling him out for being in the house with another woman. Her emotions were high, and I could see the fire in her eyes. As I sat in the car, watching the situation unfold, I started to feel uneasy. I had only wanted to support my sister, but I was beginning to question whether this was the right way to do it. The Bible says, *"A gentle answer turns away wrath, but a harsh word stirs up anger"* (Proverbs 15:1). I prayed silently, hoping that things wouldn't escalate and that everyone would remain calm. But this wasn't the kind of situation that stayed calm for long.

## A Connection Through Letters

After returning home, I found myself scrolling aimlessly through Facebook. It had been a long day, and I needed a distraction. As I scrolled, a notification popped up—a message in my inbox. It simply said, "Hey." Curious, I clicked on the message and saw it was from a guy I didn't know. I looked at his profile, wondering if I should respond. I thought to myself, *why not? I'm not talking to anyone right now, and I could use someone to talk to.* We started chatting, and it wasn't long before he told me that he was currently locked up. Strangely, that didn't bother me. Life had already thrown so many unexpected things my way, and I figured everyone deserves a chance to connect with someone, regardless of their situation. The Bible says, *"The thief comes only to steal and kill and destroy. I came that they may have life and have it abundantly"* (John 10:10). I wanted to believe that even someone in a difficult situation like his could still find redemption and purpose. As we talked more, I found myself drawn to our conversations. They were deep, engaging, and often heartwarming. He had a way of making me feel understood, like someone finally saw me for who I was, not for the mistakes I had made or the struggles I carried.One day, he asked me if I could help him out by sending him some money for food. He explained that he could use the funds to buy items from the commissary. I hesitated for a moment but decided to help. He then asked if I had the Jpay app, which would allow us to exchange letters, send money, and stay in touch more easily. With his guidance, I downloaded the app and set up my account. It felt strange at first, navigating this new way of communicating, but soon it became something I looked forward to. When I didn't hear from him on the phone, I would write him letters through the app. His responses were so heartfelt and genuine. His words made me feel seen, valued, and connected in a way I hadn't felt in a long time. The letters became a source of comfort for me. Each one was filled with stories, encouragement, and expressions of hope for the future. It felt good to relate to someone who seemed to understand me on a deeper level. In those moments, it didn't matter where he was or what he had been through—our connection was real, and it brought a sense of joy into my life that I hadn't felt in a long time. The Bible reminds us, *"Let all that you do be done in love"* (1 Corinthians 16:14). While I didn't know where this connection would lead, I chose to approach it with an open heart, letting kindness and understanding guide my actions.

## Love Built Through Distance

As the days passed, I found myself falling deeply in love with him—even though I hadn't touched him yet. His words captivated me, and the way he expressed his desires made my heart race.

He had a way of making me feel wanted, cherished, and seen, something I had been longing for. Our connection grew stronger with each conversation. I wanted him to feel just as good about me as I felt about him, so I began sending him intimate pictures to his phone. It made him happy, and his excitement gave me a sense of confidence and fulfillment. We even had specific times set aside for video chats. Those moments became something I looked forward to, a secret escape from my reality. The calls were filled with laughter, affection, and a deep intensity that neither of us could resist. The Bible says, *"Submit yourselves, then, to God. Resist the devil, and he will flee from you"* (James 4:7). But in those moments, I wasn't thinking about resistance. The pull between us was too strong, and I found myself giving in to the desires we both shared. I started exploring a part of myself I hadn't before. I would please myself during our video chats while he watched, and he would express how much he loved every bit of it. It became our routine, a private space where we could share parts of ourselves that no one else saw. Though I knew this was unconventional and risky, I couldn't help but fantasize about what it would be like when he finally came home. I imagined our first moments together, how I would make him feel, and the love we would share. Every conversation seemed to circle back to that moment in the future, when we could finally see each other face to face. In my heart, I believed this connection was real. It felt like the beginning of something powerful, something that could change both of our lives. But in the back of my mind, I also wondered if I was setting myself up for heartbreak. The Bible reminds us, *"Above all else, guard your heart, for everything you do flows from it"* (Proverbs 4:23). I knew I needed to be careful, but I couldn't stop myself from falling deeper into this relationship, hoping that it would lead to something beautiful.

## Disrespect and Determination

The next day, he called me, and I told him about my plans to attend Zone 6 Day with my godmother. It was a big community event, and I was excited to spend time with her. I explained that I was getting ready and promised to call him back once I got there. When I arrived at the park, my godmother and I set up everything at her spot. It was a beautiful day, filled with energy and excitement as people gathered. Everything seemed to be going as planned. I kept my promise and called him to let him know what was going on and who all was there. As we talked, everything changed in an instant. Out of nowhere, I heard gunshots. Chaos erupted as people scattered, running for safety. My heart was pounding, and I could barely process what was happening. Still holding the phone, I told him, "I'm going to call you back. I can't talk right now. "What happened next shocked me. Instead of showing concern or offering support, he called me out of my name—for the first time. I froze, unable to believe what I had just heard. In that moment, I realized he wasn't even worried about my safety or what I was going through. He was only thinking about himself. I was hurt and upset. In a moment when I needed reassurance and comfort, he had disrespected me. Once the. The situation at the park calmed down, I called him back to confront him. I asked him why he had spoken to me like that, but instead of apologizing, he responded with attitude. This was our first real argument, and it was over something so unnecessary. The Bible says, *"God is our refuge and strength, an ever-present help in trouble. Therefore, we will not fear, though the earth gives way, and the mountains fall into the heart of the sea, though its waters roar and foam and the mountains quake with their surging"* (Psalm 46:1-3). In that moment, I reminded myself that God was my refuge, even when people let me down. Later, he asked me when I was going to come and see him. Despite everything, I decided to make it happen. I reached out

## The First Meeting

This was our first time seeing each other in person. As I arrived, my heart raced with anticipation. When our eyes met, I smiled at him, and he smiled back, it was one of the sweetest moments

I had ever experienced. We spent the visit talking, laughing, and simply enjoying each other's company. It felt so real, so genuine. For the first time in a long while, I felt an overwhelming sense of happiness. The connection we had built through letters and phone calls was now tangible. But as the visit came to an end, my heart sank. Saying goodbye was harder than I anticipated. I hugged him tightly, not wanting to let go, and told him that I couldn't wait for him to come home. I reassured him that I had a place ready for him—a home where we could finally be together. Before I left, we took family pictures, capturing the precious memories of our first meeting. As I was riding for two hours back home, I couldn't stop thinking about him. My mind replayed every moment, every smile, and every word. Months later, he called me with exciting news. He told me that he didn't have much time left in prison and that he would soon be transitioning to a halfway house. My heart leapt with joy at the thought of him finally being back in the real world. The Bible says, *"Give your worries to the Lord, and He will take care of you. He will never let good people down"* (Psalms 55:22). I held on to this promise as I prepared for the next chapter in our journey together. Around the same time, I received another incredible blessing. The landlord I had been working with called to let me know that my application for a townhome had been approved. I was officially moving into a house—a real home for me and my daughter. I couldn't contain my excitement. This wasn't just a house; it was a symbol of hope and progress. It was a new beginning, a chance to create a stable environment where my daughter and I could thrive. As I unpacked boxes and settled into the new space, I felt an overwhelming sense of gratitude. The journey hadn't been easy, but each step brought me closer to the life I had been praying for. The Bible reminds us, *"Trust in the Lord with all your heart and lean not on your own understanding; in all your ways submit to Him, and He will make your paths straight"* (Proverbs 3:5-6). I knew God was guiding me every step of the way, opening doors and creating opportunities where there seemed to be none.

## A New Beginning

I couldn't believe it—I was finally in a house; a place I could call home. It was everything I had ever wanted and prayed for. My daughter and I settled in quickly, exploring every corner of the space that was now ours. There was a sense of peace and excitement as we began to get comfortable and imagine all the memories we'd create here. I was eager to make this house a reflection of us. Decorating became my favorite task, turning the empty rooms into a warm, welcoming sanctuary. To celebrate this new chapter, I hosted a housewarming party. Friends and family came, filling the space with laughter, love, and joy. It was a reminder that even after all the hardships, there was light and hope on the other side. With the holidays approaching, I was determined to bring my family together for a special dinner at my new home. I invited my aunt, uncle, and sisters, wanting to create a sense of unity, even if things hadn't always been perfect between us. Regardless of how they felt about me or the ways they had treated me in the past, I still loved them and wanted to share this milestone with them. The Bible says, *"Above all, love each other deeply, because love covers over a multitude of sins"* (1 Peter 4:8). I held on to this verse, believing that love and forgiveness could mend even the most broken relationships. During this time, I also called my boyfriend to tell him about my move. We had made our relationship official, and I wanted him to know about this new beginning for me and my daughter. Sharing this part of my life with him felt like a step toward building a future together. While everything seemed to be falling into place, I found myself struggling with my daughter's behavior. She was acting out more and more, and it was becoming overwhelming. Her defiance and lack of focus at school were frustrating, and I felt powerless to guide her in the right direction. Her actions began to take a toll on me. I found myself losing jobs, peace, and even my sanity. I didn't know how to handle the situation, and it was breaking my heart. I loved my daughter deeply, but I was starting to feel disconnected. The Bible reminds us, *"Fathers, do not provoke your children to anger, but bring them up in the discipline and instruction of the Lord"* (Ephesians 6:4). I tried to remind myself to lead with patience and love, but it wasn't easy. I found myself getting upset with her, feeling like I was failing as a parent. The weight of the situation was heavy, and I knew I needed guidance—both spiritually and emotionally. Even in the midst of these struggles, I knew that this home represented a fresh start, a chance to reset and build a better future for both of us. I prayed for strength, wisdom, and the ability to show my daughter the love and guidance she needed.

## Seeking Help And Building Connections

The weight of everything was becoming too much for me to bear. It was overwhelming and draining trying to manage my daughter's behavior alone. I felt like I was drowning in frustration, constantly asking myself where I had gone wrong. Deep down, I knew I needed help—specifically, the kind of guidance and support a father figure could provide. I decided to seek professional help and took her to a therapist. After observing her, they diagnosed her with ADHD and a developmental delay. Hearing this was hard for me. They explained that she would need medication to help manage her symptoms, and though I wasn't entirely comfortable with it, I trusted their expertise and started her on the prescribed treatment. Her behavior continued to embarrass me at times, especially in public. I felt ashamed, not of her as a person, but because I didn't understand how to handle her unique needs. I constantly questioned myself, wondering, *why is my child this way? What am I doing wrong?* I wrestled with feelings of inadequacy, but I pressed on because I knew she needed me. The Bible says, *"Cast all your anxiety on Him because He cares for you"* (1 Peter 5:7). I reminded myself of this promise, trusting that God saw my struggles and would guide me through this season. In the midst of these challenges, my boyfriend introduced me to his sister. We planned to meet at the halfway house during one of my visits with him. I was excited to build a connection with someone from his family, hoping it would strengthen our bond. When I arrived to see him, he informed me that his sister couldn't make it that day because she had other commitments. While I was a little disappointed, I took the opportunity to spend quality time with him. It was bittersweet—we laughed, talked, and cherished every moment we had, but time flew by too quickly. Saying goodbye always felt like leaving a piece of my heart behind. Before I left, he gave me his sister's number so we could connect later. I reached out, and we began talking. At the time, she was pregnant and not feeling her best, so we didn't meet right away. Eventually, when she was feeling up to it, we arranged to meet in person.

From the moment we met, I liked her. She was kind, warm, and easy to talk to. I felt happy to finally connect with someone from his family who seemed genuine and supportive. It gave me hope for the future and a sense of belonging that I hadn't felt in a while. The Bible reminds us, *"A friend loves at all times, and a brother is born for a time of adversity"* (Proverbs 17:17). Meeting her felt like a blessing, and I was grateful for the opportunity to grow closer to the people who mattered to him.

## Seeking Support And Understanding

My boyfriend's sister quickly became someone I valued deeply. She was so sweet, and we would often spend time together, building a bond that felt genuine. Her son even started calling me "auntie," and it warmed my heart. I thought to myself, *this is going to be my family.* However, as my relationship with her blossomed, my struggles with my daughter's behavior continued to worsen. Her outbursts were becoming more frequent and more intense. I felt overwhelmed, unsure how to handle her, and deeply concerned that there might be something more serious going on. One day, I called my aunt and shared my concerns. I told her that I suspected my daughter might have autism, and I asked if she could accompany me to the doctor. To my surprise, she mentioned that I used to display the same behavior when I was young, which made me feel less alone in my worries. The Bible says, *"Now may the God of hope fill you with all joy and peace in believing, that you may abound in hope by the power of the Holy Spirit"* (Romans 15:13). This verse reminded me that God could bring peace and clarity, even in the midst of my confusion and fear. My aunt and uncle supported me by coming to the doctor's appointment. They even pointed out that I had acted in a similar way when I was younger. While that gave me some comfort, I couldn't shake the feeling that something was wrong with my daughter. At the doctor's office, they ran evaluations and informed me that my daughter didn't show any signs of autism. While that should have been reassuring, I left the appointment feeling defeated. Deep down, I knew there was still something going on, and I was determined to get to the bottom of it. During this challenging time, my friend from the daycare center invited me to several gatherings at her house. I attended a few, hoping they might offer a distraction or some comfort. However, I often found myself angry and overwhelmed, unable to enjoy myself because my daughter's behavior was constantly on my mind. Without adequate support from my family or friends, I felt like I was carrying the weight of the world on my shoulders. The frustration and pain inside me began to spill out, and I found myself taking my anger out on my daughter. I hated that I was doing it, but the guilt and rage inside me made it hard to stop. My friend would often tell me, "You need to stop talking to her like that. She's just a child." While I knew she was right, I couldn't see past my own pain. I felt like no one truly understood the depths of my mental and emotional exhaustion. The Bible reminds us, *"Let us not become weary in doing good, for at the proper time we will reap a harvest if we do not give up"* (Galatians 6:9). This verse encouraged me to keep going, even when it felt like I was at my breaking point. I desperately needed help with my daughter, but I also realized I needed help for myself. The anger and hurt I carried from my past were spilling into my present, and it was affecting how I showed up as a mother. I prayed for strength, healing, and the wisdom to navigate this season of my life.

## Finding Strength In The Struggle

As I continued to struggle with my daughter's behavior, the weight of my emotions became unbearable. I felt like I was in a constant battle trying to parent, manage my own mental health, and heal from all the pain I carried inside. I was angry, hurt, and overwhelmed, but most of all, I was scared. Scared that I was failing my daughter, scared that I couldn't give her the love she needed, and scared that I was losing myself in the process. I realized I needed to make some changes. I started seeking help, not just for her but for myself. I began to pray more intentionally, asking God to guide me and give me the strength to be the mother she deserved. The Bible says, *"The Lord is close to the brokenhearted and saves those who are crushed in spirit"* (Psalms 34:18). In those quiet moments of prayer, I felt a flicker of hope a reminder that God was with me, even in my darkest hours. I began to reflect on myself.

## A Test of Faith and Patience

All I ever wanted was for my daughter to thrive and be the best version of herself. Despite the struggles, I kept pushing forward, determined to create a better life for both of us. Just when I thought things were stabilizing, my boyfriend called me one day to let me know about a BBQ his family was hosting. He asked me to pick him up so we could attend together. I was always ready to support him, so without hesitation, I went to pick him up. I wanted to be there for him and show him that I was willing to stand by his side. I believed in being a supportive partner, even when things between us weren't perfect. The BBQ started off well—laughter, food, and the buzz of family gatherings surrounded us. However, I couldn't shake an uneasy feeling. Something felt off. My instincts were screaming at me that there was more to his demeanor than he was letting on. Soon, my worst fears were confirmed. I discovered that he had been involved with another woman, and not only that—he had gotten her pregnant. The revelation hit me like a ton of bricks. I felt my heart shatter into a million pieces. I immediately confronted him, demanding answers. I was furious, hurt, and betrayed. Rage boiled within me as I tried to process how someone I trusted could do something so devastating. I wanted to scream, to cry, and to lash out all at once. Every ounce of pain I had ever experienced seemed to rise to the surface in that moment. The Bible says, *"The Lord will fight for you; you need only to be still"* (Exodus 14:14). But in that moment, being still was the last thing on my mind. I was ready to fight him and the other woman. My anger took control of me. I started blowing up his phone, desperate for explanations. I even looked for the girl's social media page, determined to let her know that he wasn't as committed to her as she might think. But even as I acted out of anger, a quiet voice in the back of my mind reminded me that this wasn't the answer. The Bible also says, *"Refrain from anger, and forsake wrath! Fret not yourself; it tends only to evil"* (Psalms 37:8). I knew I needed to take a step back, breathe, and focus on my own healing rather than chasing after explanations from someone who had already shown me his true colors. That night, as I sat in my car crying, I began to pray. I asked God to take the hurt and bitterness out of my heart and replace it with peace. I prayed for clarity, for the strength to walk away from toxic relationships, and for the wisdom to focus on what truly mattered—my daughter and my own well-being. This situation taught me a hard but valuable lesson: not everyone who claims to love you will honor you. But that doesn't mean you're unworthy of love. It means you must protect your heart and trust God to lead you to the relationships He has prepared for you. The Bible reminds us in *Romans 8:28, "And we know that in all things God works for the good of those who love Him, who have been called according to His purpose."* Even this betrayal, as painful as it was, would ultimately work for my good. I didn't have all the answers yet, but I knew one thing for sure—I deserved better. My daughter deserved better. And I was determined to let this be a turning point, not a setback

CHAPTER

# CORRUPTED
# SITUATIONS

*"Everything that is hidden will become clear,*
*and every secret will be made known" (Luke 8:17).*

L ove can blind you to truths you don't want to face.
No matter how much I tried to convince myself that
things were fine, the truth about his lies and betrayal
came crashing down. It was like being caught in a storm with no
shelter. I kept telling him he was wrong—that his actions were
hurting me deeply—but he didn't care about my feelings. Instead
of offering an apology or showing remorse, he doubled down.
One day, he sent me an ultrasound picture, claiming it was proof
that the other woman was pregnant with his child. Seeing that
image sent me into a rage. My heart pounded, my mind raced,
and I was filled with anger and hurt. *How could he do this to me? How*

*could he betray me in this way?* But as I looked closer at the image, something didn't sit right. I did some investigating and found out it wasn't even real—it was a fake ultrasound she had sent him to manipulate him. I confronted him immediately, thinking this revelation would bring us closer or at least clear the air. I told him she was lying, expecting him to side with me. Instead, he lashed out, accusing me of being jealous and petty. His words cut deep. *Jealous? Petty? After all I've done for you?* The man I loved had not only betrayed me but was now gaslighting me into thinking I was the problem. It felt like he had taken a knife to my heart and twisted it. Still, I stayed. I stayed because my love for him ran so deep, I thought I could fix what was broken. I held onto the hope that he would change, that he would see how much I cared and finally choose me over the lies and chaos. Looking back, I realize how much of myself I sacrificed for someone who wasn't willing to do the same for me. The Bible says, *"But I say to you who hear, love your enemies, do good to those who hate you, bless those who curse you, pray for those who mistreat you"* (Luke 6:27-28). That verse became a lifeline for me. I learned that loving someone doesn't mean you allow them to mistreat you. It means you pray for them, release them to God, and let Him handle what you cannot. Every time he lied, I forgave him. Every time he betrayed my trust, I stayed. But with every hurtful word, every deceitful action, a piece of me broke. I began to lose myself in the process of trying to love someone who didn't value me. The storm I was living in was relentless. Lies, accusations, and manipulation were constant companions in our relationship. But even in the middle of all that chaos, God was whispering to my heart, *"This is not the love I have for you.* "It took time, but I began to see the truth. God doesn't want us to stay in situations where we're being mistreated, undervalued, or betrayed. His love is pure, kind, and sacrificial, not full of manipulation and lies. As I reflect on this chapter of my life, I realize it was part of my journey to understanding what true love looks like. Love doesn't hurt, deceive, or tear you down. Love builds you up, reflects Christ, and draws you closer to Him. The Bible reminds us in *Romans 8:28,* *"And we know that in all things God works for the good of those who love Him, who have been called according to His purpose."* Even the pain and betrayal I endured were part of a greater plan to shape me into the woman God intended me to be. I was still in the middle of my storm, but I began to hold onto the hope that God would deliver me. I prayed for strength, clarity, and the courage to walk away if it ever became too much.

## A Collision Of Faith And Reality

He continued to believe the lies of the other woman, hanging onto every fabricated story she told him. Despite my constant efforts to show him the truth, it seemed like my words fell on deaf ears. When he showed me the fake ultrasound, I had no choice but to confront him with the evidence that it wasn't real. I explained to him that it was created using an app and showed him proof. Finally, he believed me and stopped talking to her, but the damage to our relationship was undeniable. The trust I had in him was shattered, and even though he apologized, I couldn't shake the pain of being doubted and betrayed. Still, I stayed because I loved him, believing that love could mend what had been broken. The Bible says, *"Love bears all things, believes all things, hopes all things, endures all things"* (1 Corinthians 13:7). I held onto this scripture, praying it would guide me through the chaos. One morning, he called me and asked if I could pick him up from the gas station where his coworkers met before work. He wanted me to come early so we could spend the day together. Despite the tension in our relationship, I was excited to spend time with him, hoping it would bring us closer. I picked him up, and we went back to my house to rest for a while. Later that morning, he asked me to drive him to his cousin's house to grab something he needed. Then he told me we had to take the expressway I froze. I had never driven on the expressway before, and just the thought of it terrified me. The cars moved too fast, and the idea of merging into that chaos made my palms sweat. But because I wanted to please him, I agreed. I gripped the steering wheel tightly, silently praying as I merged into the speeding traffic. The Bible says,

*"Do not fear, for I am with you; do not be dismayed, for I am your God. I will strengthen you and help you; I will uphold you with my righteous right hand"* (Isaiah 41:10). I repeated this verse in my mind, holding onto the promise that God was with me, even in my fear. Out of nowhere, a large truck swerved into my lane. Panic set in as I tried to steady the car, but the truck was too close. My hands gripped the wheel so tightly that my knuckles turned white. I felt completely out of control. In that moment, I thought I was going to die. I closed my eyes, bracing for the worst, and whispered a silent prayer. All I could hear was the sound of screeching tires and his voice screaming. He wasn't calming me down; he wasn't reassuring me. Instead, he was yelling in panic, which only made the situation worse. I tuned out his voice and focused on the silence of my prayer, begging God to protect us. The car spun into a 360-degree turn. When I opened my eyes, I saw that the car had miraculously stopped, now facing the fast lane. To my astonishment, every car had come to a halt. It was as if the entire world had paused just to protect me. In that moment, I knew I was covered by God's angels. There was no other explanation for how I had survived without a scratch. Tears streamed down my face as I whispered, "Thank you, Lord." The Bible says, *"For He will command His angels concerning you to guard you in all your ways"* (Psalm 91:11). I knew that his divine protection had saved me. When I finally managed to gather myself, I pulled the car to the

shoulder of the road, trembling and overwhelmed by what had just happened. Instead of comforting me or acknowledging the miracle we had just witnessed, he began to blame me. He said I shouldn't have gotten on the expressway if I wasn't confident. His words stung deeply. I had faced one of my biggest fears for him, and instead of gratitude or support, I was met with blame. It was a painful realization that no matter how much I gave, it would never be enough for him. The rest of the drive home was silent, but my mind raced with thoughts. The accident wasn't just a physical collision; it was a wake-up call. It made me realize how much I had been putting myself at risk emotionally, mentally, and now physically, just to keep him happy. I thanked God for His protection and asked Him for clarity about my relationship. The Bible says, *"Trust in the Lord with all your heart and lean not on your own understanding; in all your ways submit to Him, and He will make your paths straight"* (Proverbs 3:5-6). I needed His guidance more than ever. That day, I learned that while love requires sacrifice, it should never come at the cost of your own safety and well-being. God's love for me was greater than anything I had been chasing in this relationship, and I had to trust Him to lead me to the love and peace I truly deserve

## A Strained Connection

After the accident, I was focused on getting him home safely so he wouldn't get into any trouble. I thought that once we were back at the house, we'd have a moment to process what had happened and maybe even come together in gratitude for being spared. But as soon as we arrived, he called a friend to pick him up. He told me he was still scared the police might come to my house. I couldn't believe it. I had just gone through one of the most terrifying experiences of my life, trying to help him and ensure his safety, and now he was leaving me to deal with the aftermath alone. I looked at him and asked, *"Why would you leave me like this? I'm the one who got hit on my side. I'm the one who could have died today.* "It hurt deeply. I had been trying to help him, support him, and be there for him, but it felt like all my efforts were in vain. Instead of appreciation or care, I felt drained, emotionally and physically. I wanted so badly to see him better himself, but his actions made it clear that he wasn't willing to change. The Bible says, *"Do not give dogs what is sacred; do not throw your pearls to pigs. If you do, they may trample them under their feet and turn and tear you to pieces"* (Matthew 7:6). Looking back, I realized I was giving my love and energy to someone who didn't value it. Even after all this, we continued to see each other. His sister picked him up from the halfway house one day, and I met her to spend some time with him. I was holding onto the hope that things would improve, but some weekends were good while others were unbearable. We argued constantly. Most of our fights stemmed from his dishonesty. He was always on his phone, and I'd catch him in lies about what he was doing or who he was talking to. It wasn't hard to uncover the truth, but each discovery chipped away at the trust I had in him. I'd confront him, and he'd deny everything, making me feel like I was overreacting or imagining things. One night, I told him how distant he had become. He wasn't affectionate or intimate with me like he used to be, and that hurt me. I felt rejected and unwanted, and it created even more tension between us. I asked him, *"Why won't you love me the way you used to? Why won't you touch me like before?"* But he had no answer. The Bible says, *"Love is patient, love is kind. It does not envy, it does not boast, it is not proud. It does not dishonor others, it is not self-seeking, it is not easily angered, it keeps no record of wrongs"* (1 Corinthians 13:4-5). I had been trying to live by these principles, pouring love and forgiveness into the relationship, but it wasn't being reciprocated. Instead, I was left feeling empty and unworthy. I started questioning myself. *Was I not enough? Was I doing something wrong?* But deep down, I knew the problem wasn't me. It was the situation. I was trying to force something that wasn't meant to be. I wanted so badly for him to change, to love me the way I deserved, but his actions made it clear that his priorities were elsewhere. This cycle of love, betrayal, and hurt had taken a toll on me. I knew I needed to make a change, but I wasn't ready to let go just yet. I kept holding on, hoping that the next day, the next week, or the next month would be different. The Bible says, *"The Lord is close to the brokenhearted and saves those who are crushed in spirit"* (Psalm 34:18). In my lowest moments, I leaned on this promise, trusting that God saw my pain and would guide me toward healing.

## False Hopes And Shattered Expectations

I confronted him one night, unable to keep my suspicions to myself any longer. *"You're cheating on me,"* I said, looking him straight in the eyes. *"There's no way we're together, and you're not even trying to please me. Something isn't right.* "His response didn't do much to calm my fears. His actions, his distance, and his disinterest made it impossible for me to believe otherwise. I felt invisible, like my needs and feelings didn't matter to him. Yet, I still clung to hope—hope that things could change, that love could be rekindled. Deep in my heart, I wanted to build a family with him, hoping that it would create a stronger bond between us. I told him, *"I want a baby—a son."* He agreed without hesitation, but his words felt empty, as though he was only telling me what I wanted to hear. The Bible says, *"Watch and pray so that you will not fall into temptation. The spirit is willing, but the flesh is weak"* (Matthew 26:31). Looking back, I realized that I had let my desires cloud my judgment. We began trying for a child. Every time we were together, we didn't use protection, and I eagerly hoped for the day I'd see a positive result. When nothing happened, I decided to take matters into my own hands. I downloaded a pregnancy app to track my ovulation, thinking it would increase our chances. I was determined to make this dream a reality, believing that a child might finally bring us closer together. But things between us only grew worse. Our arguments became more frequent and intense, and eventually, we parted ways. The separation left me feeling empty and defeated, but I still held onto the possibility of a better future. One day at work, everything changed. I noticed that I had missed my period, and my heart raced with anticipation. I took a pregnancy test, and when the result came back positive, I was overcome with joy. Tears filled my eyes as I thought about the life growing inside me. Despite our separation, I called him immediately to share the news. *"I'm pregnant,"* I said, my voice trembling with excitement. He seemed happy, even excited. This was his first child, and he even picked out a name for our baby boy. In that moment, I felt a spark of hope. *Maybe this will change him,* I thought to myself. *Maybe now he'll step up and become the man I know he can be.* I began to dream about the life we could build together. I pictured us as a family, raising our son in a home filled with love and stability. But as time went on, the reality of the situation became painfully clear. Instead of drawing us closer, my pregnancy seemed to push him further away. The Bible says, *"The Lord is near to the brokenhearted and saves the crushed in spirit"* (Psalm 34:18). In the midst of my excitement and hope, I found myself turning to God, praying for strength and guidance. I needed Him more than ever as I faced the challenges ahead. What I thought would be a new beginning turned out to be the beginning of something even more difficult. Despite my joy at becoming a mother, I was left to navigate this journey alone, feeling betrayed and abandoned by someone I thought would stand by my side.

## Shattered Trust And Unwavering Strength

When I told him I was pregnant, I expected joy, maybe even relief that we were building a family together. Instead, his response left me in disbelief. *"You need to get an abortion,"* he said coldly. His words cut through me like a knife. *"You're the devil,"* he continued, *"and I've prayed to God that you don't have this baby.* "I froze, my heart breaking into pieces. How could he say such a thing to me, after all we had talked about and planned together? I had stayed by his side through every challenge, offering him my love and support, and now he was turning his back on me and the life growing inside me. Rage bubbled up within me. I cursed him out, letting him know exactly how worthless his words made me feel. I wanted him to understand the pain he had caused, but deep down, I knew I couldn't change his mind or his heart. I was devastated. The Bible says, *"The Lord gives his people strength; the Lord blesses them with peace"* (Psalms 29:11). I clung to this promise, knowing that I would need God's strength to navigate the road ahead. Despite his harsh words, I knew in my heart that I hadn't done anything wrong. I loved him deeply, supported him mentally and physically, and stayed by his side even when it hurt me. But he couldn't do the same for me. I only wanted to love him, to build a future together, despite everything he had put me through. When it was time for him to transition from the halfway house, I decided to show him just how much I cared. I planned a surprise welcome home party for him, inviting his friends and family to celebrate his new beginning. I cooked his favorite dishes, decorated the house, and poured my heart into making the day special. When he arrived, his face lit up with surprise. For a brief moment, it felt like we were on the same page again, like we were the couple I had always hoped we could be. He enjoyed himself, laughing and talking with everyone who came to celebrate. And for a little while, we got along. Later that evening, I sat him down to talk about the future. I told him about the bills I needed help with and the responsibilities we would need to share to build a stable home for our baby. I hoped that this would be the start of a new chapter for us, one where we could work together as partners and parents. The Bible says, *"Trust in the Lord with all your heart, and lean not on your own understanding. In all your ways, acknowledge Him, and He will make your paths straight"* (Proverbs 3:5-6). I prayed silently, asking God for guidance and strength. I wanted so badly for this to work, to give my child the stable, loving home I had never had. But deep down, I couldn't ignore the nagging feeling that things were far from where they needed to be.

## False Promises and Unmet Expectations

He finally agreed to help me, and for that, I was grateful. Watching him put in applications and facing rejection after rejection because of his record was frustrating, but I tried to encourage him. I reminded him not to give up and assured him that we'd find a way together. Determined to help, I started asking around for job opportunities. I reached out to my uncle and shared my concerns about him not being able to find work. My uncle told me he could get him a job at a club since he knew the owners there. Excited, I told him about it, and he went down to meet with the owner. To our delight, they hired him on the spot. I was overjoyed. After months of searching, he had finally found a job. This felt like a breakthrough not just for him, but for us as a family. His employment meant stability and the possibility of sharing responsibilities more equally. At the same time, I decided to take a leap of faith and started selling plates, combining my passion for cooking with a way to bring in extra income. The pandemic was still in full swing, and my regular job hadn't reopened due to COVID-19 restrictions. So, I poured my heart into my cooking business, obtaining my LLC and creating meals that brought joy to others. To my surprise, it turned out to be a success. I was making a good amount of money doing something I genuinely loved, and for the first time in a long while, I felt empowered. His job at the club had him working night shifts, so I rarely saw him until the early morning hours. On his first night, he came home at 4 a.m. and proudly counted over $1,000 in front of me. I felt a surge of hope—finally, things were looking up. But that hope was short-lived. I asked him if he planned to contribute to the bills, and his response crushed me. *"I need to save my money,"* he said casually. I reminded him of his promise to help me, to be a partner in this life we were trying to build. He shrugged it off, handing me only a small amount of money, barely enough to make a dent in what I needed to cover the household expenses. Night after night, he came home drunk, counting stacks of cash in front of me. Each time, the anger and frustration in me grew. I was doing everything I could to provide for our home, pouring my heart into my business and sacrificing sleep and peace for the sake of our family. And yet, he didn't seem to care about the strain I was under. The Bible says, *"Bitterly she weeps at night, tears are on her cheeks. Among all her lovers there is no one to comfort her"* (Lamentations 1:2). That verse described exactly how I felt. Here I was, trying to build something meaningful with someone who seemed content to take advantage of my love and effort. I wanted him to see the bigger picture—to see that his selfishness was hurting not just me, but the foundation we were supposed to be building together. Yet, no matter how much I explained or pleaded, his priorities remained the same: himself and his money. Despite my frustration and anger, I turned to God for guidance and strength. I prayed for clarity, for wisdom to know what to do next. The Bible says in *Proverbs 3:5-6, "Trust in the Lord with all your heart and lean not on your own understanding; in all your ways submit to Him, and He will make your paths straight.* "Even though I was angry and felt betrayed, I knew I couldn't carry the weight of this burden alone. I needed to trust that God had a plan for me and that this season of disappointment and hurt would lead to something greater.

## Welcoming My Miracle

I desperately needed support—mentally, physically, and emotionally. Each day felt heavier than the last. I was constantly sick, miserable, and drained, longing for some form of escape or relief. During this difficult time, I began talking to a friend who lived across the street from my grandmother's house. We were both pregnant, and we were both dealing with the pain of being mistreated by our children's fathers. Our shared struggles brought us closer, and we quickly became a source of comfort for each other. We met up regularly, alternating between each other's homes, and poured our hearts out about the challenges we faced. She was incredibly supportive and kind, and in her presence, I found a bit of solace amidst the chaos of my life. She had her baby before me, and seeing her strength through it all gave me hope. Then came my turn. One evening, while I was home, I felt a sudden rush of water. My heart raced as I realized my water had broken. My baby wasn't due until October, and I wasn't prepared for this moment to come so soon. I called my aunt and uncle, desperately trying to figure out who could take care of my daughter while I rushed to the hospital. After a few phone calls, my uncle's sister arrived to pick her up. By the time I arrived at the hospital, my son's father had left work and met me there. I was relieved to have him by my side, even with all the struggles we had faced. The doctor explained that I would need to be induced and that my son could come at any moment. The anticipation was overwhelming, and though I was nervous, I prayed for a safe delivery. When the time came, it all happened so fast. My son was ready to enter the world before the doctor even made it back into the room. It was just me and his father. I felt a pressure I couldn't ignore and asked him to check if the baby was coming. His face said it all as he nodded and quickly left to find the doctor. Before I knew it, my son entered the world—a month early, with a head full of hair and weighing just 4 pounds. The moment was surreal. The rush of emotions was overwhelming—excitement, gratitude, and an indescribable love filled my heart. The Bible says in *Psalm 127:3*, *"Children are a gift from the Lord; they are a reward from him."* I knew in that moment that my son was a miracle, a precious gift entrusted to me. They placed him in my arms for just a brief moment before taking him away for additional care. My heart ached as I watched him leave my embrace, but I understood the importance of him receiving the attention he needed. He was so tiny, so fragile, but I knew that God was watching over him. *Psalm 46:1* reminds us, *"God is our refuge and strength, an ever-present help in trouble."* I clung to this promise, trusting that my baby boy would thrive. This experience, though overwhelming, reminded me of the strength God had given me. Holding my son, even for that fleeting moment, filled me with a new sense of purpose. No matter the challenges I faced, I was determined to provide for him, love him, and protect him with everything I had.

## "A New Life, A New Challenge"

The Bible states in (Joshua 1:9), "Have I not commanded you? Be strong and courageous. Do not be afraid; do not be discouraged, for the Lord your God will be with you." I was so sad because this same thing happened to my daughter. They took him and told me that they had to keep him to monitor him before he could go home. I had to accept that he wasn't coming home, but I went up there every day to see my precious baby. They finally called me and told me that he could come home, this was the best news ever. I took him home, and I loved every moment of my son's presence. My family was complete. I got my boy and my girl. A month after I came home with my son, I caught COVID during the pandemic, and I had no help. I was in bed trying to get myself together while taking care of a 1-month-old and my daughter. My son's father was there, but he was not helpful at all, so I had to deal with this by myself. I was sick. I felt like I was going to die—literally. I prayed to God to give me the strength to take care of my children. Every day was a battle, but I managed to push through it. The Bible reminds us in (Isaiah 40:31), "But those who hope in the Lord will renew their strength. They will soar on wings like eagles; they will run and not grow weary, they will walk and not be faint." I relied on God's promises to keep me going because, without His strength, I wouldn't have made it. Though I was physically drained and emotionally broken, my love for my children kept me motivated. I reminded myself daily that I had come too far to give up. My son's little cries and my daughter's innocent laughter gave me moments of peace in the storm. I knew that this was a season, and seasons eventually change. When I finally recovered, I felt a renewed sense of purpose. I realized that God had been with me through every trial and had given me the strength to endure. I started to focus on creating a stable, loving environment for my children. I knew that even though their father wasn't fully supportive, God had given me everything I needed to raise them. The Bible says in (2 Corinthians 12:9), "But he said to me, 'My grace is sufficient for you, for my power is made perfect in weakness.' Therefore, I will boast all the more gladly about my weaknesses so that Christ's power may rest on me." I leaned into this truth, knowing that my struggles were shaping me into the mother and woman God called me to be. Looking back, I see that this was a defining moment in my life. It was in the darkest times that my faith grew the most. God used this experience to remind me that I am never alone and that His grace is always sufficient. My children became my driving force, and through it all, I found hope, resilience, and a deeper connection to God.

## A Mark of Heartbreak

He came home from work drunk, and as he came up the stairs, he gave my daughter, my son, and me a kiss. I was on the phone at the time, with my back turned to my children. After he kissed me, I turned around to look at my children and saw my daughter's face was bloodshot red. I asked him what he did to my daughter. He said that he gave her a kiss. I told him that he gave my daughter a hickey. I was angry, emotional, and embarrassed. I wanted revenge. He really did this. I was ready to call the police on him. I didn't trust him, and I was confused because he didn't do anything like that to me or my son. Seeing the mark on my daughter's face filled me with rage and heartbreak. He kept denying that he had done it intentionally, telling me it was an accident. But I couldn't shake the uneasy feeling that something deeper was wrong. That mark stayed on her face for a while, a painful reminder of a moment I couldn't erase. I was overwhelmed, questioning how things had spiraled so far out of control, and praying for clarity and strength to navigate through this storm. The Bible states in **(Psalms 9:9)**, *"The Lord is a refuge for the oppressed, a stronghold in times of trouble."* I needed His refuge more than ever.

## A Breaking Point

I wanted to kill him in my head, but a part of me still loved him. My emotions were in turmoil. I told my daughter to go to the neighbor and tell them to call the police, but he blocked the door so she couldn't leave. Then he took my phone so I couldn't call for help because he was on legal papers and didn't want any trouble. He grabbed my son from the room and walked outside as if nothing happened, heading off on foot. Thank God I had another phone upstairs. I called the police and explained what had happened. They came, took a report, and left, but the damage to my heart and spirit lingered. Later, he called his sister, twisting the situation and making it seem like I was the problem. She believed his lies and told him to pack his things, promising to send an Uber to take him to her house. In my head, I was furious and hurt. How could no one see the pain I was in? I had gone through so much to support him, yet no one offered me comfort in my darkest moment. He was wrong, and I was exhausted from dealing with his narcissistic behavior and lies. Despite everything, I had wanted to help him, to see him become the man I thought he could be. But it was never enough. The Bible states in **(Isaiah 41:10),** *"So do not fear, for I am with you; do not be dismayed, for I am your God. I will strengthen you and help you; I will uphold you with my righteous right hand."* This verse became my lifeline as I realized I needed to let go. I told him he couldn't come back to my home. He started staying with his uncle, and though we were still in contact, I knew I had made the right decision. For a while, things seemed better. We even spent Valentine's Day together, exchanged gifts, and had a good time. But later that night, I saw a female on his social media story. When I asked him about it, he claimed she was just a friend he met at the gas station. My heart ached again. Why couldn't he just be honest? Why couldn't he value the love and sacrifices I had given him? I was tired of the endless cycle of betrayal, but I also knew God was preparing me for something greater, teaching me that my worth was not dependent on someone else's validation.

## Unveiling The Truth

I tried to let it go, but things started to feel strange. One day, I got on his Instagram page and saw a comment from a female that made it seem like they were talking. Feeling uneasy, I messaged her, letting her know that he and I were together and had a child together. I asked her what was going on. She shocked me with her response, claiming that they were in a relationship and that she was pregnant by him. The Bible says in **(Ephesians 5:11)**, *"Take no part in the unfruitful works of darkness, but instead expose them."* This scripture rang in my heart because I felt betrayed once again. How could he do this to me, especially after the last incident with the fake pregnancy? I continued to talk to her, but as she shared details about their relationship, my anger consumed me. This was the second time he had led me astray, and now he was dragging someone else into the chaos. I didn't know if her pregnancy was real, but her words pierced my heart. My son needed his dad, yet he wasn't stepping up—only showing interest when he wanted to post pictures of our son to showcase him in cute clothes. Jealousy and hurt boiled within me as she detailed their relationship. I started to lash out at her, calling her names and even wishing harm on her pregnancy. It wasn't the person I wanted to be, but the pain had a way of overtaking me. He kept calling me, telling me he loved me and wanted his family back. I wanted to believe him so badly that I ignored the lies he fed me to soothe his guilt. Instead of confronting him directly, I began to focus my anger on her. I called her out, bringing up her name in every conversation, hoping to make her feel the weight of the pain she had unknowingly or knowingly been a part of. He, in turn, complained to me about her, painting her as the villain. And somehow, I allowed myself to take his side, disliking her based on the things he told me about her. The betrayal wasn't just from him anymore; it felt like a web of deceit I couldn't untangle myself from. My heart ached for my son, for the family I had envisioned, and for the peace I so desperately craved. But through it all, I reminded myself of the truth in **(Psalm 34:18)**: *"The Lord is close to the brokenhearted and saves those who are crushed in spirit.* "Though I was hurting, I knew God had a purpose for me, even in this brokenness. It was a painful reminder that trusting the wrong people can bring heartache, but trusting God would bring healing and clarity in His time.

## Obsession and Heartbreak

Whatever he told me, I couldn't let go. I was completely obsessed with him, even though he continued to hurt me in unimaginable ways. When I found out she was pregnant, my heart was consumed with anger and pain. The Bible says in **(Ephesians 4:26)**: *"Don't sin by letting anger control you. Don't let the sun go down while you are still angry."* I clung to this verse, but in those moments, my emotions were overwhelming. I called her and confronted her about the situation. I told her the hard truth—that he didn't even take care of his son. I asked her why she would want to bring a child into a situation like this. But she didn't care. She refused to believe anything I said, blinded by her own obsession with him. She, too, was caught up in his manipulation. To make matters worse, he kept calling me, claiming he wanted to come back home. I could tell they were both trying to provoke me. Despite my better judgment, I let him come over because he made it seem like he wanted to make things right. While he was at my house, she called, and he told her he was only there to see our son. That was a lie. He told me to be quiet so she wouldn't suspect anything, and I went along with it, just to avoid more drama. After he left, I finally said enough is enough. I put him on child support, knowing I had to stand up for myself and my son. I later found out that he and this woman had moved in together. The news hit me like a ton of bricks. I was devastated, angry, and confused. How could he move in with someone he barely knew? The Bible says in **(Genesis 5:1):** *"When God created man, he made him in the likeness of God."* This verse reminded me of my worth, even though I felt discarded and unappreciated. He started blaming me for his actions, saying it was my fault that things ended up the way they did. But deep down, I knew it wasn't true. As if the betrayal wasn't enough, he completely stopped supporting our son after moving in with her. The weight of it all crushed me. I wanted my son to have a father who loved and cared for him, but instead, I had to carry the burden alone. Through the heartbreak and disappointment, I leaned on my faith. The Bible says in **(Isaiah 41:10):** *"Do not fear, for I am with you; do not be dismayed, for I am your God. I will strengthen you and help you; I will uphold you with my righteous right hand."* I knew that even when people failed me, God never would.

## A Spring Break To Remember

I didn't hear much from him unless he and his girlfriend were arguing, and only then would my phone ring. By this point, I was completely over him. When my Godmother invited me and my children to join her and her family for spring break in Florida, I gladly accepted. I desperately needed a mental break from everything I had been enduring. She brought her children, a friend, and her boyfriend along. While the idea of the trip was exciting, her boyfriend seemed so uptight and mean, which immediately set the tone for tension. I didn't know why, but we weren't seeing eye to eye from the start. To make matters worse, my daughter's behavior was out of control during the trip. I was already on edge, and her constant outbursts only heightened my frustration. The other kids would come to me, complaining about her behavior, and I felt embarrassed. I pulled her aside to talk, but in my frustration, I called her out of her name. I was deeply upset, feeling like she was embarrassing me in front of everyone. Her behavior didn't improve throughout the trip, and I found myself battling irritation and anger the entire time. The Bible says in **(Matthew 12:36-37):** *"I tell you, on the day of judgment people will give account for every careless word they speak, for by your words you will be justified, and by your words you will be condemned."* This verse echoed in my heart as I reflected on my harsh words toward my daughter. By the time it was time to pack up and leave, I felt a mix of exhaustion, guilt, and frustration. This trip, which was supposed to be a chance for me to relax and recharge, had turned into yet another stressful experience. I was reminded once again how much I needed to lean on God for strength, wisdom, and patience during these difficult times.

## A Moment of Reckoning

On our way back to Atlanta, my daughter was acting out in the back seat, doing something she wasn't supposed to be doing. I lost my temper and went off on her. All the emotions I had buried from my past—the pain, the frustration, the anger—came flooding to the surface. I couldn't hold it in anymore, and I lashed out. My Godmother's boyfriend, who was sitting in the front seat, turned around and yelled at me to watch how I was talking to my daughter. His words cut through me like a knife. I knew, deep down, that he was right. But in the moment, it didn't feel like that. It felt like another person judging me without understanding the weight I was carrying. I was overwhelmed with emotions, shame, and exhaustion. I snapped back at him because he didn't know my story. He didn't know what it was like to fight through years of trauma, neglect, and pain while trying to raise children and keep your own sanity intact. I felt like no one truly understood the battle I was fighting. After everything settled down, we rode the rest of the way in tense silence. When they dropped me off at home, I told my Godmother goodbye, but the interaction felt cold and distant. She left, and I sat in my house, consumed by guilt and regret. I felt terrible about how things had escalated on the ride back. A few days later, I discovered that my Godmother had blocked me, cutting off all communication, because we had words. My heart broke because she had always been a source of support for me, and now that connection was gone. I replayed the argument in my head over and over again, wishing I had handled things differently. The Bible says in **(Colossians 3:13):** *"Bear with each other and forgive one another if any of you has a grievance against someone. Forgive as the Lord forgave you."* I realized I needed to ask for forgiveness—not just from my Godmother, but also from myself and my daughter. I had been carrying so much pain from my past that I was letting it dictate my reactions in the present. This moment became a turning point for me. I began to understand that healing wasn't just about surviving my past—it was about releasing it, forgiving it, and learning to respond to life from a place of love instead of hurt. I had to find a way to stop letting the wounds of yesterday control my today. Even though I didn't hear from my Godmother for a while, I started to pray for reconciliation and for God to soften both of our hearts. I also started to pray for patience and strength to love my daughter the way she deserved to be loved, despite my struggles. **(2 Corinthians 12:9)** reminds us, *"My grace is sufficient for you, for my power is made perfect in weakness."* I clung to this promise, believing that even in my weakest moments, God's grace was enough to carry me through. This experience taught me that the journey to healing is not a straight path. It's filled with setbacks and lessons, but every step is an opportunity to grow closer to the person God created me to be. I was determined to keep moving forward—not just for myself, but for my children. They deserved a mother who was whole, loving, and free from the chains of her past.

# UNGODLY
# SITUATIONSHIPS
# / FAMILY

*"Don't be wise in your own eyes. Have respect for the Lord and avoid evil. That will bring health to your body. It will make your bones strong." (Proverbs 3:7-8)*

I was officially single, but my heart was burdened with unresolved pain. Instead of taking the time to heal and grow, I sought comfort in all the wrong places. I started having sex with different people because I was emotionally broken and desperate to feel loved by someone. I wasn't seeking a genuine relationship; I simply wanted to fit in and numb the ache inside me. I was doing what the world was doing, chasing after temporary fixes instead of lasting peace. The Bible says in (Romans 12:12), *"Do not conform to the patterns of this world but be transformed by the renewing of your mind. Then you will be able to test and approve what God's will is—His good, pleasing, and perfect will."* Yet, in my brokenness, I couldn't see that I was conforming to the world's standards, trying to fill a God-shaped void with people who were never meant to complete me. I was searching for affirmation in others when all I needed was already available in God. The world often glamorizes quick fixes and temporary pleasures, but those things never address the deeper wounds inside us. I thought that connecting with others physically would mend the emotional damage I had endured, but every fleeting connection left me feeling even more lost and empty. I longed for love, but I wasn't seeking it from the One who is the very definition of love. The Bible reminds us in (Proverbs 4:23), *"Above all else, guard your heart, for everything you do flows from it."* But instead of guarding my heart, I left it wide open, vulnerable to further hurt. I exposed my emotions to situations that brought more harm than healing. I was allowing my past pain to dictate my present decisions, and I realized I couldn't continue like this. Despite my struggles, God's love never wavered. His grace was constant, even in the midst of my mistakes. The Bible says in (Lamentations 3:22-23), *"The steadfast love of the Lord never ceases; His mercies never come to an end; they are new every morning; great is your faithfulness."* This verse reminded me that no matter how far I had wandered, God's mercy was waiting for me. His love was a safe haven, a place where I could heal and be made whole again. I poured myself into my business, hoping to find a sense of purpose. Cooking brought me joy, and it felt like a small ray of light in the midst of my emotional storm. Yet, even as I found moments of peace in my work, I knew I needed to address the deeper issues within my heart. My business could provide temporary relief, but only God could bring lasting healing. The Bible says in (Psalm 34:18), *"The Lord is close to the brokenhearted and saves those who are crushed in spirit."* This verse resonated deeply with me. I was brokenhearted, but I realized I was not alone. God was near, waiting for me to turn to Him and trust Him with my pain. I began to take small steps toward God, acknowledging my need for His guidance and love. It wasn't an easy journey. Healing required me to confront the wounds I had been avoiding and to surrender my brokenness to Him. But as I leaned into God's grace, I started to feel the weight of my burdens lift. I also began to understand that my worth wasn't tied to my past mistakes or the opinions of others. My identity was rooted in Christ, and He saw me as His beloved child. The Bible says in (Ephesians 2:10), *"For we are God's handiwork, created in Christ Jesus to do good works, which God prepared in advance for us to do."* This truth reminded me that my life had purpose, and my pain could be transformed into a testimony of God's faithfulness. Letting go of the unhealthy patterns I had created was challenging, but it was necessary. I realized that the temporary comforts I had sought were only distractions from the true healing I needed. As I embraced God's love and allowed Him to renew my mind, I began to see glimpses of hope and restoration. The Bible says in (Isaiah 61:3), *"To all who mourn in Israel, He will give a crown of beauty for ashes, a joyous blessing instead of mourning, festive praise instead of despair. In their righteousness, they will be like great oaks that the Lord has planted for His own glory."* This verse reminded me that God specializes in turning ashes into beauty. He was taking the broken pieces of my life and creating something beautiful for His glory. This chapter of my life wasn't about perfection; it was about progress. It was about learning to let go of the past, embrace God's grace, and take steps toward healing and peace. God was showing me that His love was more than enough to fill the void in my heart, and His plans for my life were far greater than anything I could imagine.

## A Story To Share

*"I can do all things through Christ who strengthens me."*
*(Philippians 4:13)*

I reached out to *Voyage ATL* to see if I could share my story about how I started my business. When they responded saying they were able to share it, I felt an overwhelming sense of excitement. This was a significant moment for me—a reflection of how far I had come. I wanted others to know that no matter the challenges, it's possible to rise above and accomplish great things if you're determined and stay focused. This opportunity felt like a breakthrough, proof that I could do anything if I put my mind to it. But even as I celebrated my growth, I found myself struggling emotionally. I called my aunt, hoping for support, and confided in her about how difficult things had been. I told her I felt like giving up, especially because my daughter's behavior was becoming more overwhelming by the day. Instead of offering the comfort and encouragement I was looking for, she brought up my past, reminding me of a time when I wrote a suicide letter as a child. Hearing her words stung deeply. I had called for understanding, but her response only reopened old wounds. She reminded me that I had written the letter because I didn't have any friends, and I wanted to end my life. But in my heart, I knew the truth: it wasn't just loneliness that made me feel that way back then, it was the way I was being treated, both at home and at school. That conversation hurt more than I anticipated. Instead of finding solace, I felt more broken and misunderstood. It was a painful reminder of the lack of support I had experienced growing up. I wanted to scream, "Don't you see? I needed love back then, and I need it now! "The Bible says in (Isaiah 41:10), *"So do not fear, for I am with you; do not be dismayed, for I am your God. I will strengthen you and help you; I will uphold you with my righteous right hand."* This verse reminded me that even when people fail to understand or support me, God is always present. He knows my heart and my struggles, and He promises to be my strength. Reflecting on my aunt's words, I realized something important: though others might bring up my past to shame me, God uses it to remind me of how far I've come. What was meant to break me as a child has become the foundation of my resilience and faith. My past doesn't define me; it fuels me to keep moving forward, trusting that God has a greater purpose for my life. The journey hasn't been easy, but I am learning to release the pain and disappointment that people have caused me. The Bible reminds us in (2 Corinthians 12:9), *"But He said to me, 'My grace is sufficient for you, for my power is made perfect in weakness.' Therefore, I will boast all the more gladly about my weaknesses, so that Christ's power may rest on me."* God's grace has carried me through moments when I wanted to give up. He has shown me that even in my weakest moments, His strength is enough to sustain me. Through every setback, He has been molding me into someone who can inspire and uplift others. This moment with my aunt may have reopened old wounds, but it also reinforced my determination to rise above the hurt. Sharing my story through *Voyage ATL* became more than just a business milestone—it became an opportunity to show others that God's grace is powerful enough to transform even the darkest parts of our lives into testimonies of His goodness.

I've realized that healing is a journey, and part of that journey is choosing to lean on God instead of looking for validation or comfort from people who may never understand. I will keep moving forward, trusting that God is using every part of my story for His glory and for my growth.

## Crying Out For Help

*"Whoever closes his ear to the cry of the poor will himself call out and not be answered." (Proverbs 21:13)*

I wanted my family to be there for me, to support me mentally and physically. But that didn't happen—they failed me when I needed them the most. I was overwhelmed and crying out for help, but it felt like nobody was listening. As a single mother, I was carrying the weight of everything on my shoulders. I desperately wanted to get my daughter the help she needed, but I didn't know how. My cries for help were met with silence and indifference. It hurt deeply when my aunt, instead of supporting me, brought up my past. She reminded me of things I did as a child, things I couldn't even remember, and threw them back at me during a time when I was already broken. I was furious. How could she do this when I reached out to her for comfort? I wasn't asking for a judgment; I was asking for help. The Bible reminds us in (Psalms 30:5), *"For his anger lasts only a moment, but his favor lasts a lifetime: weeping may stay for a night, but rejoicing comes in the morning."* This verse gave me a glimmer of hope, even as I wrestled with feelings of anger and betrayal. It reminded me that while people may fail me, God's favor and love endure. Her words cut deeply, and in my frustration, I let all my emotions spill out. I sent her a long text message, telling her exactly how I felt. I wasn't holding back anymore. I wanted her to feel the same hurt and sadness I was experiencing. But even as I did it, I realized it wasn't going to heal the pain inside me. I was trying to make her understand, but I was also reacting out of my own woundedness. I called her because I needed her help—not to be reminded of my mistakes as a child. It's hard when the people you expect to comfort you only add to your pain. I thought about the times she had hurt me, and it felt like history was repeating itself. I felt abandoned once again. When my diabetes began spiraling out of control and I started feeling sick, I called her again to ask if she could take my children for a little while so I could rest and recover. Her response shocked me. She told me I should call their father, knowing full well that he wasn't involved or helpful. She was my last resort, and yet she pushed me away. The Bible says in (Isaiah 41:10), *"So do not fear, for I am with you; do not be dismayed, for I am your God. I will strengthen you and help you; I will uphold you with my righteous right hand."* This verse became my anchor in the midst of the storm. When my family turned away, I reminded myself that God would never leave me. He was my strength when I had none left. I realized that sometimes, the people we expect to show up for us simply won't. It's a hard truth to accept, but it doesn't mean we are alone. God hears the cries of the weary, the desperate, and the brokenhearted. He sees every tear and understands every hurt. This season of my life taught me that while people may fail me, God's grace is sufficient. He is always present, ready to lift me up when I feel like I can't take another step. I learned to lean on Him more than ever, trusting that He would provide for me and my children in ways I couldn't imagine. Though I felt abandoned by my family, I found peace in knowing that God had not abandoned me. He was working behind the scenes, preparing a way for me. Every trial, every disappointment, was drawing me closer to Him and strengthening my faith.

## "When Family Fails"

*"When the righteous cry for help, the Lord hears and delivers them out of all their troubles. The Lord is near to the brokenhearted and saves the crushed in spirit. Many are the afflictions of the righteous, but the Lord delivers him out of them all. He keeps all his bones; not one of them is broken."*

*(Psalm 34:17-20)*

I couldn't shake the anger I felt toward my aunt. She reminded me of all the reasons I had come to believe that the phrase *"blood is thicker than water"* was nothing more than a lie. My family had made it clear that their love for me was conditional. Time after time, I was there for them, offering my help and support. Yet, when I needed them the most, they turned their backs on me. I had reached out to my aunt in a moment of vulnerability, desperate for her support, but instead, she made me feel even more alone. It wasn't just the lack of help that hurt; it was the dismissal of my struggles and the way she used my past to invalidate my present pain. I felt like I was screaming into a void, unheard and unseen by the very people who were supposed to love me. But even in my anger and disappointment, the Bible reminded me of a comforting truth: God hears the cries of the brokenhearted. He is always near, even when people fail us. The verses from (Psalm 34:17-20) gave me hope and reassurance that my pain was not invisible to Him. Feeling let down by my family, I reached out to someone else—a staff member from the group home where I once stayed. She had been someone who cared for me in the past, and I hoped she would be willing to help me again. When she showed up, I felt a wave of relief. Her willingness to step in when I was at my lowest was a blessing, and it reminded me that God places the right people in our lives at the right time. My aunt had tried to convince me that my struggles were because I didn't have friends, that I had isolated myself. Maybe there was some truth to her words, but I knew deep down it wasn't the whole story. My pain was rooted in years of rejection, loneliness, and feeling like I wasn't enough. It's hard to understand why the people we love the most can sometimes hurt us the worst. But through the anger, I began to realize that my worth was not tied to their opinions or their treatment of me. God's love was constant, even when human love faltered. He was near to me, hearing my cries, and offering the comfort and deliverance I so desperately needed. The lesson I learned in this season was painful but powerful: When family or others fail you, God never will. His love is unconditional, His support unwavering, and His presence constant. While the wounds from my aunt's lack of support hurt deeply, they also taught me to lean on God more fully and to trust that He would always make a way, even when others would not. This was a turning point for me—a realization that while people may disappoint me, my Heavenly Father would always be my refuge and strength. I didn't need to rely on anyone else to validate me or give me the support I needed, because God's grace was more than sufficient.

## "Finding My Voice"

*"And a person's enemies will be those of his own household."*
*(Matthew 10:36)*

I explained to my aunt that I didn't want to get upset with her during our conversation, so I ended the call before things could escalate. Tears flowed from my eyes as I began typing a long message to her, expressing my feelings. I made sure not to curse or be disrespectful, but I spoke honestly and openly. I believed that as adults, we should be able to communicate in a healthy and respectful way, but it seemed that my aunt didn't agree. She brought up my past, as if my growth and voice as an adult didn't matter. When I was younger, I didn't feel like I had the strength to stand up for myself, but now I did, and I think that insulted her. After I sent the message, she didn't respond directly to me. Instead, she went to the family, accusing me of being disrespectful. That broke my heart, but I reminded myself that

I had spoken my truth. The Bible says in *Matthew 10:36, "And a person's enemies will be those of his own household."* Sometimes, the deepest wounds come from those we love the most. I tried to seek comfort from my cousin, but our relationship began to feel strained as well. She would make comments about what I had, comparing her life to mine, and it felt like she was trying to bring me down. I couldn't understand why she seemed jealous of me when all I ever wanted was family. Arguments would arise, and she would call me names that hurt deeply. Eventually, I reached a breaking point and decided to distance myself. Enough was enough. Amid all the turmoil, I started working at a daycare in Stone Mountain. I gave it my best, even though I was still dealing with the weight of my personal struggles. Unfortunately, I had an argument with the owner and decided to quit. Daycare work had always been a safe choice for me because I had over 10 years of experience, but looking back, I regretted the way I handled the situation. My past trauma and inner battles had clouded my judgment, and I realized that nobody truly knew the pain I was carrying. I humbled myself, apologized, and tried to move forward with grace. The Bible says in *Philippians 4:8-9, "Keep your thoughts continually fixed on all that is authentic and real, honorable and admirable, beautiful and respectful, pure and holy, merciful and kind. And fasten your thoughts on every glorious work of God, praising Him always."* I clung to this verse, reminding myself to focus on the beauty and goodness that still surrounded me, even when life felt overwhelming.

In the midst of everything, I reached out to the man I had met at Walmart. I longed to feel loved and nurtured, and he had always been respectful and made me feel secure. When we reunited, we shared so many wonderful moments together that felt priceless and unforgettable. But our connection was inconsistent—he would disappear for weeks or months at a time without explanation. This left me feeling abandoned and frustrated, leading me to send him long, emotional messages about how he made me feel. Despite my hurt, I would apologize and unblock him, longing for the peace and happiness I felt when we were together. He would return, and we would share more beautiful moments, but it was always temporary. He called our relationship toxic, and perhaps he was right, but I didn't want to let go. I wanted him to understand that I cared for him deeply and wanted something lasting. His lack of communication left me feeling unseen, and eventually, we stopped talking all together. This chapter in my life was marked by struggles with family, relationships, and my own inner battles. Yet, through it all, I was learning to find my voice, to stand up for myself, and to lean on God for guidance and strength. Every setback reminded me that I was stronger than I realized, and every heartbreak taught me to seek healing and peace from within rather than from others. God was teaching me that even in the midst of pain, His grace was sufficient, and He would never leave me alone

## "Seeking Control, Finding Chaos"

*"If a woman has sex before marriage, she is put in the same category as a prostitute." (Deuteronomy 22:13-21)*

My sex life became my source of power and control. It was something that made me feel good, like I was in charge of my life and decisions. I was independent, paying my own bills, and doing everything on my own. I didn't need men for anything other than the physical satisfaction they brought me. But deep down, I knew this wasn't fulfilling me. The Bible's teachings weighed on my heart, reminding me that my actions were leading me further from God's path. I received shocking news that my son's father welcomed his baby boy into the world—on my birthday. We weren't together anymore, but it still hit me hard. I couldn't believe that the baby was born on my special day. This wasn't even her due date, and it felt like they planned it just to hurt me. I wrestled with feelings of disbelief, anger, and betrayal. But then, I shifted my perspective. I thought, *maybe this is a reminder that he will always remember me, no matter what.* Slowly, I accepted the situation and focused on moving forward with my life. My sister invited me to go on a trip for her birthday. One of her friends had backed out at the last minute and didn't pay their portion, so I stepped in. She told me that her boyfriend and a couple of their friends would meet us there, and I agreed to go. When we arrived and got settled, I realized I was the only single person on the trip. It felt awkward, like I didn't belong. I started to notice things that made me uncomfortable. My sister seemed more focused on her boyfriend than enjoying her birthday, and he came across as controlling. The whole situation felt off, but I kept my observations to myself because I wanted my sister to feel special. Being the only single person on a trip full of couples made me feel isolated. It was a reminder of how lonely I truly felt inside, despite the independence and control I tried to maintain in my life. Watching my sister in her relationship made me reflect on the kind of love and connection I truly desired—not just temporary moments of satisfaction, but something deeper and more meaningful. The Bible says in *Proverbs 3:5-6*, *"Trust in the Lord with all your heart, and lean not on your own understanding; in all your ways submit to Him, and He will make your paths straight."* Even in the midst of confusion and frustration, I realized I needed to surrender my control to God. I couldn't fill the emptiness I felt with fleeting pleasures or shallow connections. True peace and fulfillment could only come from him. This trip taught me more about myself than I expected. I began to see the areas of my life where I needed healing and clarity. I wasn't just searching for control—I was searching for love, validation, and peace. But the more I sought these things from the world, the emptier I felt. I knew I needed to turn back to God, to realign my heart and my actions with His will. This wasn't just a lesson about relationships—it was a lesson about faith, self-worth, and trusting God with the journey ahead.

## "A Breaking Point On The Journey"

*"Trust in the Lord with all your heart, and do not lean on your own understanding. In all your ways acknowledge Him, and He will make straight your paths." (Proverbs 3:5-6)*

When we went to the bar that evening, I noticed my sister seemed sad. As we talked, she opened up about what was going on between her and her boyfriend. I listened, and the more I heard, the angrier I became. He had left her to do whatever he wanted while she was left feeling hurt and alone. Seeing her like that brought out emotions I couldn't control—I wanted to stand up for her, but I held my tongue. The next day, we all went to a restaurant. Things were tense, and when her boyfriend made a rude comment to my sister, I couldn't take it anymore. I snapped and started arguing with him. The situation escalated, and her other friends pulled me aside, trying to calm me down. They reminded me that we were in Florida and warned me about the consequences if things got out of hand. I took a deep breath and decided to let it go for the moment. One of her friends tried to cool me down, and I eventually calmed down. But my heart broke when my sister walked over to me in tears. She was hurting, and it made me even more upset to see her like this. I didn't want her to go through the same pain I had experienced in toxic relationships. I wanted to protect her, to shield her from the heartache I knew all too well. I thought we were on the same page, but then she walked away to find him. I was stunned. After everything I did to stand up for her, she left with him, getting into an Uber and abandoning me with her other friends. I was left standing there, confused and hurt. As we rode back to the Airbnb, I replayed everything in my head, wondering why she chose him over me when I was only trying to help. I couldn't shake the feeling that this trip had turned into something I never expected. It was supposed to be a celebration, a time to bond with my sister, but it ended up revealing so much more about where we stood. I sat in silence that night, reflecting on everything. The Bible says in Psalm 34:18, "The Lord is close to the brokenhearted and saves those who are crushed in spirit." I realized how crushed I felt— not just because of this trip, but because of the countless times

I had tried to show love and loyalty to the people around me, only to feel abandoned or unappreciated. I wanted my sister to see her worth, to realize she deserved better. But it hurt deeply to see her cling to someone who caused her so much pain. This trip was a turning point for me. It reminded me that I couldn't change people, no matter how much I wanted to. I couldn't make my sister see what I saw or force her to leave a situation she wasn't ready to let go of. The only thing I could do was pray for her and trust that God would guide her in His time. The Bible says in Romans 12:12, *"Be joyful in hope, patient in affliction, faithful in prayer."* I needed to hold on to hope—for my sister, for myself, and for the relationships in my life. I needed to trust that God was working even in the chaos, that He had a purpose for everything I was going through. As I lay in bed that night, I prayed for peace and strength. I asked God to guide my steps, to help me release the anger and pain that had built up in my heart. I realized that this trip wasn't just about my sister's journey—it was about mine, too. It was about learning to let go, to trust God's plan, and to find strength in His love even when the people around me let me down.

## "A Last Straw with Family and a New Beginning"

*"The Lord is close to the brokenhearted and saves those who are crushed in spirit." (Psalm 34:18)*

I was ready to leave. The trip had left a bitter taste in my mouth, and I didn't feel like saying much to anyone. The feeling of betrayal weighed heavily on me, and as we boarded the plane back to Atlanta, I couldn't shake the frustration. My sister told me that I had ruined her trip, blaming me for what had happened when all I tried to do was help her. It was heartbreaking to hear her say that. I knew in my heart that her boyfriend was the root of the problem, but somehow, I was the one taking the fall. That trip was my breaking point. I decided I was done allowing my family to tear me down. When we returned, I found out that my sister had gone to our family and twisted the story, making it seem like I was the reason her trip was ruined. I couldn't understand why she would do that. I kept asking myself, *when will I finally be happy? When will I have a good family and a healthy relationship?* The constant pain and rejection from those closest to me left me feeling defeated. Returning to my daily routine, I tried to push the pain aside. I started a new job at a leasing office, and for the first time in a long time, I felt like I had a fresh start. The opportunity brought me hope, and I met some wonderful people while working there. However, that hope was short-lived. The management company I was working for lost their contract, and a new company took over. I was given the choice to stay with my original employer or transition to the new one. I decided to stay with the new company, hoping it would bring stability. Unfortunately, after about a month, the new manager told me I'd have to work weekends. As a single parent with no support, I knew this was going to be a problem. My daughter's behavior was out of control, and no one was willing to watch her. I couldn't manage a schedule that required weekend shifts because I had no reliable babysitter. Feeling overwhelmed and trapped, I made the decision to leave the job. I was frustrated because my circumstances made it hard for me to keep any job. The Bible reminds us in *Psalm 34:18, "The Lord is close to the brokenhearted and saves those who are crushed in spirit."* I clung to this truth, hoping God would provide a way for me to push forward. My strength was running thin, but I was determined to keep moving. Around this time, I received a message on Instagram from a man who had been in my inbox for two years. For some reason, I finally decided to respond. Maybe I was searching for a connection, or maybe I was just curious. Whatever the reason, it felt like a small light breaking through the darkness I had been carrying. I wasn't sure where this would lead, but I allowed myself to take a step toward something new. This chapter of my life was a reminder of how heavy the weight of disappointment and rejection can feel. Yet, in those moments of despair, I realized that God was still guiding me, still providing small glimpses of hope to remind me that I wasn't alone. My journey was far from over, but I held on to the belief that brighter days were ahead.

## "A Last Straw With Family And A New Beginning"

*"The Lord is close to the brokenhearted and saves those who are crushed in spirit." (Psalm 34:18)*

I was ready to leave. The trip had left a bitter taste in my mouth, and I didn't feel like saying much to anyone. The feeling of betrayal weighed heavily on me, and as we boarded the plane back to Atlanta, I couldn't shake the frustration. My sister told me that I had ruined her trip, blaming me for what had happened when all I tried to do was help her. It was heartbreaking to hear her say that. I knew in my heart that her boyfriend was the root of the problem, but somehow, I was the one taking the fall. That trip was my breaking point. I decided I was done allowing my family to tear me down. When we returned, I found out that my sister had gone to our family and twisted the story, making it seem like I was the reason her trip was ruined. I couldn't understand why she would do that. I kept asking myself, *when will I finally be happy? When will I have a good family and a healthy relationship?* The constant pain and rejection from those closest to me left me feeling defeated. Returning to my daily routine, I tried to push the pain aside. I started a new job at a leasing office, and for the first time in a long time, I felt like I had a fresh start. The opportunity brought me hope, and I met some wonderful people while working there. However, that hope was short-lived. The management company I was working for lost their contract, and a new company took over. I was given the choice to stay with my original employer or transition to a new one. I decided to stay with the new company, hoping it would bring stability. Unfortunately, after about a month, the new manager told me I'd have to work weekends. As a single parent with no support, I knew this was going to be a problem. My daughter's behavior was out of control, and no one was willing to watch her. I couldn't manage a schedule that required weekend shifts because I had no reliable babysitter. Feeling overwhelmed and trapped, I made the decision to leave the job. I was frustrated because my circumstances made it hard for me to keep any job. The Bible reminds us in *Psalm 34:18, "The Lord is close to the brokenhearted and saves those who are crushed in spirit."* I clung to this truth, hoping God would provide a way for me to push forward. My strength was running thin, but I was determined to keep moving. Around this time, I received a message on Instagram from a man who had been in my inbox for two years. For some reason, I finally decided to respond. Maybe I was searching for a connection, or maybe I was just curious. Whatever the reason, it felt like a small light breaking through the darkness I had been carrying. I wasn't sure where this would lead, but I allowed myself to take a step toward something new. This chapter of my life was a reminder of how heavy the weight of disappointment and rejection can feel. Yet, in those moments of despair, I realized that God was still guiding me, still providing small glimpses of hope to remind me that I wasn't alone. My journey was far from over, but I held on to the belief that brighter days were ahead.

## "A Season Of Heartache And Determination"

*"But I say to you, whoever looks at a woman to lust for her has already committed adultery with her in his heart." (Matthew 5:28)*

After years of ignoring his messages, I finally gave him a chance. We exchanged numbers, and he seemed nice at first. He told me he had recently moved to Atlanta from Chicago. However, something about him felt off. It wasn't long before his controlling side started to show. He began telling me what I should and shouldn't post on Instagram and even tried to dictate who I could and couldn't talk to. I wasn't even talking to him for that long, and already he was trying to take control of my life. Despite these red flags, I gave in to the attention. He asked me to come over after work, but I told him he could come to my house since I had my kids, and it was late. He made an excuse, so I ended up going to his house with my kids. We talked, and eventually, things became physical. The way he touched me made me feel desired, like I belonged to him, and I gave in because my body craved the connection. That night, we slept together. The next morning, I woke up early and left to get home before he went to work. He walked me outside, said goodbye, and that was it. I didn't hear from him after that. He didn't even check to see if I made it home safely. When I confronted him, he claimed he had to wake up for work, but deep down, I knew the truth—he only wanted me for my body. The Bible says in *Matthew 5:28*, "*Whoever looks at a woman to lust for her has already committed adultery with her in his heart.*" That verse echoed in my mind as I processed what had happened. I felt used and ashamed, and I decided to cut ties with him. I refused to continue allowing people into my life who only drained me emotionally and left me feeling empty. I moved on, but the pain lingered. I was hurt, broken, and depressed, but I didn't let it stop me. I decided to focus on finding a bigger home for me and my children. I was determined to create a better environment for us, one that was stable and filled with hope. I searched and searched, and finally, I found a house that was perfect for us. The only problem was the deposit—I didn't have the money. In desperation, I called my Godmother and explained my situation. Without hesitation, she loaned me the money I needed. Her support meant the world to me. It reminded me that even in my moments of despair, there were still people who cared and were willing to help. The Bible reminds us in *Psalm 46:1, "God is our refuge and strength, a very present help in trouble."* My Godmother's generosity was a reflection of God's provision in my life. I moved into the house, feeling grateful for this fresh start. It was a step forward in my journey toward healing and restoration—a new chapter filled with possibilities for me and my children. Even though my heart was still heavy with the weight of past experiences, I was determined not to let them define my future. This house represented more than just a place to live; it was a symbol of hope and resilience, a reminder that God's grace was sustaining me every step of the way.

## "A Dangerous Obsession"

*"Flee fornication. Every sin that a man does is without the body;*
*but he that commits fornication sins against his own body."*
*(1 Corinthians 6:18)*

We began talking, sharing our relationship struggles with one another. There was an instant connection, and we bonded over our shared stories. I told him about my business and handed him one of my cards, and he did the same, sharing his dreams and aspirations. His presence was magnetic, and I felt drawn to him in a way I hadn't experienced before. When he came to fix my garage, I gave him the code to my house since I had to work and didn't want to miss him. I kept checking my camera, watching him work hard, and I couldn't stop staring. He texted me when he finished and told me the job was done. I thanked him, grateful for his help, but what I didn't expect was how much his follow-up text the next week would brighten my day. He sent me a beautiful affirmation, and it was so thoughtful that I couldn't help but smile. Before I knew it, we were on the phone often, sharing our days and exchanging messages that quickly became a routine. I invited him over one evening and told him I needed a massage. He came, his touch soft yet strong, and the massage led to something much deeper. Our connection became physical, and I couldn't deny how amazing he made me feel. It was intoxicating, the best I had ever experienced. The Bible warns us in *1 Corinthians 6:18*, *"Flee fornication. Every sin that a man does is without the body; but he that commits fornication sins against his own body."* But in that moment, I ignored the truth. I was captivated, allowing my desires to control me instead of seeking God's guidance. I trusted him enough to let him spend the night. He had my mind completely consumed, and I couldn't get enough of him. We texted and called each other constantly, and I cooked him dinner, pouring my heart into every detail. I wanted to be the woman he could confide in, the one who made him feel safe and understood. I knew he had been through so much, and I thought that maybe I could be the one to bring him peace. I wanted to show him love and care in a way that he might not have experienced before. But deep down, I realized I was trying to fill my own void, seeking validation and comfort in someone who, at the end of the day, could never replace what I truly needed—God's love and healing. The moments with him were fleeting but powerful, and I clung to the way he made me feel. Yet, as much as I wanted to hold onto the fantasy, I couldn't escape the truth: I was losing myself in the process. It was time to reflect on whether this was truly love or just another distraction keeping me from the healing and peace I so desperately needed.

## "A False Hope in Love"

*"Trust in the Lord with all your heart and lean not on your own understanding; in all your ways submit to Him, and He will make your paths straight." (Proverbs 3:5-6)*

We began sharing special moments together, and the bond between us seemed to grow with each passing day. He would spend the night with me, and waking up next to him felt comforting, like the beginning of something real. One morning, after he left, I received a text from him saying he had left a gift on my car. I rushed outside, my heart fluttering with excitement. There it was, a thoughtful surprise just for me. I was blushing, overwhelmed by the gesture. No one had ever done anything like that for me before, and in that moment, I truly believed he might be "the one." His actions and the way he made me feel gave me hope, a feeling I had been searching for. I wanted to reciprocate, to show him that I appreciated and cared for him. I planned something special, hoping to surprise him in the same way he had surprised me. I called him and asked him to come over, telling him I had planned a night he wouldn't forget. When he arrived and walked in, the look on his face was priceless. He was shocked at the gifts and the setup I had carefully prepared for him. He told me that no woman had ever done anything like this for him, and hearing those words made me feel like I had succeeded in showing him how much I cared. I wanted him to know that I was all he needed, that I could love him in a way he hadn't experienced before. He began spending more time with me, coming over every weekend. Each visit felt like a promise; a step closer to the relationship I thought we were building. I poured my heart into those moments, believing that my efforts were creating something lasting. But as much as I gave, I couldn't shake a small voice in the back of my mind, a quiet whisper reminding me to seek clarity and wisdom. The Bible says in *Proverbs 3:5-6, "Trust in the Lord with all your heart and lean not on your own understanding; in all your ways submit to Him, and He will make your paths straight."* Yet, in my pursuit of love and validation, I was leaning on my own understanding, hoping to secure a future that wasn't guaranteed. One night, he came over again, and the comfort of his presence felt reassuring. I had placed so much hope in this relationship, yearning for it to be the love story I had always dreamed of. But deep inside, I knew that love built without God's foundation is fragile, and I began to wonder if this was truly the path, He wanted for me.

## "Unveiled Truths"

*"Love is patient and kind; love does not envy or boast; it is*
*not arrogant or rude. It does not insist on its own way; it is not*
*irritable or resentful; it does not rejoice at wrongdoing but rejoices*
*with the truth. Love bears all things, believes all things, hopes all*
*things, endures all things." (1 Corinthians 13:4-7)*

That night felt perfect, almost too perfect to be real. After
putting the kids to bed, we went downstairs, and I told him I was
hungry. Without hesitation, he cooked for me and even cleaned
up afterward. Watching him move around the kitchen, I felt like
I was living a dream. No man had ever made me feel this way—
so cared for, so seen, so appreciated. When the food was ready,
we ate together, and then he played some R&B music. Out of
nowhere, he grabbed me and pulled me close, and we started to
dance right there in the kitchen. As he held me tightly, the weight
of everything I had been through poured out of me in the form
of tears. I couldn't hold it in—I was overwhelmed by the love and
comfort I thought I had found. In that moment, I felt complete,
like all the broken pieces of my heart were finally being put back
together. But deep down, I was holding back. I wanted to tell him
my darkest secrets, to let him know every part of me, but I was
afraid. Instead, I simply told him that he made me feel whole,
something I hadn't felt in a very long time. The Bible verse from

*1 Corinthians 13:4-7* echoed in my mind, reminding me of what true love should look like—patient, kind, and enduring. I wanted to believe that this was it. He continued to do thoughtful things, like surprising me by putting up my daughter's bed and helping around the house. He wasn't just a presence he was contributing, making me feel like we were building something real. One day, after helping me at home, he told me he had to leave to attend a company dinner. I believed him and didn't think much of it at the time. Later that night, we spoke briefly on the phone while he was getting ready. He said he'd call me back after dinner, but the call never came. I went to bed feeling uneasy, but I told myself not to overthink it. The next morning, I woke up and went to work, still waiting for his text or call. When my phone finally buzzed, it was a message from him—a picture of what he wore to dinner. He looked amazing, but something about the picture didn't sit right with me. His outfit didn't seem like something you'd wear to a company dinner. It felt more intimate, like he had dressed up for a date. My intuition told me to investigate, so I went on social media and searched the page of a woman I had noticed before—someone who had been tagging him and liking his posts. What I saw shattered me. She had posted a picture from the night before, and in the photo, I recognized his arm, his phone, and two wine glasses on the table. My heart sank. This wasn't a company dinner, it was a date, and he had lied to me. I sat there in disbelief, replaying everything in my head. The dancing in the kitchen, the sweet messages, the moments that felt so real—were they all just lies? I wanted to believe that he was different, that he was genuine, but now I wasn't so sure. The Bible says in *Luke 8:17, "Everything that is hidden will become clear, and every secret will be made known."* The truth had been revealed, and as painful as it was, I knew I couldn't ignore it. I deserved honesty, respect, and love—the kind of love that God promises, not the kind that leaves you questioning your worth. In that moment, I realized that love isn't just about how someone makes you feel; it's about how they honor you, respect you, and align their actions with their words. This wasn't love, it was deception, and I knew I had to confront the truth, no matter how much it hurt.

## "Deception and Disarray"

*"For all that is in the world—the lust of the flesh, the lust of the eyes, and the pride of life—is not of the Father but is of the world."* (1 John 2:16) I texted him back, letting him know we needed to talk. He could already tell from my voice that I was upset. My mind was racing, and I couldn't focus at work. What I had seen on social media was consuming my thoughts. I decided to leave work early because my anger and confusion were too overwhelming. When I got home, I received a text from him asking if I liked seafood.

I replied yes, even though I was still upset. I waited for him to arrive at my house, playing the conversation, I wanted to have with him over and over in my head. Finally, he came, and we went upstairs. I asked him directly if he had been with another woman the night before. Instead of coming clean, he got defensive. He brushed it off, saying she was just a coworker. Deep down, I knew he was lying, but I let it slide for a moment. I wanted to confront him, but I also didn't want to push him away completely. To make up for the tension, he told me to get ready so he could take me out to eat. I reluctantly agreed. At dinner, we laughed, talked, and had a good time. He bought me a drink, and for a moment, it felt like we were back on good terms. By the end of the night, I was drunk, tired, and emotionally drained. When we got back to the house, he wanted to be intimate, but I couldn't. I was too weak and exhausted. The next morning, we both woke up wanting each other, and we had the most passionate makeup sex. For a brief moment, it made me forget what I was angry about. But reality soon crept back in. Afterward, he told me he had to leave to pick up his daughter and promised to take me on a date later that day. I was happy because I felt like he owed me this time together. However, as the day went on, he called to say he had to work and that our date would have to be postponed. I couldn't hide my disappointment and suspicion. I told him I hoped he was really working and not doing something else. He became defensive, told me he would call me later, and hung up. My emotions were in turmoil. I didn't know what to believe or how to feel. The Bible reminds us in *1 John 2:16* that the temptations of this world—the lust of the flesh, the lust of the eyes, and the pride of life—are not of God. I was caught in a cycle of emotional highs and lows, trying to hold onto someone who wasn't being truthful with me. That night, I waited for his call, but it never came. The silence spoke louder than any words he could have said, leaving me feeling hurt, confused, and alone. My heart was heavy with the weight of unanswered questions, and I knew deep down that something wasn't right.

## "Seeking Love, Finding Heartache"

*"Be strong and courageous. Do not be afraid or terrified because of them, for the Lord your God goes with you; He will never leave you nor forsake you." (Deuteronomy 31:6)*

My sister called and invited me over for a get-together. I agreed, hoping to take my mind off the whirlwind of emotions I was feeling. Despite trying to distract myself, my thoughts were still consumed by him. I dressed up in my most flattering outfit, snapped a few pictures, and uploaded them to Instagram, knowing he would see them. He looked but didn't say anything.

I checked his story and found myself spiraling into feelings of hurt and longing. I went to my sister's house, hoping to vent and find some relief. I told her about everything that had happened, and before I realized it, she grabbed my phone and texted him. I was shocked and furious. Her impulsiveness only made things worse. He blocked me on everything, and I felt an overwhelming sense of rejection and worthlessness. The days that followed were tough. I would log into Instagram from another account just to see his page, desperate to hold on to some connection. I missed us—our time together, the way he made me feel. I questioned everything. Was it my fault? Did I do something wrong? I blamed myself for everything, carrying the weight of guilt and confusion. Eventually, I realized I had to let it go. The Bible says in *Deuteronomy 31:6*, "Be strong and courageous. Do not be afraid or terrified because of them, for the Lord your God goes with you; He will never leave you nor forsake you." This verse reminded me that I wasn't alone, and that God would never abandon me, even when others did. In an attempt to move forward, I reached out to a guy I had known for a long time, someone I once had a crush on. He replied, saying he missed me too. My hopes were high because I had always wanted a chance with him. But as time went on, I saw the truth—he was more focused on material things like cars, clothes, and jewelry. Every time we planned to meet, something would come up, and he would cancel. He stood me up more times than I could count, leaving me hurt and questioning why I kept going back to him. It was a toxic cycle that drained me emotionally. My heart longed for a real connection, for someone who would value me, but this wasn't it. The Bible says in *1 Peter 2:17*, "Show respect for all people: Love the brothers and sisters of God's family, respect God, honor the king." I realized I wasn't showing respect for myself by continuing to chase after people who didn't value me. One day, I messaged him on Facebook about a meal he had posted, asking if he had cooked it. He replied, admitting he had been lurking on my page and complimenting me on my looks. We exchanged numbers, and the conversations started up again. This gave me a glimmer of hope, but deep down, I knew his words didn't align with his actions. Not long after, I attended a fish fry at a friend's sister's house. While I was there, I slipped and fell, breaking my foot. The pain from the injury was physical, but it also mirrored the emotional pain I was carrying. It was a harsh reminder that I needed to slow down, heal, and focus on myself instead of seeking validation and love in the wrong places. The fall was yet another challenge, but I clung to God's promises. I knew I needed to rebuild my life with Him as my foundation. The healing process—both physical and emotional—would take time, but I was determined to find strength and courage through my faith.

## "Broken Trust, Healing Hearts"

*"Be kind to one another, tenderhearted, forgiving one another, as God in Christ forgave you." (Ephesians 4:32)*

I sent him pictures and a video of my foot, hoping he would show some care or concern, but his response was distant. He simply told me he hoped I felt better. I wanted more from him—I wanted him to come and take care of me, to show me that he cared. But he didn't, and the pain wasn't just in my foot; it was in my heart. My birthday was approaching, and I felt crushed knowing I wouldn't be able to go out of town to celebrate the way I had planned. The thought of being stuck at home with a broken foot on my birthday left me feeling defeated. In an effort to still celebrate, I decided to throw a small party at my house with a few people. It wasn't what I had envisioned, but I was determined to make the best of it. I arranged for one of my coworkers to watch my kids for the weekend. She agreed, and I dropped them off, grateful for the opportunity to enjoy myself for a little while. The party went well, and I tried to focus on having a good time, but the weight of everything I had been dealing with still lingered in the background. When it was time to pick up my children, my coworker mentioned something that left me shaken. She said my children had "unclean spirits." I didn't know what to say. I was confused, scared, and hurt by her words. I told her that I pray over myself and my kids every day, but her comment lingered in my mind, sowing seeds of fear and doubt. The Bible warns in *1 Timothy 4:1, "The Spirit clearly says that in later times some will abandon the faith and follow deceiving spirits and things taught by demons."* I clung to my faith, knowing that God's love and protection were over me and my children, but it was hard to shake off the fear her words had planted. Around the same time, my relationship with my godmother fell apart. I had trusted her with so much—my secrets, my pain, and my hopes. I saw her as a mother figure, a mentor, and a friend. I always spoke highly of her, even when others didn't. So, when I found out she had been talking about me behind my back, it felt like a betrayal deeper than anything I had experienced before. She had shared my darkest secrets; the things I had confided in in her during my most vulnerable moments. Her words painted me as someone I wasn't, and it hurt more than I could express. I couldn't understand why she would do this to me. In my anger and pain, I lashed out. I said things I now regret. The argument we had created a chasm between us that felt impossible to bridge. It broke my heart because I loved and respected her so much. Losing that relationship felt like losing a piece of myself. The Bible says in *Ephesians 4:32, "Be kind to one another, tenderhearted, forgiving one another, as God in Christ forgave you."* Those words felt heavy, especially when forgiveness seemed so far away. But deep down, I knew that holding onto anger and pain would only hurt me more. I prayed for God to soften my heart, to help me find the strength to forgive, even if the wounds were still fresh. I didn't know how to move forward, but I knew that with God's help, healing was possible. This chapter of my life was a painful reminder of the importance of guarding my heart and choosing to respond to hurt with grace and forgiveness. Through all the pain, I held onto the hope that God would guide me through. I had to trust that even in moments of betrayal, He was working to bring healing and restoration to my life.

## "Betrayed by Trust"

*"Blessed is the man who trusts in the Lord, whose trust is the Lord." (Jeremiah 17:7)*

The guy I was talking to at the time asked if he could borrow my car, and without hesitation, I trusted him. It was Halloween night, and he came over so we could spend time together. We shared a bottle, and as the night went on, he fell asleep while I cooked us dinner. I woke him up to eat and told him it was time for him to head to work. He was visibly drunk, stumbling as he tried to stand. I pleaded with him not to go to work in that condition, but he insisted he could handle it. As he walked out the door, I reminded him to be safe and to call me when he arrived. Hours passed, and I didn't hear from him. Worry crept in, so I texted him to ask if he made it to work. His response was a voice message that shattered me—he admitted he had wrecked my car. He explained that the car was in the road, and the transmission was damaged. My heart sank. I immediately called him, anger and frustration overwhelming me. I needed that car for everything—work, my children, and daily responsibilities. I demanded to know why he didn't just stay home as I had suggested. He told me to call my insurance and report the damage as caused by road debris. Reluctantly, I followed his advice, and my insurance arranged for the car to be towed. When he came back to my house, I was furious, but I let it go because I didn't have the energy to fight anymore. He promised to call his stepdad in the morning so I could borrow a car to take my children to school. Exhausted, I went to bed, praying for strength. *"Blessed is the man who trusts in the Lord, whose trust is the Lord."* (Jeremiah 17:7). I had to put my faith in God because my situation felt out of my control. The next morning, I woke up at 6 a.m., went downstairs, and reminded him to call his stepdad as promised. He was still drunk, slurring his words, and being disrespectful. To my disbelief, he hung up the phone mid-conversation with his stepdad. My anger boiled over, and we got into a heated argument. Frustrated and irresponsible, he packed up his things and walked out, leaving me stranded without a car or any help. I couldn't believe I had trusted him. I was beyond upset. I replayed the situation in my mind, asking myself why I had let him drive my car in the first place. This is what happens when you try to be nice, I thought to myself bitterly. Hours later, he returned to pick me up so I could get a rental car, but I was done. I didn't even want to speak to him. We agreed on what he owed me for the damage to my car, including the deductible, but things quickly spiraled. Our arguments grew worse, and I threatened to come to his house to demand the money he owed me. Instead of taking responsibility, he blocked me, leaving me to deal with the financial burden alone. A call from the body shop delivered the final blow—the car was totaled. I was devastated. I called him to inform him of the situation, hoping he would follow through on his promise to help. Instead, he lied, avoided me, and never gave me a dime toward the car. I was left without transportation and had no idea how I was going to replace my car. I felt betrayed, used, and abandoned. The situation taught me a painful lesson about trust and boundaries. I had given him the benefit of the doubt, but his actions showed me that not everyone deserves my kindness or my trust. In the midst of my anger and despair, I turned to God for comfort. The Bible says, *"The Lord is near to the brokenhearted and saves the crushed in spirit."* (Psalm 34:18). This experience left me feeling brokenhearted and crushed, but I knew God was still with me, guiding me toward healing and restoration. This was another trial in my life, but I refused to let it break me. I placed my faith in God, trusting that He would make a way when there seemed to be none.

## "Blessings Through Faith"

*"Those who sow in tears shall reap with shouts of joy."*
*(Psalms 126:5)*

Still stuck in a rental car, I was trying to figure out my next steps. I couldn't allow this setback to stop me. I clung to God's promises, believing that better days were ahead. Work had been steady—I had started with a temp agency, caring for adults who couldn't care for themselves. It wasn't easy, but I did my best. One of the young men I cared for started to show interest in me, but I set clear boundaries. I explained that I was there to work, and I couldn't entertain those conversations. Although the job had its challenges, I remained focused. He often vented his frustrations about his situation, and I reminded myself that his anger wasn't about me—it was about his circumstances. I leaned on God for patience and strength to continue showing up with grace, even when things were tough. One day after work, I made a call that would change everything. I contacted a dealership and explained my situation. I told the woman on the line that I only had $500 to put down, and I was desperate for any car she could put me in. She promised to call me back by Friday. When the call came, I went to the dealership hopeful, but my excitement quickly turned to frustration when my job delayed my paycheck for another week. I arrived with no money and had to explain my situation. The woman told me if I could come up with the $500, she could put me in a 2021 SUV. Hearing those words filled me with a mix of hope and determination. I had been praying for an SUV for two years, and now it seemed like God was answering my prayers. I just needed to figure out how to come up with the money. I reached out to my homegirl, explaining my situation, and she graciously loaned me $250. I was so grateful for her help, but I still needed the other half. I hesitated but decided to call the guy I had been talking to earlier in the year. To my surprise, he agreed to lend me the remaining $250. With their help, I was able to make the down payment and drive off the lot in the SUV I had prayed for. God is so good! Not only did I get the car, but the dealership gave me my first month's payment free. *"Hallelujah!"* God truly hears the cries of His children. The Bible says in *Genesis 50:20-22, "As for you, you meant evil against me, but God meant it for good."* Even when it seemed like everything was falling apart, God turned my situation around for my good. This experience strengthened my faith and reminded me of *Hebrews 11:1, "Faith is confidence in what we hope for and assurance about what we do not see."* I couldn't see how things were going to work out, but I held onto my faith, and God provided a way. Through every trial, He has been my provider, showing me that nothing is impossible when I trust in him. This SUV was more than just a car—it was a symbol of God's faithfulness and my perseverance through the storm. I knew I had to keep trusting, keep praying, and keep moving forward because God had more blessings in store for me.

## "Tangled in Lust"

> *"Flee from sexual immorality. Every other sin a person commits is outside the body, but the sexually immoral person sins against his own body. Or do you not know that your body is a temple of the Holy Spirit within you, whom you have from God? You are not your own, for you were bought at a price. So, glorify God in your body." (1 Corinthians 6:18-20)*

The guy who had loaned me the money for my SUV told me there was an "interest" added to his loan. That interest wasn't financial—it was physical. I wasn't offended, though, because deep down, I wanted it too. I agreed, and he came over to my house. When he spent the night, it was like we had stepped into a time machine. The connection between us brought back all the emotions, memories, and desires that I thought were behind me. That night, my feelings for him reignited. I convinced myself that this was love, but in truth, it was lust and emotional longing masquerading as something deeper. The intimacy between us wasn't just physical—it felt like his soul was tied to mine, creating a bond I couldn't break. I began to call him frequently, acting as if we were in a relationship, even though that wasn't the reality. The connection we had in those moments blinded me to the truth of our situation. I thought the passion between us was a sign of something deeper, but I was ignoring the warning signs. The Bible reminds us to *"flee from sexual immorality"* because it entangles us in ways that harm us spiritually, emotionally, and even physically. I wasn't protecting my heart or my spirit. Instead, I allowed the temporary pleasure to dominate my thoughts and actions, making it harder to let go. When Thanksgiving came around, I wanted to focus on family and friends. I invited my friend, her boyfriend, another friend, and her children over for dinner. We shared a wonderful time playing games, laughing, and enjoying each other's company. As everyone left, he stayed behind and spent the night with me again. The cycle continued intimacy followed by deeper feelings and emotional attachment. Each encounter blurred the line between what I wanted and what I needed. That morning, we relaxed together, watching movies, eating snacks, and talking. It felt like the perfect picture of companionship, but there was an undercurrent of doubt. He often spoke about his child's mother, saying things about her that weren't kind or respectful. Though I listened, grateful that he wasn't talking about me, his words were a red flag. The Bible in (Proverbs 18:21) says, *"The tongue has the power of life and death, and those who love it will eat its fruit."* His words reflected his heart, and I began to realize that if he could speak this way about someone else, he could one day speak the same way about me. Still, I stayed, convincing myself that I could love him enough to change his ways. This season of my life was filled with confusion, longing, and the pursuit of something that couldn't truly satisfy my heart. I was chasing love and validation in the wrong places, all while ignoring the love and purpose God had for me. I was allowing my desires to cloud my judgment, but deep inside, I knew that I needed something more, something real and lasting. God's Word reminded me that my body is a temple, a sacred vessel that should be honored and cherished. I wasn't living in alignment with that truth, and I knew it was time to reflect, reset, and seek God's guidance for the next steps in my life.

## "Revealing Truths and Finding Purpose"

*"The Lord your God is in your midst, a mighty one who will*
*save; He will rejoice over you with gladness; He will quiet you by*
*His love; He will exult over you with loud singing."*
*(Zephaniah 3:17)*

A week ago, I found myself questioning everything about my connection with him. He had posted some disturbing things on Instagram, and when I confronted him about it, he denied everything. Instead of addressing my concerns, he told me that all I was good for was sex and food. His words cut deeply, stirring anger and resentment within me. I blocked him, determined to move forward. The Bible in (Zephaniah 3:17) reminded me that even in the midst of rejection and pain, God's love is steadfast. I needed that love to quiet my heart and renew my strength. At work, things took a chaotic turn. A friend of my client's mother confronted me about not wanting to engage with a man who was bisexual. The conversation made me uncomfortable, especially when he started talking about hoodoo practices from Louisiana. I tried to remain calm, but when my client asked for help, and I told him to wait, the man jumped up, called me out of my name, and got in my face. The situation escalated quickly, and I decided it was time to leave. I slammed the door behind me and walked away, knowing that this was not an environment I could thrive in. I called my boss and informed her that I wasn't coming back. The Bible in (Romans 8:28) says, *"And we know that in all things God works for the good of those who love Him, who have been called according to His purpose."* Though the situation felt overwhelming, I trusted that God was moving me toward something better. Later that week, my friend's boyfriend reached out to me on Facebook, asking if I could help make her birthday special. He wanted me to cook dinner for her, and I happily agreed. I went to T-Mobile to get her the iPhone 15, something she had been wanting, and I picked him up so we could go shopping for other surprises. We both wanted her to feel celebrated and loved. When the evening came, I decorated my house and made everything look beautiful for her. I cooked a special dinner, pouring my heart into every detail. When she arrived and saw what we had done, her smile was everything to me. Her joy reminded me of the importance of being there for others, even in the midst of my own struggles. The Bible says in (Galatians 6:9), *"Let us not become weary in doing good, for at the proper time we will reap a harvest if we do not give up."* Seeing her smile reminded me of the joy that comes from serving others with a genuine heart. Despite the challenges I faced, moments like this showed me that God was still working in my life, guiding me toward healing and purpose. This chapter of my journey wasn't just about the hardships—it was about recognizing the glimpses of God's grace and finding joy even in the small victories.

## "Strength in the Storm"

*"He gives strength to the weary and increases the power of the weak." (Isaiah 40:29)*

That night, we had such a wonderful time. I picked up my son from school, and he had a cold, but I thought it was nothing more than a common one. I gave him some cough medicine, hoping it would help. I took my daughter out to eat, and my friend joined us as we celebrated and enjoyed ourselves. Everything felt normal, like life was finally starting to look up. After we returned home, I went to bed feeling content. But the next morning was a completely different story. I woke up feeling like I was on my deathbed—weak, overwhelmed, and consumed by an illness that came out of nowhere. I couldn't figure out what was wrong. Fear set in as my body felt like it had been overtaken. I quickly gathered my strength and took me and my children to the doctor, hoping for some answers. When the doctor returned, the news hit me like a ton of bricks: we had COVID-19. It was four days before Christmas. I was devastated. How could this happen at a time when my children deserved joy and celebration? I was weak, physically and emotionally, unsure of how I was going to pull through for them. I sat there feeling helpless and defeated. But in that moment, Isaiah 40:29 resonated in my spirit. God gives strength to the weary and increases the power of the weak, and I clung to that promise with all my heart. I shared on Instagram that I was feeling too weak to even take care of my basic needs and asked if someone could bring something to my house. My friend stepped up; the only person who brought me the help I needed. She dropped off supplies at my door, and it reminded me of the beauty of having even one person who truly cares. Her kindness gave me the encouragement I needed to keep going. Every day, I forced myself to get up and move around, fighting through the pain and exhaustion. I knew my children were watching me, and I wanted them to see strength even in the midst of struggle. Christmas was just around the corner, and I was determined to make it special for them, even with the weight of illness on my shoulders. The Bible in (Philippians 4:13) reminds us, *"I can do all things through Christ who strengthens me."* That truth carried me as I prepared to give my kids the best Christmas I could manage under the circumstances. I wanted them to know that even in times of difficulty, love and joy can prevail. This moment taught me about resilience, faith, and the power of leaning on God when life feels unbearable. It reminded me that, even when we feel completely drained, God's strength is made perfect in our weakness.

## "Healing and Resilience"

*"Who his own self bore our sins in his own body on the tree,*
*that we, being dead to sins, should live unto righteousness; by*
*whose stripes ye were healed." (1 Peter 2:24)*

Even in my weakest moments, I knew I couldn't let my children feel the weight of what I was going through. I wanted them to experience joy, especially during the holidays, a time meant for love and togetherness. My body was drained, my mind overwhelmed, and my spirit weary, but I pressed on. There were times when I doubted if I could make it. The illness left me feeling powerless, but I clung to the promise of healing found in God's Word. 1 Peter 2:24 reminded me that through His stripes, I was healed—not just physically but emotionally and spiritually too. This truth was my anchor, steadying me in the storm. As the days wore on, I began to feel a glimmer of hope. God was restoring me. With every breath, I could feel His strength returning to me, and I realized that healing wasn't just about recovering from sickness. It was about finding the courage to keep going, to love despite pain, and to trust that God was working everything for my good. I reflected on the love and perseverance God instills in us. Even when I felt alone in my struggle, I wasn't truly alone. God's hand was on me, guiding me through. When my friend brought over the supplies I desperately needed, I saw it as a reminder that God sends help in unexpected ways. It was a small act of kindness, but to me, it felt monumental. I saw His grace through the people who cared enough to show up. As Christmas arrived, I made it my mission to ensure my children felt joy and love, despite the challenges we faced. I saw their smiles as gifts from God, reminders of the beauty in life even when things feel broken. This wasn't just about surviving; it was about finding purpose and joy in the midst of hardship. The Bible says in Isaiah 40:29, *"He gives strength to the weary and increases the power of the weak."* And He truly did. Every moment I got up and moved, every smile I saw on my children's faces, and every ounce of strength that returned to my body was evidence of His faithfulness. This season reminded me that trials don't define us. It's how we trust God through them that shapes our character. I learned that God's healing isn't just physical— it's transformative. It renews our faith, strengthens our hope, and fills our hearts with gratitude. Looking back, I see that this chapter wasn't just about enduring a difficult time. It was about learning to trust God in every circumstance, knowing that He would carry me through. It was about discovering that even in the darkest nights, His light shines brightly, guiding us toward a better tomorrow.

I am stronger because of what I endured, and I know that with God, I can face whatever comes next. His love heals, restores, and renews, and for that, I am forever grateful.

# CHAPTER 10

# SPIRITUAL HEALING / JESUS SAVED ME

*"God is spirit, and those who worship him must worship in spirit and truth." (John 4:24)*

December 28th marked a turning point in my life. I reached out to a lady who was known as a praise worshiper, and I told her that I wanted to give myself to God. My heart was yearning for transformation and a deeper connection with Him. She responded warmly, telling me that she offered one-on-one classes and assured me that I was making the right decision. However, when she mentioned a $150 fee, I felt conflicted. I thought to myself, *"Why should I pay to give myself to God? Isn't His love freely given?* "The Bible reminds us in (1 John 4:1), *"Do not believe every spirit but test the spirits to see whether they are from God, because many false prophets have gone out into the world."*

This verse spoke to me, urging me to seek discernment and stay rooted in God's truth. Salvation is a gift of grace, not something we can purchase or earn. On January 5th, 2024, something stirred in my spirit. I felt a divine nudge to set my alarm and prepare myself and my children for church that Sunday. I couldn't explain it fully, but it was as if God Himself was guiding me. The Bible says in (Titus 3:5), *"He saved us, not because of works done by us in righteousness, but according to His own mercy."* I knew this wasn't about me earning His love, it was about surrendering to His mercy and letting Him lead. When Sunday morning arrived, I woke up with a joy I hadn't felt in a long time. I was excited and eager to worship. A lady from my daughter's school had previously mentioned her church to me, so I decided to visit. Little did I know that decision would be the start of something life changing. Walking into the church, I felt an overwhelming sense of peace. The music, the worship, and the Word of God being preached spoke directly to my heart. I cried tears of release, surrendering all my pain, struggles, and fears to Him. It was as if God Himself wrapped me in His arms and said, *"You are mine, and I will never leave you.* "The Bible says in (Psalm 34:18), *"The Lord is close to the brokenhearted and saves those who are crushed in spirit."* And that day, I truly felt His closeness. I realized that no matter how far I had strayed, His love never wavered. He had been waiting for me with open arms, ready to restore and heal me. That Sunday marked the beginning of my journey toward spiritual healing. I made a commitment to not only attend church but to actively seek a deeper relationship with God. I began reading the Bible, praying daily, and surrounding myself with people who encouraged and uplifted me in my faith. Through this process, I learned that true healing starts with surrender—giving God all the broken pieces of your life and trusting Him to create something beautiful. My journey wasn't perfect, and I faced challenges along the way, but I held onto the promise in (Philippians 1:6): *"Being confident of this, that He who began a good work in you will carry it on to completion until the day of Christ Jesus."* Jesus saved me—not just from my sins but from myself. He showed me that my worth isn't tied to my past mistakes or the approval of others. My worth comes from being a child of God. This chapter of my life is a testimony to His faithfulness, His grace, and His power to transform even the most broken hearts. As I continue this journey, I am reminded daily of His love and mercy. I am not the same person I used to be, and for that, I give all the glory to God. Through Him, I found peace, purpose, and a new beginning. My life is a testament that no matter how far you've fallen, God is always there, ready to pick you up and lead you into His light.

## A New Beginning: Embracing Faith and Healing

*"God is spirit, and those who worship him must worship in spirit and truth." (John 4:24)*

A friend mentioned a church she had been attending for years, so I decided to visit. It had been such a long time since I'd stepped foot in a church, and I wasn't sure how I would feel, but I knew I wanted to reconnect with God. When my children and I arrived at the church, a minister greeted us warmly. He was so kind and welcoming that it eased some of my nervousness. As we sat down, I noticed the same minister came and sat behind us. At first, I didn't think much of it. When the pastor called for an offering and invited anyone who wanted to come to the altar, the minister encouraged me to go. I hesitated—I wasn't sure if I was ready to take that step. But he insisted, saying he would go with me. Reluctantly, I went, bringing my children along. When we returned to our seats, my daughter began to cry. She told me she didn't want to be there, and her tears left me confused. I couldn't understand why she felt that way, but I comforted her as best as I could. Despite this moment, I knew deep down that this was where God wanted us to be. We joined the church that day, and I made the decision to have both myself and my children baptized. I wanted a fresh start, a commitment to truly getting to know Jesus on a personal level. The Bible says in (Philippians 3:10-12), *"That I may know him and the power of his resurrection, and may share his sufferings, becoming like him in his death, that by any means possible I may attain the resurrection from the dead. Not that I have already obtained this or am already perfect, but I press on to make it my own, because Christ Jesus has made me his own.* "This scripture resonated deeply with me. I wasn't perfect, and I knew I had a long way to go, but I was determined to press forward. Jesus had claimed me as His own, and that truth gave me strength to begin this new chapter of my life. As soon as I made this commitment, I started noticing challenges and distractions trying to pull me away from my newfound faith. People from my past began reaching out, trying to re-enter my life. Old temptations resurfaced, and I felt the weight of my struggles pressing down on me. Yet, I clung to the promises of God. The Bible says in (James 4:7), *"Submit yourselves, then, to God. Resist the devil, and he will flee from you."* I realized that these challenges were tests—opportunities to grow stronger in my faith. The more I pressed into God, the more I felt His presence guiding me. Deciding to follow Jesus wasn't the end of my journey; it was the beginning of a new one. It was a journey of healing, transformation, and learning to trust God in every area of my life. I wasn't perfect, but I was willing to grow. I wanted to show my children what it meant to live a life dedicated to God, to give them a foundation of faith that would carry them through their own lives. This experience reminded me that God's love is constant and unwavering, no matter how far we may have strayed. He welcomes us back with open arms, ready to heal our wounds and guide us into His light. This was the start of my spiritual healing, and I knew that with Jesus by my side, I could face whatever came my way. Through it all, I held onto the truth in (2 Corinthians 5:17): *"Therefore, if anyone is in Christ, he is a new creation. The old has passed away; behold, the new has come."* My old life didn't define me anymore. Jesus had given me a new beginning, and I was ready to walk boldly into the future He had planned for me.

## A Divine Revelation: Trusting God's Guidance

*"Beware of the false prophets, who come to you in sheep's clothing, but inwardly are ravenous wolves." (Matthew 7:15)*

One evening, as I was sitting and reading my Bible, my son's father called me. Normally, my reaction would have been frustration, and I would have cursed him out. But something was different this time—I felt a calmness wash over me, and my voice was soft and kind. Even he was shocked by the change in my tone. I told him that I had started my journey with God, and to my surprise, he claimed that he was a prophet. I didn't think much of it at first, but then he began to say things that unsettled me. He told me about seeing devil angels and said that a bird watching over him was actually his child's spirit protecting him. He even said that the universe was trying to bring us back together. I responded calmly, saying, "If it is the Lord's will." I sent him positive messages about trusting God and drawing closer to Him, but my spirit remained uneasy. As I shared this conversation with someone on the phone, I felt a nudge in my spirit to open my Bible. When I did, my eyes landed on (Matthew 7:15): *"Beware of the false prophets, who come to you in sheep's clothing, but inwardly are ravenous wolves.* "At that exact moment, he called me again. My heart raced, and I couldn't bring myself to answer the phone. I whispered, "God, you are talking to me." The timing was too perfect to ignore, and I knew it was a divine warning. I began reflecting on the importance of discernment and trusting God's guidance. Not every voice is from God, and sometimes the enemy disguises himself to distract us from the truth. As I prepared for my son's dedication to the Lord, I felt a renewed sense of purpose. I reached out to friends and family, asking them to come and support us during this important moment. I wanted to give my son a foundation of faith, one that would guide him through life. Later that day, I dropped my daughter off at the YMCA and sat in my car scrolling through my phone. I came across a live video from a prophet on TikTok. Curious, I joined the live. What she said left me in tears: She spoke about how God had revealed to her that some ministries were engaging in witchcraft and warned us to be cautious. She asked everyone on the live to pray. As she spoke, I could feel the presence of God so strongly. I began crying and praising Him right there in my car for over an hour. The Bible says in (1 John 4:1), *"Beloved, do not believe every spirit, but test the spirits to see whether they are from God, for many false prophets have gone out into the world."* This experience reminded me of the importance of staying close to God and seeking His truth above all else. Through these moments, I felt God teaching me to trust Him more deeply. He was showing me how to listen for His voice and rely on His wisdom to navigate the uncertainties of life. I realized that no matter how confusing or overwhelming things may seem, God's Word is the ultimate guide, providing clarity and peace. This was a pivotal moment in my spiritual journey. It was a reminder that God is always speaking to us if we're willing to listen, and His guidance is a light in the darkest of situations. He was protecting me and drawing me closer to Him, and for that, I am forever grateful.

# A Divine Encounter and The Power of Prayer

*"Commit your way to the Lord; trust in him, and He will act."*

*(Psalms 37:5)*

As I sat praying in my car, pouring my heart out to God, I looked up to the sky. What I saw took my breath away—the sky opened before me, and I felt the undeniable presence of God. In that moment, I knew He was listening, reassuring me with His gentle reminder: *"I'm right here, daughter."* It felt so real, so comforting, and I was overwhelmed with peace. The Bible says in (Psalms 37:5), *"Commit your way to the Lord; trust in him, and He will act."* I left the TikTok live and continued to sit in my car, praying and seeking clarity. I asked God to reveal to me if the church I had been attending was truly where I was meant to be. I didn't want my son to be dedicated at a church that wasn't aligned with God's will. Later that evening, around 8:00 pm, one of the ladies from the church called me. Her tone was harsh, and she informed me that I would need to be a member for six months before receiving any assistance from the church. She was rude and abrupt, and when she hung up, I felt hurt and confused. But I chose to leave it in God's hands, trusting that He would guide me. The Bible reminds us in (1 Corinthians 14:33), *"For God is not the author of confusion but of peace."* Her words may have shaken me momentarily, but I knew that God's peace would always guide me to the right path.

As I continued reading my Bible later that night, my son's father called, asking to speak to his son. I told him that I would let him talk to him later. Instead of understanding, he disrespected me, called me out of my name, and hung up the phone. The old me would have reacted, ready to argue and defend myself, but I knew that wasn't the right way. Instead, I prayed and asked God to handle the situation. I recognized that this wasn't just a battle between me and him—it was a spiritual battle. The Bible states in (Ephesians 6:12), *"For we are not fighting against flesh-and-blood enemies, but against evil rulers and authorities of the unseen world, against mighty powers in this dark world, and against evil spirits in the heavenly places."* With God's strength, I chose not to fight back. I realized that the devil wanted me to react, to step out of the peace God was giving me, but I refused. I listened to my Heavenly Father, stayed calm, and focused on what mattered most. To celebrate my son's dedication, I got myself and my children ready, taking them out to eat as a way to honor this special moment. Before we left, I prayed over my son, asking God to protect him, guide him, and bless his life. And I know God heard my prayer. Moments like these reminded me that God is always near, even when life feels overwhelming. He is the One who opens the sky to show

His presence, calms our hearts in the face of disrespect, and gives us the wisdom to choose peace over conflict. *"Be still and know that I am God."* (Psalms 46:10) This journey is teaching me that no matter the challenges or confusion, God's peace will always lead me forward. Trusting God Through the Storm *"The Lord will rescue me from every evil attack and will bring me safely to his heavenly kingdom. To Him be the glory forever and ever."* (2 Timothy 4:18-20) One evening, I told my daughter to go downstairs to get me something to drink because my blood sugar was low. Moments later, she called out my name, saying the floor had flooded. I rushed downstairs to find water overflowing, flooding the entire floor. Panic rose within me as I realized I didn't know how to stop it. I immediately called my cousin for help, and she said she was on her way. While waiting, I sat on the stairs, feeling helpless yet determined to trust in God. I closed my eyes and prayed, telling Him, *"Lord, I trust you. I put this situation in Your hands."* I decided to let go of my worries and trust that He would provide a solution. When my cousin arrived, we searched everywhere to find the water shut-off valve but couldn't locate it. Desperation led us to call the police, who sent the fire department. They arrived quickly, found the valve, and turned off the water. It was a blessing to have their help in a moment of chaos. Despite the flooding, which left two inches of water covering my kitchen and garage floors, we cleaned up the mess and didn't let it ruin the day. I reminded myself that sometimes delays and disruptions are God's way of protecting us from something worse. Perhaps He was keeping me safe from harm outside the house during that time. The Bible says, *"This too shall pass."* While cleaning, I kept repeating those words in my mind. Later, when we made it to the restaurant for my son's celebration, he had an outburst. A kind lady smiled at me and softly said, *"This too shall pass."* Her words touched me deeply, reminding me that every trial, no matter how difficult, is temporary. When things are bad, remember it won't always be this way. Take one day at a time. And when things are good, cherish every moment, because those times are precious. This experience became a significant turning point in my journey with God. Through the flooding, the delays, and the challenges with my son, He was teaching me to trust Him fully. He was opening my eyes to see His guidance, even in the storms. I began to journal every day, pouring out my thoughts, prayers, and reflections on what I was learning from the Bible. I wanted to understand His Word more clearly and apply it to my life. Each page became a testimony of how God was working in my heart, healing me, and helping me grow. Life isn't perfect, but with God, I've learned that every challenge has a purpose. He's teaching me patience, resilience, and trust. And even in the floods—literal or figurative—He shows up to rescue me. *"Be still and know that I am God."* (Psalms 46:10)

## Trusting God Through the Storm

*"The Lord will rescue me from every evil attack and will bring me safely to his heavenly kingdom. To Him be the glory forever and ever." (2 Timothy 4:18-20)*

One evening, I told my daughter to go downstairs to get me something to drink because my blood sugar was low. Moments later, she called out my name, saying the floor had flooded. I rushed downstairs to find water overflowing, flooding the entire floor. Panic rose within me as I realized I didn't know how to stop it. I immediately called my cousin for help, and she said she was on her way. While waiting, I sat on the stairs, feeling helpless yet determined to trust in God. I closed my eyes and prayed, telling Him, *"Lord, I trust you. I put this situation in Your hands."* I decided to let go of my worries and trust that He would provide a solution. When my cousin arrived, we searched everywhere to find the water shut-off valve but couldn't locate it. Desperation led us to call the police, who sent the fire department. They arrived quickly, found the valve, and turned off the water. It was a blessing to have their help in a moment of chaos. Despite the flooding, which left two inches of water covering my kitchen and garage floors, we cleaned up the mess and didn't let it ruin the day. I reminded myself that sometimes delays and disruptions are

God's way of protecting us from something worse. Perhaps He was keeping me safe from harm outside the house during that time. The Bible says, *"This too shall pass."* While cleaning, I kept repeating those words in my mind. Later, when we made it to the restaurant for my son's celebration, he had an outburst. A kind lady smiled at me and softly said, *"This too shall pass."* Her words touched me deeply, reminding me that every trial, no matter how difficult, is temporary. When things are bad, remember it won't always be this way. Take one day at a time. And when things are good, cherish every moment, because those times are precious. This experience became a significant turning point in my journey with God. Through the flooding, the delays, and the challenges with my son, He was teaching me to trust Him fully. He opened my eyes to see His guidance, even in the storms. I began to journal every day, pouring out my thoughts, prayers, and reflections on what I was learning from the Bible. I wanted to understand His Word more clearly and apply it to my life. Each page became a testimony of how God was working in my heart, healing me, and helping me grow. Life isn't perfect, but with God, I've learned that every challenge has a purpose. He's teaching me patience, resilience, and trust. And even in the floods—literal or figurative—He shows up to rescue me. *"Be still and know that I am God."* (Psalms 46:10)

## Guarding My Spirit and My Temple

*"Let marriage be held in honor among all, and let the marriage bed be undefiled, for God will judge the sexually immoral and adulterous." (Hebrews 13:4)*

As I continued my spiritual journey, I noticed changes not only in myself but in my daughter. Her behavior started to improve remarkably, and she was doing better in school—even without medication. I knew it was the power of prayer and God's hand guiding us both. But just as I began to feel peace, the enemy tried to disrupt my life. Out of nowhere, people I hadn't talked to in years began to reach out, saying they missed me. Among them was a man I had known in 2023. He expressed interest in rekindling our connection, and at first, I thought maybe this could be a chance to move forward. I told him about my spiritual journey and my commitment to walking with God. I made it clear that my life had changed, and I was focused on growing in my faith. He seemed to say all the right things. He told me he wanted to marry me, attend church with me, and even start a family. At first, it was tempting to believe him, but as we spoke more, I began to see the truth. His actions didn't align with his words, and his intentions weren't genuine. He started trying to manipulate me into giving in to his desires, suggesting we could have a child to "bring us closer" and that if I aborted it, God would forgive me.His words were unsettling, and I knew deep in my spirit that this was not a man of God. I firmly told him I wouldn't compromise my values or my body for anyone. He tried to pressure me, even questioning my faith by asking if I was a Jehovah's Witness. I confidently told him, *"I'm a believer in Christ.* "When he realized I wouldn't give in, he said he'd call me back but never did. I didn't mind because I knew God was protecting me from someone who wasn't meant to be in my life. The Holy Spirit gave me discernment to see through his lies, and I realized he was only interested in satisfying his own desires. The Bible states, *"Flee from sexual immorality. Every other sin a person commits is outside the body, but the sexually immoral person sins against his own body. Or do you not know that your body is a temple of the Holy Spirit within you, whom you have from God?"* (1 Corinthians 6:18-19). For the first time in my life, I truly understood the importance of this verse. I began to see my body as sacred, a temple for God's Spirit, and I refused to let anyone disrespect it. In the past, I never fully grasped why God designed sex to be reserved for marriage. Now I understand that sex outside of marriage elevates human desire over God's wisdom. It mocks His will and diminishes the sanctity of something He created to be beautiful within the covenant of marriage. As I continued seeking God, something incredible happened I lost the desire for casual relationships and sexual encounters. I asked myself one day, *Why don't I have that feeling or urge to want to have sex anymore?* The answer was clear: God was transforming me. He was teaching me to align my desires with His will and showing me the joy of living a pure and focused life. The enemy may try to tempt us, but God's grace is greater. I am learning to guard my spirit and my heart, trusting God to lead me toward relationships that honor Him. The journey wasn't easy, but it has been worth it. I am no longer defined by past mistakes or worldly desires. Instead, I am being renewed by the Spirit, walking confidently in the knowledge that I am a daughter of the King. *"Do not conform to the pattern of this world but be transformed by the renewing of your mind. Then you will be able to test and approve what God's will is—His good, pleasing and perfect will."* (Romans 12:2)

## Trusting God Through Temptation and Fear

*"You are not your own, for you were bought at a price. So, glorify God in your body." (1 Corinthians 6:19-20)*

As I read my Bible and grew closer to God, I began to understand His commandments more clearly. I realized that sex before marriage was something He did not approve of, and it was time for me to align my life with His will. This understanding was not just a rule to follow but a call to honor the body God gave me, a temple of His Spirit. I knew now that I had given myself to the Lord, and everything I did would require me to seek Him first. God, the one who gave me life and created me, now had full access to my heart and my decisions. This realization left me feeling clean and refreshed—a deep sense of renewal I had never felt before. But as with any spiritual journey, temptation tried to creep back in. The devil wanted me to fall, to return to the behaviors and choices I had left behind. The Bible states, *"The temptation in your life is no different from what others experience. And God is faithful. He will not allow the temptation to be more than you can stand. When you are tempted, He will show you a way out so that you can endure."* (1 Corinthians 10:13). Every time temptation came, I felt God grab my hand and say, *"No, this is not for you.* "In obedience, I listened to His guidance. The more I leaned on Him, the more I realized that His plans were far better than anything I could imagine. It wasn't always easy—there were moments when I felt the pull to go back, but God's faithfulness gave me the strength to stand firm. During this time, my anxiety began to overwhelm me. My heart raced, and my mind was consumed with fear, especially when my children began exhibiting unusual behaviors. My daughter came into my room one night, claiming to see marks on her brother that weren't there. Her words sent chills down my spine. I was so scared, questioning what was happening and why these things were unfolding in my home. My children finally went to sleep, but the weight of it all remained heavy on my heart. In desperation, I called a friend and asked him to stay on the phone with me until I could fall asleep. As fear gripped me, I turned to God in tears, crying out for His help. I went to the bathroom and poured my heart out to Him like a child seeking comfort from a parent. *"God,"* I prayed, *"help me with my anxiety. I don't want to feel this way.* "The Bible reassures us in *2 Timothy 1:7, "For God has not given us a spirit of fear but of power, love, and self-control."* I clung to this promise, knowing that fear was not from Him. In that moment of prayer, I felt His presence surround me, reminding me that He was in control. He whispered to my heart that I didn't have to carry these burdens alone, that He was with me every step of the way. This was a pivotal moment for me. God was teaching me that no matter how overwhelming life may seem, He is always nearby. He reminded me that when I surrender my fears and anxieties to Him, He replaces them with peace, strength, and clarity. My journey is still unfolding, but I know that God is walking with me, guiding me through every challenge. And as I continue to trust Him, He is transforming my heart and mind, leading me into the fullness of His love and purpose.

*"Cast all your anxiety on Him because He cares for you."*

*(1 Peter 5:7)*

## God's Presence and Protection

*"For God speaks again and again, though people do not recognize it. He speaks in dreams, in visions of the night, when deep sleep falls on people as they lie in their beds…He makes them turn from doing wrong; He keeps them from pride."*

*(Job 33:14-17)*

That night, I was consumed with fear. I lay down with the cover over my head, trembling in my own home. I was too scared to close my eyes and sleep, the weight of anxiety still pressing heavily on me. But then, something extraordinary, happened God gave me a vision. In my hallway, I saw an angel. At first, I was confused and unsure. I screamed out, "Is that God?" Then, I doubted myself and said, "No, that's the devil." But as I calmed myself and reflected, I realized that it was, in fact, God. He was showing me that I was safe, that His angel was there to protect me. This was a new and unfamiliar experience for me. I didn't understand it fully, so I had questions. But God, in His loving patience, gave me answers. He wanted me to know that I didn't have to live in fear, that He was always with me, surrounding me with His protection. *"Blessed are your eyes because they see, and your ears because they hear."* (Matthew 13:16) As I continued to read my Bible and seek God, I felt the burden of anxiety lifting from me. Within a few days, my anxiety was completely gone. It was a miracle—a tangible sign that God had His hands on me every step of the way. I couldn't contain my excitement. I wanted to tell everyone about God and the vision He gave me. I felt like a new person, filled with peace, joy, and an unshakable faith. I began writing down my prayers and favorite Bible scriptures in a journal, pouring my heart out to God and documenting my spiritual journey. *"Cast all your anxiety on Him because He cares for you."* (1 Peter 5:7) Every time I said the name of Jesus, I felt stronger, more alive, and more connected to Him. My fear had been replaced with confidence, and my doubt had been replaced with unwavering belief. God had shown me that He was with me, guiding me, protecting me, and filling me with His love. This experience deepened my faith and ignited a passion within me to keep seeking Him, no matter what challenges I faced. I learned that when you call on Jesus, He answers. And when you place your trust in Him, He works everything out for your good.

*"The Lord is my light and my salvation—whom shall I fear?*
*The Lord is the stronghold of my life—of whom shall I be*
*afraid?"* (Psalm 27:1)

## Embracing Spiritual Growth and Trusting God's Plan

*"You prepare a table before me in the presence of my enemies. You anoint my head with oil; my cup overflows." (Psalms 23:5)*

Every day, it became a routine for me to walk with Jesus, and I cherished every moment of it. My spirit was genuinely seeking to forgive those who had wronged me, letting go of bitterness and embracing God's grace. As I continued this journey, God began removing people from my life—those who didn't see my worth or who didn't align with His purpose for me. At first, it was challenging, but I trusted His process. I knew that picking up my cross daily meant surrendering all to Him, regardless of the cost. *"Therefore, if anyone is in Christ, the new creation has come: The old has gone, the new is here!"* (2 Corinthians 5:17) I began to see myself as God saw me: redeemed, loved, and with a purpose. I was becoming the new Destiny—a better version of myself. With every prayer and every step of faith, I felt God shaping me into the woman He created me to be. The Bible says, *"You must believe God destined you for dominion (victory) and greatness."* Understanding that my destiny is tied to glorifying God gave me strength and confidence to move forward, even when the road seemed uncertain. I prayed for God to remove anyone who didn't mean me well, and He did just that. Though it wasn't easy, I didn't question His decisions. Instead, I trusted that He was aligning my life with His will. He showed me that He was the only one I truly needed—my provider, my guide, my best friend. *"And my God will meet all your needs according to the riches of his glory in Christ Jesus."* (Philippians 4:19) Despite submitting countless job applications and facing rejection after rejection, I held onto God's promises. I realized He was calling me to be still and trust in His timing. He wanted me to grow closer to Him, to know myself better, and to build unshakable faith. Life's challenges intensified, but I understood that God was testing me, refining me like gold in the fire. He tested my patience with my children, with others, and even with myself. When I prayed for patience, He provided opportunities for me to practice it. When I prayed for wisdom, He placed me in situations that required discernment and trust. *"Be still and know that I am God."* (Psalms 46:10) Through it all, I discovered that I had truly changed. The old me would have been overwhelmed by anger, frustration, and doubt, but the new me was anchored in God's love and promises. Nothing could separate me from the peace and purpose I found in Him. This journey wasn't just about survival, it was about transformation. It was about learning to walk in God's light, trusting Him completely, and embracing the person He created me to be. With each passing day, I found joy in the small victories and hope in the challenges. God was and always will be my strength and my salvation. *"I can do all things through Christ who strengthens me."* (Philippians 4:13)

## A Divine Encounter and a New Beginning

*"For you shall worship no other god, for the Lord whose name is Jealous, is a jealous God." (Exodus 34:14)*

That morning, I woke up, got my children ready for school, and dropped them off. As I returned home, an overwhelming wave of emotion overtook me, and I began to cry out to God, asking Him to lead me to a God-fearing church. After pouring out my heart, I went upstairs, opened my Bible, and began reading. Suddenly, I heard my doorbell ring. Looking at my camera, I saw two people standing at my door. I opened it, and without hesitation, I said, "God answered my prayers." They introduced themselves as Jehovah's Witnesses, and though I had heard warnings in the past not to engage, I felt compelled to invite them in. We sat down, and as they began sharing their message, something didn't sit right with me. While I appreciated their passion, God had already revealed to me that we are to worship no other God but Him. This moment tested my spiritual discernment and reminded me of His word:*" Give your servant therefore an understanding mind to govern your people, that I may discern between good and evil."* (1 Kings

3:9) The conversation made me realize that I was in the middle of spiritual warfare. But I stood firm, knowing God was with me, guiding me through every trial. I had faced battles since childhood, yet God had never abandoned me. Each struggle was a steppingstone for growth and a lesson in faith. Despite having no money, job, or close relationships, I felt an incredible sense of freedom. My joy was no longer tied to material things or the approval of others—it came from God. I could truly say, *"I'm free indeed." Without faith, it is impossible to please God, because anyone who comes to him must believe that he exists and that he rewards those who earnestly seek him."* (Hebrews 11:6) In a quiet moment, I reflected on my journey and the pain I had unintentionally caused my children. Tears welled up in my eyes as I called my daughter to my side. I apologized for the times I had failed her, for the hurt I had caused, and for not always being the mother she deserved. Her response was immediate—she hugged me tightly, and we both cried. It was a moment of healing and redemption, a tangible reminder of God's grace and the power of love. I knew then that I was on the right path, picking up my cross daily and walking with Jesus." *And now these three remain: faith, hope, and love. But the greatest of these is love."* (1 Corinthians 13:13) This journey isn't perfect, but it's filled with hope, restoration, and unwavering faith in the God who never leaves us. My story is still being written, but one thing is certain: I am free, forgiven, and held in His hands.

## A Divine Encounter: Trusting God's Greater Plan

*"Be kind to one another, tenderhearted, forgiving one another,*
*as God in Christ forgave you." (Ephesians 4:32)*

Sitting with my daughter, I explained to her, "Mommy was going through some things, and I had to truly find who I was." Apologizing to her was one of the hardest things I've done, but it was also one of the most necessary. It taught me humility and allowed me to experience grace in a new way. As I committed to being a better mother, I made significant changes in my life. I stopped cursing and started teaching my children about the importance of walking with Jesus, reading the Bible, and trusting Him as our Father. Yet, as I grew closer to God, challenges seemed to increase. My daughter's behavior became more erratic, and she began experiencing nightmares. Each night, I prayed over her with tears streaming down my face. I prayed over her room, over her heart, and over her spirit. Still, the nightmares persisted. I realized that when the enemy cannot reach you, he will attempt to attack those you love. I clung to God's promise in *James 4:7*, "Submit yourselves, then, to God. Resist the devil, and he will flee from you." I kept praying, refusing to let the enemy have power in our lives. One night, as I finally fell asleep after hours of prayer, I experienced the most profound moment of my life. I had an out-of-body experience. My soul floated above my physical body, and I felt a peace I had never known. In my right ear, I heard the softest, sweetest voice say, "I am the Son of God. Are you okay?" I replied, "I am blessed," and then I felt my soul gently return to my body. That experience changed me. I cried out to Jesus, overwhelmed with gratitude. I didn't want to come back down—it felt so real, so pure, and so filled with His presence. I knew that God was showing me a glimpse of the eternal joy that awaits those who trust in Him. *"Call to me, and I will answer and show you great and unsearchable things you don't know."* (Jeremiah 33:3) This experience was a confirmation of God's promises. I no longer doubted that everything in the Bible is true. I realized that God is greater than anything I could ever face, and I trust Him to fulfill every promise He has made. Through this journey, I've learned to glorify God in everything I do. Each prayer, each act of faith, and each surrender to His will brings me closer to Him. My life is no longer my own—it belongs to God, and I am honored to walk in His light.

## Experiencing God's Provision and Protection

*Ask, and it will be given to you; seek, and you will find; knock, and it will be opened to you." (Matthew 7:7)*

Embracing my journey with Jesus has transformed my life in profound ways. One day, with only $7 in my pocket, I felt a desire to visit Popeyes, trusting that God would provide. Knowing that meals typically cost more than what I had, I prayed and proceeded in faith. At the drive-thru, I inquired about any specials, and to my amazement, the attendant mentioned a $5 five-piece breast special. I asked again to confirm, and he affirmed the offer. In that moment, I knew God had heard my prayer. He provided exactly what I needed, reinforcing that faith, even in small matters, opens doors. Later, during an eye doctor's appointment, I was informed that I was a suspect for glaucoma, a condition that can lead to vision loss. Instead of succumbing to fear, I turned to prayer, telling God, "I have faith that I don't have this, and I trust You will heal my eyes." This reaffirmed my belief that God is the ultimate healer, capable of miracles beyond our understanding. That same day, I received a call from my daughter's school regarding an inappropriate comment she had made. Recognizing this as a test of my patience and growth, I chose to respond differently than I might have in the past. I prayed for guidance, refusing to let the enemy pull me back into old habits. At home, I invited my daughter to pray with me. When she hesitated, I anointed her with oil and played William McDowell's *"I Give Myself Away"*, creating an atmosphere of worship and surrender. This song, written and performed by William McDowell, emphasizes the act of surrendering oneself entirely to God's will and purpose. Its lyrics reflect a deep desire to live a life fully devoted to God, allowing Him to use us for His greater purpose. By incorporating this song into our prayer time, I aimed to teach my daughter the importance of yielding to God's will and experiencing His transformative power. Through these experiences, I've learned that faith isn't just about belief; it's about trusting God in every aspect of life. Whether it's providing a meal, healing ailments, or guiding our responses to challenges, God is ever-present, ready to support and lead us. By surrendering to Him and allowing His will to work through us, we can navigate life's trials with grace and confidence.

## Guiding My Daughter Through Spiritual Challenges

Recognizing the spiritual challenges my daughter faced, I encouraged her to cry out to Jesus, emphasizing the importance of seeking His presence and strength. Observing behaviors that seemed unlike her true self, I discerned the influence of negative forces attempting to disrupt her peace. Understanding that the enemy often targets our loved ones when he cannot reach us directly, I turned to prayer, entrusting the situation to God's capable hands.I explained to my daughter the significance of prayer and aligning her actions with God's will. We revisited the Ten Commandments together, highlighting the path God desires for us. I reassured her of God's unwavering love and protection, reminding her that while the devil may attempt to interfere, steadfast prayer and resistance would make him flee. As James 4:7 advises, "Submit yourselves therefore to God. Resist the devil, and he will flee from you." Despite these efforts, my daughter continued to face challenges, sometimes making choices she knew were not right. I reminded her that allowing negative influences could invite the enemy back into her life, and the importance of resisting such temptations. I committed to praying over my children, trusting that God understands the struggles they face and is the ultimate solution. When her teacher suggested reinstating medication due to behavioral concerns, I respectfully declined. God had revealed to me that my daughter didn't need medication but rather prayer and healing. While her teacher may not have understood my perspective, I stood firm in my faith, believing in God's power to transform without medical intervention. Over time, my daughter's behavior improved, a testament to the effectiveness of obedience to God and the power of prayer. As Psalm 103:2-3 reminds us, "Bless the Lord, O my soul, and forget not all his benefits, who forgives all your iniquity, who heals all your diseases. "Through these experiences, I learned that unwavering faith and persistent prayer can overcome spiritual challenges. By entrusting my children's well-being to God and adhering to His guidance, we navigated difficult times and emerged stronger in our faith.

## Recognizing and Removing Ungodly Influences in the Home

Embarking on a spiritual journey often brings to light influences that may have previously gone unnoticed. As I deepened my relationship with God, He began revealing items in our home that didn't align with His teachings. One such instance involved my daughter's comforter, which featured carnival imagery and unsettling phrases like "you lost." After she experienced a disturbing dream involving a carnival ride and a menacing clown, I felt compelled to remove the comforter, recognizing it as a potential source of negative influence. The Bible cautions against bringing detestable objects into our homes, as stated in Deuteronomy 7:26: "Do not bring a detestable thing into your house or you, like it, will be set apart for destruction. Regard it as vile and utterly detest it, for it is set apart for destruction." This verse underscores the importance of being vigilant about the items we allow into our living spaces. To ensure our homes remain sanctuaries of peace and godliness, it's beneficial to conduct a spiritual cleansing by: Identifying and Removing Unholy Items: Evaluate possessions for symbols or objects associated with the occult, witchcraft, or other practices contrary to Christian beliefs. This includes certain books, movies, jewelry, or decorations that may carry ungodly connotations.

1.  Praying Over Your Home: Dedicate each room to the Lord, inviting His presence to fill every corner. Anointing doorways and windows with oil while praying for protection can help create a spiritually clean environment.

2.  Staying Discerning: Regularly seek God's guidance in discerning any items or influences that may disrupt the spiritual harmony of your home.By taking these steps, we can foster an environment that honors God and provides a safe haven for our families. Trusting in His guidance ensures that our homes remain aligned with His will, free from influences that may lead us astray

## Choosing to Serve the Lord and Protecting Our Household

In our spiritual journey, it's crucial to make a conscious decision about whom we serve. Joshua's declaration, "But as for me and my house, we will serve the Lord," (Joshua 24:15) emphasizes the importance of dedicating our households to God. This commitment involves actively removing influences that do not align with His teachings. Recognizing that negative forces can infiltrate our homes through various means, it's essential to be vigilant. Engaging in regular spiritual cleansing helps maintain a peaceful and godly environment. This can include practices such as anointing doorways with oil, praying over each room, and removing items that may carry ungodly connotations. By committing ourselves and our households to serve the Lord, we create a sanctuary that honors God and protects our loved ones from spiritual harm. Regular prayer and discernment are key in maintaining this sacred space.

## Guiding Others Toward Faith

The Bible reminds us that no one knows the day or hour of Christ's return, as stated in Matthew 24:36: *"But about that day or hour no one knows, not even the angels in heaven, nor the Son, but only the Father."* This truth anchors our understanding that our journey with God is not about predicting His timing but about living in obedience, faith, and readiness for His return. I found myself in a disagreement with someone about this topic, but I stood firm in my understanding of God's word. It became clear that not everyone is willing to accept certain biblical truths, and that's okay. Even when he later messaged me, claiming God was about to return him to heaven, I realized the importance of guarding our speech. As Proverbs 18:21 says: *"What you say can mean life or death. Those who speak with care will be rewarded.* "I continued to pray for him despite our differences, showing love and compassion. His struggles were apparent, especially when he shared his concerns about his mother. He felt overwhelmed, but I immediately prayed for her well-being and asked God to intervene in her situation. When I spoke to her, I realized how deeply she desired to get closer to Jesus. Hearing her testimony and sharing mine built a connection that I knew God intended. She began calling me daily for advice and encouragement, and I answered every time. I wanted to help her see the strength and peace that come from walking with Christ. When she was upset about her roommate treating her poorly, I encouraged her to pray and trust God. I reminded her not to let negativity consume her, as trials often come to test our faith and resilience. James 1:2-4 reassures us: *"Consider pure joy, my brothers and sisters, whenever you face trials of many kinds, because you know that the testing of your faith produces perseverance. Let perseverance finish its work so that you may be mature and complete, not lacking anything.* " I reminded her that through these challenges, God was refining her, helping her grow stronger in her faith. Although her son distanced himself from me, I continued to pray for him. I knew that even when others turn away, God calls us to respond with love, understanding, and forgiveness. I didn't take his actions personally but saw them as an opportunity to extend grace, just as God has done for me. God's work in our lives often positions us to guide others toward Him. I realized that the seeds of faith I planted in his mother's life were part of His divine plan. Galatians 6:9 encourages us: *"Let us not become weary in doing good, for at the proper time we will reap a harvest if we do not give up."* Through patience and prayer, I trusted that God would continue to work in both of their lives. This journey taught me the importance of staying grounded in God's truth, remaining patient with others, and trusting His timing. Every act of obedience and kindness brings us closer to fulfilling His purpose for our lives.

## Encouraging Others to Seek God First

I reminded her that everything we go through in life is a test and that protecting her peace and energy is vital. She agreed, and after that conversation, she seemed more at ease. She called me daily to talk and seek guidance, and while I appreciated her trust, I told her that the real answer to her struggles would come from building her relationship with Jesus. I encouraged her to read her Bible, fast, and pray. The Bible assures us in Ezra 8:23: *"So we fasted and petitioned our God about this, and he answered our prayer."* I explained that having a direct relationship with God is the most powerful source of strength and peace. Jesus is the one who will carry us through life's burdens. Once we surrender everything to Him, life becomes more manageable. I shared with her the importance of prayer and trusting God to take care of her concerns. I told her, *"Make yourself a prayer closet—your sacred space—and just pour out your heart to God. Believe that He hears you and will guide you."* She took my advice, and later she called to tell me how much it helped. She said she was thankful that God had brought me into her life to steer her back onto the right path. Hearing that filled my heart with joy because it showed that God was using me as an instrument of His love and wisdom. The Bible says in Matthew 6:33: *"But seek first the kingdom of God and his righteousness, and all these things shall be added to you."* I emphasized to her that when we seek God first, He provides for all our needs in ways we couldn't imagine. One day, she called upset about her son. She was angry with how he was treating me and mentioned something he said about me that wasn't true.

I assured her that it was okay, and that God would handle the situation. I reminded her that I hadn't done anything wrong and didn't want to dwell on negativity. I told her that moving forward, our conversations should focus on her growth and not on her son or past situations that could bring negativity. She agreed, understanding my perspective, and respected my boundaries. This experience reminded me that helping others is not about solving their problems for them but about pointing them to the One who can. God is always ready to lead us through trials if we seek Him with a sincere heart. By encouraging her to build her relationship with Jesus, I was showing her how to rely on the eternal, unshakable foundation of faith. Philippians 4:6-7 says: *"Do not be anxious about anything, but in every situation, by prayer and petition, with thanksgiving, present your requests to God. And the peace of God, which transcends all understanding, will guard your hearts and your minds in Christ Jesus."* This peace is what I hoped she would continue to discover as she grew in her walk with the Lord.

## Seeking Clarity and Trusting God

I felt like her son's jealousy was misplaced because our walks with God should never be a competition. Everyone grows in their relationship with God at their own pace. It's not about who knows more or who has walked longer—it's about genuinely seeking Him and allowing His love to transform us. When she called me to tell me her son wanted to talk about Jesus, I was happy to share my testimony and offer advice. I encouraged him to build his own relationship with Jesus through prayer and faith. The next day, she called me again, explaining that her sons were now talking about me, and one of them had even shown the other a picture of me. I was confused about how something pure and faith-driven turned into confusion and jealousy. The Bible reminds us in 1 Corinthians 14:33, *"For God is not the author of confusion, but of peace."* I decided then that I wasn't going to let myself be part of this confusion. God's work is meant to bring clarity, healing, and unity—not strife. Later, I spent time with a church member friend and her kids. We went to the fair, shared a meal, and had meaningful conversations about our faith and life. It was refreshing to be around someone who shared my passion for God and could uplift me during this time. Our kids connected and wanted to be friends, which felt like another blessing. After I dropped her off, I texted her to express my gratitude for the day, and she responded with the same warmth. I thanked God for sending someone like her into my life because I had prayed for God-fearing friends who could walk with me on this journey. When I called the lady back later, she said something that left me questioning her intentions. She mentioned hearing a voice from the devil telling her I wasn't a good friend but then claimed that God told her to stay connected to me because He put us together. Her words left me feeling confused and uneasy. I didn't know whether her claims were true or if she was telling them to manipulate the situation. I turned to prayer for clarity, asking God to reveal the truth. The Bible says in James 1:5, *"If any of you lacks wisdom, you should ask God, who gives generously to all without finding fault, and it will be given to you."* I knew that God would provide the discernment I needed to determine whether this was truly from Him or just a distraction.

## Trusting God's Guidance

When faced with confusion or uncertainty, it's important to remember that God doesn't lead us astray. His guidance brings peace, not chaos. Through prayer, I asked God to direct my steps and protect me from anything that wasn't from Him. I trusted that He would continue to remove any distractions or confusion from my life and surround me with people who genuinely sought to honor Him. This experience reminded me to lean on God in every situation and to trust His timing and wisdom. While I didn't have all the answers immediately, I knew that by staying faithful, God would continue to guide me in the right direction. Proverbs 3:5-6 says, *"Trust in the Lord with all your heart and lean not on your own understanding; in all your ways submit to him, and he will make your paths straight."* I held onto that promise as I navigated these moments of uncertainty.

## Discerning God's Voice Through Faith and Trust

I began questioning the situation even further, reaching out to others for advice. Many reminded me of the biblical truth in 1 Corinthians 14:33, *"God is not the author of confusion, but of peace."* They said if I had to second-guess the situation, then it likely wasn't from God, but a distraction from the enemy. That resonated with me deeply, so I decided to leave it alone and trust God to guide me. On Sunday, I went to church, and my pastor prophesied over me, saying that God was going to use me in a mighty way. I cried like a baby because I knew it was confirmation of what I had been feeling in my spirit. God had been using me to share my testimony with others, and now it was clear that He had a purpose for my life. After service, one of the church leaders invited me to a Thursday prayer meeting. I told her I would come, and I left feeling uplifted and ready to walk further in my purpose. I prayed to God for protection as I didn't have insurance on my car, but I trusted that He would cover me. The Bible reassures us in Matthew 17:20, *"If you have faith as small as a mustard seed, you can say to this mountain, 'Move from here to there,' and it will move. Nothing will be impossible for you."* With faith as my foundation, I knew I could trust God to keep me safe. That Thursday, I went to Stone Mountain Park and decided to walk to the top of the mountain. The climb was challenging, and when my water bottle dropped, I didn't have the strength to pick it up. As I considered turning back, a man walking up the mountain encouraged me to keep going, saying it would only take five more minutes. I pushed forward but eventually decided I was too tired and started making my way back down. Strangely, the same man appeared beside me not even three minutes later. It felt odd, but I remained polite and engaged in conversation with him. As we walked down, I shared my testimony with him, telling him how God had transformed my life and how my pastor had recently prophesied over me. I even showed him a video of the prophecy, expecting him to share my excitement. Instead, his demeanor changed, and he seemed skeptical. He commented that my pastor appeared to be throwing shade, which didn't sit right with me. His words suggested doubt about God's ability to fulfill His promises in my life, and it made me uneasy. Then, he pulled out a picture and asked me who I thought it looked like. I couldn't really tell who it was, and the situation started to feel even stranger. At that moment, I knew I needed to distance myself from this conversation and focus on what God had already confirmed to me.

## Trusting God's Plan Despite Distractions

This experience taught me that not everyone will understand or support the work God is doing in your life. When people sow seeds of doubt, we must remember to lean on God's truth and the promises He has already spoken over us. The Bible says in Proverbs 3:5-6, "Trust in the Lord with all your heart and lean not on your own understanding; in all your ways submit to him, and he will make your paths straight. "Not everyone who appears on our path is sent by God, but through prayer and discernment, He will reveal their intentions. This situation reminded me to guard my heart and stay focused on God's plan for me, no matter who tries to discourage me. God's promises are true, and His word will never return void. Isaiah 55:11 says, "So is my word that goes out from my mouth: It will not return to me empty but will accomplish what I desire and achieve the purpose for which I sent it."I prayed for clarity and thanked God for continually guiding me. Even when the enemy tries to bring confusion, God's peace will always prevail. Through faith and obedience, I trust that God will continue to lead me on this journey, shaping me into the person He created me to be.

## God's Provision Through Trials

So, I thanked God for the blessing He had provided. **The Bible states in Matthew 6:8**, *"Do not be like them, for your father knows exactly what you need even before you ask him."* This verse reminded me that even when others fall short in understanding, God never does. He knows our needs before we even voice them, and He is faithful to provide. Two weeks later, I went back to Thursday prayer and approached the same lady who had helped me with my car insurance. I asked if she could help me again since I was still without a job. She looked at me and said, "I don't know; I just paid my bills." Her response felt dismissive, but I said "OK" and left without any ill feelings. I went home, got my kids ready for bed, and prayed to God for strength and guidance. Later that evening, I received a phone call from the church leader and the lady I had asked for help. They told me that I needed to find a job and suggested a few options. While I appreciated their intention, the way they communicated felt disrespectful and unruly, leaving me hurt and upset. To avoid reacting in a way I would regret, I hung up the phone and took my frustrations to God in prayer. One of the leaders called me back, attempting to explain what they were trying to say, but I wasn't ready to hear it. I felt confused and dismissed, and it only deepened my frustration. After going back and forth for a moment, she eventually she told me that she would send me the money for my insurance and wished me a good night. I was grateful for her help because I knew this was God stepping in, even though the tension and misunderstanding. **The Bible says in Luke 1:37**, *"For nothing will be impossible with God."* That night, I cried out to God, asking Him why I was being treated this way and seeking His peace to calm my restless heart.

## Encouragement Through Patience and Faith

This experience taught me that God works even in difficult situations. While the words and actions of others may hurt, God uses everything for His purpose. **Romans 8:28** reminds us, *"And we know that in all things God works for the good of those who love him, who have been called according to his purpose."* Sometimes, the people we rely on for support may not meet our expectations, but God's provision is never late. His blessings often come through unexpected channels, reminding us to keep our faith and trust in Him alone. That night, as I wrestled with my emotions, I realized that these challenges were refining me. They were teaching me patience, humility, and a deeper dependence on God. **The Bible states in James 1:2-4**, *"Consider it pure joy, my brothers and sisters, whenever you face trials of many kinds, because you know that the testing of your faith produces perseverance. Let perseverance finish its work so that you may be mature and complete, not lacking anything."*

I thanked God for His provision, even though the struggle, and resolved to keep walking in faith, trusting that His plans for me were greater than anything I could imagine.

## Faith in the Midst of Betrayal

I poured my heart out to my pastor, explaining how the actions and words of the church leaders had hurt me deeply. I needed her to know how I felt, and thankfully, she addressed the situation. At that moment, I chose to leave the matter in God's hands. **The Bible says in Exodus 14:14,** *"The Lord shall fight for you, and ye shall hold your peace."* This verse reminded me to release my burdens and let God take control of the battles I couldn't fight on my own.It felt as though betrayal was coming from every direction. People I thought would support me had turned away or let me down. Yet, through it all, I clung to the promise that God would never leave or forsake me. His love was constant, even when the people around me failed. **The Bible says in Hebrews 13:5,** *"Never will I leave you; never will I forsake you."* These words became my refuge during those difficult moments, reassuring me that I was never alone.

## Finding Joy in His Presence

Instead of focusing on the pain, I began to pour my heart into prayer. Not because I wanted something from God, but because I simply loved Him. I wanted to spend time in His presence. The more I prayed, the more peace I felt. My relationship with Jesus became my anchor, and His love became my comfort. **The Bible says in 1 Thessalonians 5:16-18,** *"Rejoice always, pray continually, give thanks in all circumstances; for this is God's will for you in Christ Jesus."* I found joy not in what I received, but in the fact that God was with me every step of the way. He was my protector, my provider, and my friend. Even when people left, I found solace in knowing that Jesus never would.

## A Heart Transformed by Love

I prayed not only for myself but for the people who had wronged me. I prayed for God to bless them and heal their hearts. **The Bible says in Matthew 5:44,** *"But I tell you, love your enemies and pray for those who persecute you."* As I prayed, I felt my heart softening. I began to see people not through the lens of their mistakes, but through the eyes of grace and compassion. Every prayer brought me closer to understanding what it truly means to walk in forgiveness and faith. I asked God to help me see the best in people, to forgive without hesitation, and to trust Him completely with the future.

**The Bible says in Proverbs 3:5-6,** "Trust in the Lord with all your heart and lean not on your own understanding; in all your ways submit to Him, and He will make your paths straight." This became my daily mantra, guiding me to put God at the center of my thoughts and actions.

## Unwavering Devotion

I thanked God every day for His unwavering love. Even when life felt heavy, His presence brought me peace. I didn't care who left my life as long as Jesus stayed by my side. **The Bible says in Psalm 16:11,** *"You make known to me the path of life; you will fill me with joy in your presence, with eternal pleasures at your right hand."* This truth kept me going, reminding me that in Him, I had everything I needed. Through it all, I learned that Jesus was my rock and my refuge. No matter what challenges came my way, I would continue to love and trust Him with all my heart. He was the one who never failed me, and His love was more than enough. I held onto this thought: *Always pray to have the eyes that see the best in people. A heart that forgives the worst. A mind that forgets the bad. And a soul that never loses faith in God.*

# 11

# DON'T GIVE UP!

*"No weapon that is formed against me shall prosper; and every tongue that shall rise against thee in judgment thou shalt condemn." (Isaiah 54:17*

## Faith Amidst Adversity

I kept trusting and believing in Jesus, even when life seemed unbearable. Every morning, day, and night, I prayed with tears streaming down my face, laying my burdens at the feet of my Father. It felt like the weight of the world was pressing down on me, but prayer was my refuge and my strength. I spoke to God about everything that troubled me, and in those moments, I felt His peace washing over me. **The Bible says in Revelation 22:21,** *"The grace of the Lord Jesus be with God's people."* I clung to this truth and reminded myself that each day was a gift from the

Lord—a day to rejoice and be glad in. Even as the challenges mounted, I chose to rejoice in His grace and faithfulness.

## Staying the Course in Church

Though I faithfully attended church, serving and participating in every way I could, I faced mistreatment from some of the people there. It hurt deeply, but I didn't allow their actions to deter me. I kept showing up to prayer on Thursdays and church every Sunday because I knew I wasn't doing it for them—I was doing it for God. **The Bible says in Galatians 6:9,** *"Let us not grow weary of doing good, for in due season we will reap, if we do not give up."* This verse became my anthem as I pushed through the hurt, trusting that God would reward my faithfulness in His perfect timing

## Finding Strength Through Prayer

In those moments of discouragement, I turned to prayer like never before. I cried out to God to help me remain steadfast and to soften my heart so I wouldn't let bitterness take root. I knew that no weapon formed against me would prosper, and I trusted that God was working everything out for my good. **The Bible says in Romans 8:28,** *"And we know that in all things God works for the good of those who love Him, who have been called according to*

*His purpose.*" I reminded myself of this promise every time I felt overwhelmed, knowing that God's plan for my life was greater than any trial I faced.

## Encouragement to Persevere

Even when life feels heavy, don't give up. Remember that God's grace is sufficient for every trial, and His strength is made perfect in your weakness. When people mistreat you or life feels unfair, keep your eyes fixed on Jesus. He sees your heart, your struggles, and your faithfulness. **The Bible says in 2 Chronicles 15:7,** *"But as for you, be strong and do not give up, for your work will be rewarded."* Hold on to this truth and trust that God will honor your perseverance.

## A New Perspective

Through every challenge, I learned that adversity is an opportunity to grow closer to God. It's a chance to lean on His strength, to trust His plan, and to see His faithfulness in action. My journey wasn't easy, but it was worth it because it drew me closer to the heart of Jesus. **The Bible says in James 1:2-3,** *"Consider it pure joy, my brothers and sisters, whenever you face trials of many kinds, because you know that the testing of your faith produces perseverance."* These words remind us that every trial has a purpose, and every struggle is shaping us into the people God has called us to be.

## Never Give Up on God

No matter how hard life gets, never give up on God. He is with you in every moment, fighting for you and loving you through it all. When you feel like you can't take another step, lean on Him. Pray, trust, and believe that He will carry you through. **The Bible says in Matthew 11:28-30,** *"Come to me, all you who are weary and burdened, and I will give you rest. Take my yoke upon you and learn from me, for I am gentle and humble in heart, and you will find rest for your souls. For my yoke is easy and my burden is light."* Let these words be your comfort and your strength as you continue to walk in faith. Keep pressing forward, trusting that God's plan for your life is greater than anything you can imagine. With Him, all things are possible, and no weapon formed against you will ever prosper.

## Obedience Over Distraction

"I also asked if I could help in the kid's ministry because I love children and wanted to help them know Jesus more and more. The Bible states in (Matthew 19:14): *Jesus said, 'Let the little children come to me, and do not hinder them, for the kingdom of heaven belongs to such as these.'* I found myself asking God over and over if I was supposed to be at this church, especially after everything I had encountered there. Even though I faced challenges, I still went to church with a smile on my face and continued to do what God told me to do. I began to feel more connected with one of the leaders at the church who helped me as a friend. I appreciated her for the words she spoke over my life while I was there. God constantly reminded me to never give up and to keep pushing forward. I obeyed Him, even when it was difficult, and continued this walk with Him with tears in my eyes. One day, I met a man on TikTok who started a conversation with me. Before responding to him, I prayed and asked Jesus, *"Who is this person? Reveal his intentions for me."* After praying, I felt peace and wrote back to him. We started talking, and I asked him if he believed in Jesus and if he had a relationship with Him. He said yes, so I continued the conversation. However, as we talked, he began to ask me questions that made me uncomfortable. His responses didn't sit well with me, and I started to feel annoyed by his intentions. I decided to pause our communication, telling him I was going on a fast and would get back to him afterward. He agreed, but something still didn't feel right. Three weeks later, I received a text message from an old friend. She told me she had a dream about me and that God instructed her to warn me about a man sent to distract me from Him. She told me this man only wanted one thing and was not sent by God. She said she wanted to be obedient to God by sharing this message with me. I thanked her, and in obedience to God, I immediately stopped communicating with him.

## A Good Woman Stands Strong in the Lord

I am reminded of the value and strength of a woman walking in faith. A good woman is a blessing and a gift. She may be single now, but she will eventually find her person. A good woman is *protected by God*. She cannot be denied or destroyed. She will manifest her biggest dreams, reclaim everything that was taken from her, and achieve even greater blessings.

For every door that closes, God opens another with better opportunities. For every person who walks out, someone better walks in. A good woman walks by faith, knowing God's plans are greater than her own. She doesn't lose; she gains. In the end, a good woman always wins. I am determined to serve the Lord with all my heart. As the Bible states in (1 Samuel 15:22): *And Samuel said, "Has the Lord as great delight in burnt offerings and sacrifices, as in obeying the voice of the Lord? Behold, to obey is better than sacrifice, and to listen than the fat of rams."* Obedience is key. This experience taught me that not every person or situation is sent by God, but through prayer and discernment, He always reveals the truth. I will continue to walk by faith and trust His guidance, knowing He has a greater purpose for my life.

## Faith Through Every Season

Having faith and serving the Lord is not something you do only when it feels convenient. No, it's a commitment—a lifestyle. When you accept the Lord into your heart and life, you become His child, and as His child, you must follow His will and His rules for your life. Faith is not situational. You can't choose to serve God only when things are going well. You must serve Him at all times, whether life is smooth or challenging. Standing strong in faith means worshiping God through every season of life— good or bad. That is what it means to truly be a child of God. Some days were harder than others for me. As a single parent of two, trying to do everything God asked me to do wasn't easy. There were times when life felt overwhelming, but I never said "no" to God. I continued to worship Him through sickness, disappointment, betrayal, tears, pain, happiness, and excitement. Through it all, I gave my father the glory. There were moments when I would cry out of nowhere, not because of sadness but because the Holy Spirit would remind me of how far Jesus has brought me. Those tears were a reminder of His mercy and grace. I could have been dead. My children could have been dead. But God is a loving, caring, and patient Father. He has walked with me every step of the way, taking His time to shape and mold me into who I am today.

## God's Perfect Timing

The Bible states in (Revelation 22:13): *"I am the Alpha and the Omega, the Beginning and the End, the First and the Last."* This truth resonates deeply in my life because God's timing has always been perfect. He knew the exact day I would surrender my life to Him and never look back. Every time my bills were backed up, I prayed, and I trusted God to make a way. And every single time, He provided. He reminded me that as His child, I am never alone. He knows my needs before I even speak to them, and His provision is always right on time.

## Faith Through the Storm

Faith is not just about praising God in the light; it's about trusting Him in the dark. There were times when I felt completely overwhelmed, unsure of how I would make it through. But God never left my side. He taught me that His strength is made perfect in my weakness, and through every trial, He has shown me His faithfulness. When I cried out in pain, He comforted me. When I felt betrayed, He reminded me of His unfailing love. When I was sick, He was my healer. When I faced financial struggles, He was my provider. And when I felt lost, He was my guide.

## Living for His Glory

Through all the ups and downs, my faith has grown stronger because I have learned to put my trust completely in God. I know that He is the Alpha and Omega, the Beginning and the End. Everything in my life is under His control, and because of that, I have peace.

I will continue to worship Him through every season of life, knowing that He is worthy of all the glory. My journey has not easy, but it has been worth it because it has brought me closer to my father. The Bible states in (Philippians 4:19): *"And my God will supply every need of yours according to His riches in glory in Christ Jesus."* I am a living testimony of His provision, His grace, and His love. No matter what comes my way, I will stand strong in my faith and continue to walk with Jesus. He has never failed me, and He never will.

## Walking by Faith, Not by Sight

I prayed and gave everything to God. I didn't worry because I trusted Him completely, and He always provided for me. God is so good, and His love for us is immeasurable. All He asks is that we trust Him and obey His will. Every day is a fresh start. Though we may fall short sometimes, God wants us to get back up, lean on Him, and keep moving forward. The Bible reminds us that His mercies are new every morning (Lamentations 3:22-23). It's easy to get stuck in routines, doing the same things day after day, but God is constantly working to do something new in our lives. The Bible states in (Isaiah 43:19): *"See, I am doing a new thing! Now it springs up; do you not perceive it? I am making a way in the wilderness and streams in the wasteland."* This new thing might involve changes in our behavior, relationships, or even stepping into areas we never thought possible. God's process often requires us to step out of our comfort zones, to take risks, and yes, sometimes even to fail. But every stumble is a lesson, and every step of obedience brings us closer to the purpose He has for us. Do not be afraid to try new things or embrace the unknown. When we allow God to lead, He transforms us and the path ahead.

## Trusting God to Renew and Guide

I often pray, asking Jesus to renew my mind and my ideas, to align my thoughts with His will. The Bible says in (Romans 12:2): *"Do not conform to the pattern of this world but be transformed by the renewing of your mind. Then you will be able to test and approve what God's will is—His good, pleasing, and perfect will.* "I ask Him daily to use me as His vessel, and in doing so, I find myself blessing others—sometimes through a word of encouragement, a hug, or simply by being present and listening. It's in those moments of giving to others that I, too, feel encouraged. God's work through me strengthens my faith and reminds me that His purpose for my life is greater than anything I could ever imagine.

## Faith in Action

Life may bring challenges, but this is when we must trust, believe, and walk by faith—not by sight. When we focus on God and not on our circumstances, we see His hand guiding us. The Bible states in (2 Corinthians 5:7): *"For we walk by faith, not by sight."* Faith isn't about what we can see in the natural; it's about trusting God's promises, knowing that He is working behind the scenes for our good. I encourage you to give everything to Him—your worries, your fears, and your dreams. God wants to do amazing things in your life, but it requires you to trust Him fully. Let Him lead you and watch as He transforms not only your circumstances but also your heart. God loves you, He sees you, and He has great plans for you. Keep walking by faith, and know that His timing is perfect, His provision is sure, and His love is unending.

## Seeking God's Guidance Through Fasting and Prayer

Christians are called to trust in God's promises and guidance rather than relying on their own understanding or experiences. The Bible reminds us in (Proverbs 3:5-6): *"Trust in the Lord with all your heart and lean not on your own understanding; in all your ways submit to him, and he will make your paths straight."*

In October 2024, I felt the need for clarity in my life. I decided to embark on a 7-day fast, seeking God's direction for where He wanted me to be, especially concerning my job and the church I was attending. I was asking Him for wisdom, discernment, and peace about the decisions I needed to make. Fasting and prayer became my way of surrendering to His will, as I knew I couldn't navigate life's challenges on my own.

## Facing Challenges During the Fast

Three days into my fast, I was called in to work. I walked into the classroom I was assigned and tried to do my best, even though I wasn't familiar with the setup. I asked one of the ladies working there for guidance, but her response was cold and unkind. I reminded myself to stay calm and patient, even though her attitude made it difficult. I interacted with the child I was instructed to monitor and continued to ask questions so I could do the job well. I also sought help from another colleague, who kindly explained what needed to be done. Despite the tension with the first lady, I remained polite and tried not to let her negativity affect me.

## An Unexpected Call to the Front

As I was working, the same woman left the classroom, saying she would be back. Thirty minutes later, I was called to the front. Confused, I walked to the office, wondering what I had done wrong. When I arrived, I was met with laughter from the staff at the front desk. One of them explained her perspective on the situation and reassured me. I shared my side of the story, and she understood where I was coming from.She asked me to return to the classroom, and I did so, trying to maintain a calm and professional demeanor. However, as I opened the door, the first lady greeted me rudely and sarcastically asked, *"Do you need anything?"*

## Relying on God's Strength

At that moment, I could have let frustration or anger take over, but I remembered that my fast was about seeking God's will, not reacting to negativity. I silently prayed for strength and wisdom, asking God to guide my actions and words. The Bible reminds us in (James 1:19-20): *"My dear brothers and sisters, take note of this: Everyone should be quick to listen, slow to speak, and slow to become angry, because human anger does not produce the righteousness that God desires.* "Through this experience, I realized that the enemy often tries to test us during moments of spiritual growth. However, fasting and prayer gave me the resilience to stay grounded in my faith.

## Encouragement Through Trials

Challenges like these are reminders to lean on God even more. When we seek Him with all our hearts, He provides clarity and strength to endure difficult situations. The Bible promises in (Isaiah 40:31): *"But those who hope in the Lord will renew their strength. They will soar on wings like eagles; they will run and not grow weary; they will walk and not be faint."*

This situation taught me patience, humility, and the importance of relying on God's guidance in every aspect of my life. While people may disappoint us, God remains faithful and will never leave or forsake us. I encourage anyone facing similar trials to trust God completely, knowing that He is working everything out for their good. Stay rooted in prayer and faith and remember that no matter how challenging life may seem, God is always in control. As (Romans 8:28) says: *"And we know that in all things God works for the good of those who love him, who have been called according to his purpose."*

## Enduring Trials with Grace and Faith

Sometimes life places us in situations that test our character and faith. These moments, though painful, are opportunities for growth and a deeper connection with God. The Bible reminds us in (Philippians 4:7), *"And the peace of God, which transcends all understanding, will guard your hearts and your minds in Christ Jesus.* "I faced a situation where I felt unjustly treated at work. After being told to leave my position without explanation, I stood confused and heartbroken. As I walked to my car, tears streaming down my face, I cried out to God, asking for clarity and peace. While I didn't fully understand why this was happening, I trusted that God was still in control.

## Shifting Focus to What Matters

Instead of letting the incident consume me, I decided to focus on something that brought me joy—spending time with my daughter. I drove to her school and had lunch with her, cherishing that precious moment. It reminded me of the importance of appreciating the blessings right in front of me, even when life feels overwhelming. The Bible teaches us in (Isaiah 41:10): *"So do not fear, for I am with you; do not be dismayed, for I am your God. I will strengthen you and help you; I will uphold you with my righteous right hand."* God's strength carried me through, helping me to redirect my energy and find peace in Him.

## Challenges at Church

Sunday came, and I was eager to hear a word from my pastor. Yet, as I walked into the sanctuary, I felt a heaviness in my spirit. People I normally spoke to didn't acknowledge me, and I couldn't help but question what I might have done wrong. My heart felt burdened, and I sought answers. I approached someone I considered a friend to ask if I had offended her. Her response was hurtful—she accused me of being a "hater" and told me we couldn't be friends unless I "told the truth." The conversation left me feeling betrayed and confused, but instead of retaliating, I chose to walk away and pray.

## Turning to God for Strength

In moments like these, it's easy to feel defeated, but I knew I had to turn to God for strength. The Bible says in (Romans 12:19): *"Do not take revenge, my dear friends, but leave room for God's wrath, for it is written: 'It is mine to avenge; I will repay,' says the Lord.* "I lifted my hands in prayer during the service, asking God to guide me through this storm. I trusted that He was working behind the scenes, even if I couldn't see it at the time.

## Encouragement Through Faith

These experiences reminded me of the importance of perseverance and grace. While people may misunderstand or mistreat us, our ultimate hope lies in God. The Bible says in (James 1:2-4): *"Consider it pure joy, my brothers and sisters, whenever you face trials of many kinds, because you know that the testing of your faith produces perseverance. Let perseverance finish its work so that you may be mature and complete, not lacking anything.* "Through prayer and reflection, I've learned to lean on God's promises and remain steadfast in my faith. These trials have shaped me into a stronger, more compassionate person, and I know that God is using them to prepare me for something greater. No matter what you're going through, remember that God sees your pain, hears your prayers, and is always with you. Keep trusting in Him, and He will bring you through every challenge, stronger and more resilient than before.

## Finding Peace in God's Guidance

Life can sometimes lead us into situations that test our patience, faith, and resilience. That day at church, I found myself in an unexpected confrontation during what was supposed to be a peaceful meeting. My children, arguing over a juice box, had led me to decide to keep the peace between them. Yet, instead of resolution, I found myself in a heated exchange with a staff member, right there in front of others. The Bible reminds us in (1 Corinthians 14:33), *"God is not the author of confusion, but of peace, as in all the churches of the saints."* But at that moment, there was no peace in my heart. I felt overwhelmed, embarrassed, and unsupported as the situation escalated. My pastor's lack of intervention left me feeling unseen, and I couldn't help but question if this was where I was meant to b

## A Moment of Reflection

After the confrontation, I stayed behind to share my concerns with a leader and the pastor. Through tears, I expressed how I felt. Yet, even as I spoke, I felt my feelings being dismissed. The pastor reassured me that what I was experiencing was the enemy trying to discourage me. Still, his words did little to comfort me, and I left the meeting feeling more confused and defeated than before. Driving home, I poured out my heart to God, asking for forgiveness for the way I had responded and for clarity about whether this church was the right place for my family. My children had witnessed the entire incident, and I couldn't shake the unease I felt about their experience in the children's ministry.

## Seeking God's Direction

In moments like these, I've learned to turn to God for answers. I prayed fervently, asking Him to reveal His will for me and my children. I needed to know if staying in this church was part of His plan or if it was time for us to move on. The Bible reminds us in (James 1:5), *"If any of you lacks wisdom, you should ask God, who gives generously to all without finding fault, and it will be given to you.* "In moments like these, I've learned to turn to God for answers. I prayed fervently, asking Him to reveal His will for me and my children. I needed to know if staying in this church was part of His plan or if it was time for us to move on. The Bible reminds us in (James 1:5), *"If any of you lacks wisdom, you should ask God, who gives generously to all without finding fault, and it will be given to you.*

"God is not the author of confusion. He brings clarity and peace, even in the most challenging situations. As I continued to pray, I felt Him reminding me that my focus should always be on Him, not on the actions or words of others.

## Letting Go of the Burden

I knew I couldn't carry the weight of that day's events on my own. I had to release the hurt, frustration, and confusion to God. I asked Him to guide me, to provide clarity, and to help me find the peace I so desperately needed. The Bible says in (Matthew 11:28-29), *"Come to me, all you who are weary and burdened, and I will give you rest. Take my yoke upon you and learn from me, for I am gentle and humble in heart, and you will find rest for your souls. "*This experience taught me the importance of relying on God for direction and trusting Him to guide my steps. Even when people fail us, God never does. He remains steadfast, always working for our good and leading us toward His perfect plan.

## A New Perspective

As I reflect on that day, I realize it wasn't just about a confrontation or feeling unsupported. It was a test of my faith, patience, and ability to trust God in the midst of adversity. I may not have all the answers yet, but I know that God is working in my life, shaping me for His greater purpose. If you find yourself questioning your place or your path, remember to turn to God. Ask Him for clarity, and trust that He will provide it in His perfect timing. Keep your eyes fixed on Him, and let His peace guide your heart.]

## Trusting God's Direction and Finding Peace

Thursday arrived, and the Holy Spirit gently led me to reach out to a spiritual friend. I shared everything I was experiencing—the confusion, the hurt, and the decision I felt God guiding me toward. She reminded me of something so simple yet profound: *God will not place you in an environment where confusion reigns.* Her words gave me the reassurance I needed to trust what I already felt in my spirit.

With that clarity, I made my decision to move forward. I prayed to God, thanking Him for removing me and my children from an environment that was not aligned with His plan for us. I knew His timing was perfect, and I trusted Him to guide my next steps. The Bible says in (Proverbs 3:5-6), *"Trust in the Lord with all your heart and lean not on your own understanding; in all your ways submit to him, and he will make your paths straight."*

## Seeking God's Wisdom

During my fast, God revealed so much to me. He showed me truths I needed to see and gave me peace in my decision. I prayed for the right words to say to my pastor and reached out to her, thanking her for everything she and her ministry had done for me. I explained that I needed to explore other options that better aligned with my spiritual needs and those of my children. Her response, however, was disheartening. Rather than addressing my well-being or asking what had happened, her message focused on her feelings and her ministry. She expressed disappointment in how I communicated, emphasizing that she deserved more than an Instagram message. While her words could have upset me, I chose not to respond. I knew God wanted me to remain still and silent.

## Obedience Over Validation

God often calls us to obedience, even when it's difficult or misunderstood by others. The Bible reminds us in (1 Corinthians 15:33), *"Do not be misled: 'Bad company corrupts good character.'"* God will never lead us astray; He will reveal what we need to know, who we need to be around, and where we need to be. Sometimes, this means letting go of people or places that no longer align with

His purpose for us. It's not always easy. The world may question your decisions, and people may misunderstand your actions. But when you walk with God, you trust in His plan, not the approval of others. The Bible says in (Proverbs 24:16), *"For a just man falleth seven times, and riseth up again: but the wicked shall fall into mischief."* This verse reminded me that no matter what challenges come my way, I belong to God, and He will always lift me back up.

## Victory in Christ

I reflected on how far I had come. The battle between good and evil had already been won through Jesus Christ. He conquered death, rose from the grave, and gave us victory. Because of Him, I don't have to live in fear or confusion. I am a child of God, and He has already declared me a winner. The Bible reassures us in (Romans 8:37), *"No, in all these things we are more than conquerors through him who loved us."* I knew that my decision to move on was part of God's greater plan for me and my family. His protection, provision, and guidance were always with me, even when the path seemed uncertain.

## Moving Forward in Faith

As I ended my fast, I felt peace settle in my heart. God had spoken, and I was obedient. I didn't need validation from others because I had already received confirmation from the One who matters most. I continue to trust Him to lead me, knowing that His plans are always for my good. This chapter of my life is a testament to the power of faith, prayer, and obedience. No matter how many times I fall, I will rise again because I belong to a victorious God. As I walk forward, I do so with confidence, knowing that His promises are true, and His love never fails.

## Walking in Victory Through Christ

This is why you, too, are a conqueror of death—because through Jesus' actions, you have received eternal life. When you feel defeated or scared, take a deep breath and remind yourself that you are on the winning side—Jesus' side. He fights for you, He intercedes for you, and He gives you victory. Because of Him, you are not only surviving, but you are thriving, and you have eternal life in Him. I am not ashamed to say that I am a young, praying woman, and I wouldn't have it any other way. God has opened my spiritual eyes, allowing me to see things I never saw before. The Bible teaches us that there is a veil over our eyes until we believe, but even after that, we must be vigilant and guard our hearts against pride. The Bible states in (Joshua 24:15), *"As for me and my household, we will serve the Lord.* "God, Jesus, and the Holy Spirit led me to write my story—my testimony of how I overcame life's challenges through faith. I wrote about my life, my trauma, and the battles I had to endure. Day by day, I poured my heart onto paper, spending six hours a day writing. Sometimes I would wake up, pray, and listen to worship music to give me strength. With God's help, I finished my book in just one and a half months.

## Embracing My Journey

I am not embarrassed by anything I have been through. Yes, I struggled. I've been hurt. I've been betrayed by people I loved. I've been broken, mismanaged my money, and cried in the darkest of times. I've experienced heartbreak, made mistakes, and faced emotional battles. But through it all, I picked myself up, carried my cross, and walked with Jesus. Every trial the enemy threw at me only strengthened my resolve and faith.

As I healed and gave myself to the Lord, He taught me how to forgive those who hurt me. He showed me His love, so I could extend that love to others. He turned my heart away from evil and gave me the strength to surrender every worry, fear, and burden to Him. Now, I am made new in Christ. The Bible declares in (2 Corinthians 5:17), *"Therefore, if anyone is in Christ, the new creation has come: The old has gone, the new is here!"*

## A New Creation

Jesus has been by my side every step of the way. He has been my protector, my provider, and my guide. I am no longer defined by my past mistakes or the pain I endured. I am a new creation in Christ, filled with His love, grace, and peace. I am living proof that with God, all things are possible. No matter what comes my way, I trust in His promises and remain steadfast in my faith. I now walk boldly in the knowledge that I am His child, loved and chosen, and that He is working everything out for my good.

## Don't Give Up

Giving my life to God was the best decision I ever made. Through every trial, tear, and triumph, He has been my rock and my redeemer. So, I encourage you to call on Jesus. We all need Him every minute, every second, every hour. Jesus loves you! No matter how far you think you've strayed, His arms are always open, ready to welcome you back. The devil is a liar, and

I already won! I know the relationship I have with my Father in heaven, and nobody will ever change my mind or shake my faith, no matter what comes my way. He is worthy of being praised. Every day I stand firm in my trust in Him, knowing that He fights my battles. The Bible states in (Exodus 14:14), *"The Lord shall fight for you, and ye shall hold your peace.* "The devil and his spirits try to put evil thoughts in your head, bringing up every mistake, every regret, and every bad decision you've made in your life. But here's the truth: Jesus has already defeated the enemy, and He's been fighting for you since the beginning. Oh, how the devil hates that! He tries to destroy everything God has ordained for you to have, but no weapon formed against you shall prosper. Jesus loves you so much, and He wants you to walk in victory, not defeat. No matter how heavy life feels, trust that God is working things out for your good. The Bible states in (Romans 8:31), *"If God is for us, who can be against us?* "I still love my Father in heaven with all my heart. Every day I choose to walk by faith, not by sight. He is my protector, my provider, my healer, and my everything. Through Him, I am stronger, wiser, and more at peace than I have ever been. So, to anyone reading this, I encourage you: Don't give up. Call on Jesus. Let Him into your heart and watch how He transforms your life. With God, all things are possible.

## A Victorious Ending: Walking in Faith

This journey has taught me the true meaning of faith, resilience, and surrender. God has been my anchor, my light, and my refuge in every storm. I now see that every trial, every heartache, and every setback were all part of His divine plan to mold me into the person I am today—a new creation walking boldly in His purpose. The Bible declares in (Romans 8:28), *"And we know that in all things God works for the good of those who love him, who have been called according to his purpose.* "I have learned to embrace my story, not as a series of defeats but as a testimony of triumph through Christ. I no longer see my struggles as punishments but as steppingstones to greater faith and understanding. Each tear shed was a seed planted, and now I am witnessing the harvest of joy, peace, and restoration that only God can provide.

## God's Faithfulness

There were times when I felt like giving up—when the weight of life's challenges seemed unbearable. But every single time, God showed up. He reminded me that He is faithful, even when I felt weak. The Bible assures us in (Isaiah 41:10), *"So do not fear, for I am with you; do not be dismayed, for I am your God. I will strengthen you and help you; I will uphold you with my righteous right hand.* His presence has been my constant source of strength. When I had no one to turn to, He was there. When I felt like I couldn't take another step, He carried me. He provided for me in ways I could never have imagined, reminding me that He is Jehovah Jireh, my provider. He healed my wounds, both seen and unseen, and made me whole again.

## Choosing Faith Over Fear

I've come to realize that faith is not the absence of fear—it's choosing to trust God despite the fear. It's stepping out in obedience even when the path ahead is unclear. It's believing in His promises even when life feels uncertain. The Bible in (Hebrews 11:1) reminds us, *"Now faith is confidence in what we hope for and assurance about what we do not see.* "I've seen firsthand how God works in mysterious ways. He has opened doors I never expected, closed doors that weren't meant for me, and guided me through every season of my life. Through it all, He has remained faithful, loving, and unchanging. He is the same God yesterday, today, and forever.

## A New Chapter

As I close this chapter of my life, I am stepping into a new season with unwavering faith and confidence in God's plan for me. I know there will still be challenges ahead, but I am no longer afraid. I've been equipped with the armor of God, and I am ready to face whatever comes my way. The Bible says in (Ephesians 6:10-11), *"Finally, be strong in the Lord and in his mighty power. Put on the full armor of God, so that you can take your stand against the devil's schemes."*

This is not the end of my story—it's only the beginning. My life is a testament to God's grace, mercy, and power. I will continue to walk in faith, trusting Him to lead me every step of the way. I will continue to share my testimony, to be a light for others, and to glorify His name in all that I do.

## Don't Give Up

To anyone reading this, I want you to know that no matter what you're going through, don't give up. God sees you. He hears your prayers. He knows your pain. Trust Him with your heart, your struggles, and your dreams. He has a plan for you that is greater than anything you could ever imagine. The Bible states in (Jeremiah 29:11), *"For I know the plans I have for you," declares the Lord, "plans to prosper you and not to harm you, plans to give you hope and a future.* "Keep praying, keep believing, and keep pressing forward. You are not alone, and you are deeply loved by the Creator of the universe. Remember, no weapon formed against you shall prosper, and no obstacle is too big for God to overcome. I am living proof that God can take a broken life and turn it into something beautiful. If He did it for me, He can do it for you. Hold on to His promises, walk in His truth, and never stop seeking His presence. With God, all things are possible.

This is my testimony, and it's only the beginning.

## Songs That Strengthened My Spirit

Throughout my journey, music played a pivotal role in reminding me of God's faithfulness, uplifting my spirit, and encouraging me to press on. These songs ministered to my heart and became anthems of hope, healing, and worship. I pray they touch your heart as they did mine.

1. **Tasha Cobb Leonard** - *Gracefully Broken*
2. **Lady Harmony** - *I Owe It All to You*
3. **Koryn Hawthorne** - *Down Goes Rome*
4. **Doe** - *When I Pray*
5. **Fred Hammond** - *We're Blessed*

6. **Fred Hammond** - *Give Me a Clean Heart*

7. **Koryn Hawthorne** - *Cry*

8. **Jekalyn Carr** - *Greater Is Coming*

9. **Jekalyn Carr** - *You Carried Me*

10. **Jekalyn Carr** - *Jehovah Jireh*

11. **Jekalyn Carr** - *Curse Breaker*

12. **Marvin Sapp** - *He Has His Hand on You*

13. **Marvin Sapp** - *Never Would Have Made It*

14. **Mary Mary** - *Can't Give Up Now*

15. **Smokie Norful** - *I Need You Now*

16. **Le'andria Johnson** - *Better Days*

17. **Marvin Sapp** - *My Testimony*

18. **James Fortune** - *I Trust You*

19. **Bri Babineaux** - *Make Me Over*

20. **Tasha Cobb Leonard** - *You Know My Name*

21. **Tasha Cobb Leonard** - *Your Spirit*

22. **William McDowell** - *I Give Myself Away*

23. **Quandra Banks** - *You Are My God*

24. **Donnie McClurkin** - *Speak to My Heart*

25. **Jason Nelson** - *Nothing Without You*

26. **Pastor Mike Jr.** - *Amazing*

27. **Kierra Sheard** - *Grace*

28. **Kierra Sheard** - *Praise Through*

29. **Kierra Sheard** - *All Yours*

30. **Kierra Sheard & Tasha Cobb Leonard** - *Something Has to Break*

31. **Fred Hammond** - *You Are the Living Word*

32. **Koryn Hawthorne** - *Look at God*

33. **Koryn Hawthorne** - *Won't He Do It*

34. **Shekinah Glory Ministry** - *Praise Is What I Do*

35. **Harmony Dobson** - *Yes*

## Heavenly Father

God, You are so good.

I love You, Jesus.

I adore You.

Thank You for life.

Thank You for the good days.

Thank You for the bad days.

Thank You, God, for being the same God.

Thank You for grace.

Jesus, You are my rock.

Jesus, You are wonderful.

Jesus, You are the same today, yesterday, and forever.

Thank You, Holy Spirit. Without You, I'm nothing, but with You, I'm absolutely everything and more—and for that, I'm grateful.

Give God thanks in everything you do.

The God I serve is able.

## Prayer of Gratitude

Heavenly Father,

I never would have made it; I never could have made it without You by my side. Thank You, Lord, for Your mercy that kept me when I thought I couldn't go on. You saw the best in me when everyone around me saw the worst. You are the God who says "yes" when the world says "no." Hallelujah! Thank You, Jesus, for setting my soul free. I am healed, redeemed, and whole. It's in the past—it's over—and it's finished.

Thank You for the good days.

Thank You for the bad days.

Thank You, God, for being the same yesterday, today, and forever.

Thank You for Your grace.

Jesus, You are my rock.

Jesus, You are wonderful.

Holy Spirit, without You, I am nothing—but with You, I am absolutely everything.

Give thanks to God in everything you do, because the God I serve is able!

## Prayer for Guidance

Lord Jesus,

I seek Your guidance and wisdom in every area of my life. Direct my steps, and let Your Word be a lamp unto my feet and a light unto my path. Help me to hear Your voice clearly and to follow Your will. If I stray, draw me back to You. Teach me to trust in Your timing and to surrender my plans to Your perfect purpose. Lead me, Lord, for You are my Shepherd, and I will follow wherever You take me. In Jesus' name, Amen.

## Prayer for Forgiveness

Merciful Father,

I humble myself before You, asking for Your forgiveness. Wash me clean of my sins, Lord, and create in me a pure heart. Teach me to forgive others as You have forgiven me. I release any anger, resentment, or bitterness I hold in my heart. Fill me with Your love and grace, so I may walk in the freedom and peace that only You can give. Thank You for the sacrifice of Your Son, Jesus, who has made me righteous in Your sight. In Jesus' name, Amen.

## Prayer for Healing

Father God,

You are Jehovah Rapha, the God who heals. I pray for healing over my mind, body, and spirit. Restore me completely, Lord, and take away any pain or sickness that is within me. I pray for healing over my family, friends, and anyone who is struggling right now. By Your stripes, we are healed. I trust in Your power to bring wholeness and restoration. Thank You for being the ultimate healer, and I give You all the praise for what You are about to do. In Jesus' name, Amen.

## Prayer for Protection

Almighty God,

I pray for Your divine protection over my life, my family, my home, and my loved ones. Cover us with Your blood and shield us from every attack of the enemy. Guard our hearts and minds from fear and doubt. Surround us with Your angels to guide us and keep us safe. I declare that no weapon formed against us shall prosper. Thank You, Lord, for being our refuge and fortress. In Jesus' name, Amen.

## Prayer for Peace

Lord Jesus,

You are the Prince of Peace, and I ask You to fill my heart and home with Your peace that surpasses all understanding. Calm my anxious thoughts and quiet my restless soul. Let Your peace rule in my heart and guide me through every storm. I cast all my burdens and cares on You, for You care for me. Thank You for being my peace in the midst of the chaos. In Jesus' name, Amen.

## Prayer for Faith

Dear God,

Strengthen my faith in You. Help me to trust You even when I don't see the way forward. Remind me of Your promises and help me to stand firm on Your Word. Increase my faith, Lord, so that I may walk boldly, knowing that You are in control. Thank You for being a faithful God who never leaves or forsakes me. In Jesus' name, Amen.

## Prayer for Purpose

Father,

You have created me with a purpose, and I ask that You reveal it to me. Show me how to use my gifts and talents to glorify You and to help others. Let Your will be done in my life, and give me the courage to walk in my calling. I trust that Your plans for me are good and that You will guide me every step of the way. Use me, Lord, for Your glory. In Jesus' name, Amen.

## Closing Prayer

Lord God,

Thank You for always hearing my prayers and for walking with me every step of the way. I surrender my life completely to You. Fill me with Your Spirit, guide me with Your Word, and use me as Your vessel. I trust you with my past, my present, and my future. Let my life be a testimony of Your love, grace, and power. In the mighty name of Jesus, I pray, Amen.

## Closing Prayer

I never would have made it; I never could have made it without God on my side. If you have problems, just know you can't fix it—give it to God. The devil thought he had me, but God's mercy kept me. He saw the best in me when everyone around me saw the worst in me. When the world says no, my God said yes. Hallelujah! Thank you, Jesus. He set my soul free, and I'm healed. It's in the past; it's over.

# NOTES